# THE ESSENTIAL
# CHRISTMAS
# COOKBOOK

# THE ESSENTIAL
# CHRISTMAS
# COOKBOOK

THUNDER BAY
P·R·E·S·S

San Diego, California

**Thunder Bay Press**
An imprint of the Advantage Publishers Group
5880 Oberlin Drive, San Diego, CA 92121-4794
www.thunderbaybooks.com

All notations of errors or omissions should be addressed to Thunder Bay Press, Editorial Department, at the above address. All other correspondence (author inquiries and permissions) concerning the content of this book should be addressed to Murdoch Books®, a division of Murdoch Magazines Pty Ltd, GPO Box 1203, Sydney NSW 2001, Australia.

ISBN 1-57145-999-5
Library of Congress Cataloging-in-Publication Data available upon request.

Printed by Toppan Printing Hong Kong Co. Ltd. PRINTED IN CHINA
First published in 2000. Reprinted 2001, 2003.
1 2 3 4 5    07 06 05 04 03

Series Editor: Wendy Stephen.  Managing Editor: Rachel Carter.  Editorial Director: Diana Hill.
Designer: Michèle Lichtenberger.  Design Concept: Marylouise Brammer.
Managing Food Editor: Jane Lawson.  Food Director: Jody Vassallo.
Stylist (cover and special features): Mary Harris.
Photographer (cover and special features): Chris Jones.
Home Economists: Michelle Earl, Kathy Knudsen, Michelle Lawton.
Picture Librarian: Anne Ferrier.  Indexer: Russell Brooks.

Chief Executive: Juliet Rogers.
Publisher: Kay Scarlett.

OUR STAR RATING: When we test recipes, we rate them for ease of preparation.
The following cooking ratings are used in this book:
☆ A single star indicates a recipe that is simple and generally quick to make—perfect for beginners.
☆☆ Two stars indicate the need for just a little more care, or perhaps a little more time.
☆☆☆ Three stars indicate special dishes that need more investment in time,
care, and patience—but the results are worth it. Even beginners can make these
dishes as long as the recipe is followed carefully.

IMPORTANT: Those who might be at risk from the effects of salmonella food poisoning
(the elderly, pregnant women, young children, and those suffering from immune deficiency diseases)
should consult their physician with any concerns about eating raw eggs.

# CHRISTMAS

*Have yourself a merry little Christmas*

*Let your hearts be light*

*From now on, our troubles will be out of sight*


*Have yourself a merry little Christmas*

*Make the Yuletide gay*

*From now on, our troubles will be miles away*

*Here we are as in olden days*

*Happy golden days of yore*

*Faithful friends who are dear to us*

*Gather near to us once more*


*Through the years we all will be together*

*If the fates allow*

*Hang a shining star upon the highest bough*

*And have yourself a merry little Christmas now*

Composed by Hugh Martin and Ralph Blane for the 1944 musical
'Meet Me in St Louis'. It was first sung by the incomparable Judy Garland.

# CONTENTS

## SPECIAL FEATURES

# PLANNING FOR CHRISTMAS

Christmas is such a wonderfully nostalgic time of year, giving us that extra spring in our step as we happily look forward to celebrating with our family and friends. Any discipline we might normally display over diet or spending habits is quickly forgotten as the air of expectation becomes more and more infectious. It's impossible not to remember the excitement we felt as children, almost bursting with impatience as the pile of mysterious bundles under the tree grew ever larger.

Christmas Day can start alarmingly early when there are children in the house. And understandably so. Having put so much thought into their letters to Santa, children are most anxious to see the results of their labour. While the Christmas stocking goes some way towards occupying the very early morning hours, it brings with it an added complication. How can you possibly fall asleep on Christmas Eve when you know perfectly well that a round, white-haired gentleman will be slipping into your room to fill your stocking with exciting treasures? A terrible struggle, as any child knows, because Santa won't visit unless you are asleep. All thoughts of enjoying a last secretive squeeze of the presents under the tree must be banished.

For those of us doing the work (always a labour of love!) planning and list-making starts long before Christmas Eve. To succeed in the eternal struggle to have a calm and stress-free Christmas with all your favourite people, organization is the key. We all know this, yet somehow we still find ourselves battling the crowds, hysterically trying to buy the last few essential items that will make the celebrations perfect. Then angrily fighting our way home, cursing the jostling hordes and vowing to *really* plan ahead next year. And so it goes on, year after year, but somehow these minor irritations become quite hazy with time so you only remember the happiness and excitement of the Christmas season.

It's so satisfying to know you've bought just the right present for someone you love—especially if you've managed to achieve this well before panic buying sets in. And when you have a specific gift in mind for yourself, it's always helpful to let people know. Needless to say, this message must be conveyed with skill and subtlety. Start by dropping hints, then move on to the next step of leaving catalogues carelessly lying around, propped open at the appropriate page. If time is running out, you may need to actually accompany your intended benefactor on a shopping expedition, casually admire the item in question, then feign interest in a diversion. Allow plenty of time for them to make a note of the details or if you're very lucky, they may even dash into the shop then and there to buy this wonderful 'surprise' for you!

Decorating the house is another happy chore in the days and weeks leading up to Christmas Day. Nothing beats that moment when the familiar baubles and tinsel are on the tree and it's time to turn on the lights. And parents can always be counted on to produce those rather squashed and lopsided decorations we made as children—they won't hear of throwing them away, no matter how far we feel our artistic abilities have progressed since then. It's the warm cosiness of family and childhood memories that make Christmas such a special time.

Generously opening your house to as many people as possible based on the 'more the merrier' philosophy can be a great character-building exercise. Lessons learned over years of experience vanish into thin air and yet again you find yourself pink-faced and flustered as you serve up ham for twenty. No amount of forward planning can erase that panic-stricken moment, it seems, but at the end of the day, what does it matter? The goodwill at this time of year is all-encompassing and the great Christmas feast is always a resounding success. The care you have taken to set a beautiful table, with all the best table linen, glassware and cutlery is appreciated by all. This sophistication, this polish and style that you have brought to the occasion can only be enhanced by the loud and boisterous pulling of Christmas crackers. Once the coloured hats are on and the same old jokes have been groaned at, all there is left to do is relax and enjoy being together.

# Menu Suggestions

## Traditional Menu

### Nibbles

Chicken liver and Grand Marnier
pâté page 18

Herb cheese log with crackers
page 20

### Main

Your choice of

Traditional roast turkey with
stuffing page 59

Glazed ham page 60

Roast leg of pork page 72

Sauces and accompaniments 68–71

### Accompaniments

Selection of roast vegetables
page 138 and 144

### Dessert

Your choice of

Steamed Christmas pudding
page 192

Boiled Christmas pudding
page 208

Custard or brandy butter
page 198–199

### With coffee

Rum truffles page 258

Fruit mince tarts
page 195, 244, 245

Scottish shortbread page 251

## Seafood Menu

### Nibbles

Oysters page 98–99

Lemon prawn pâté page 25

### Main

Your choice of

Whole poached ocean trout page 94

Barbecued seafood platter
page 110

Lobster with parsley mayonnaise
page 105

### Accompaniments

Tomato and bocconcini salad
page 160

Caramelized onion and potato
salad page 163

Caesar salad page 166

### Dessert

Your choice of

Ice cream Christmas pudding
page 210

Summer berries in Champagne jelly
page 216

Mango sorbet page 211

### With coffee

Mini fruit truffle puddings
page 258

Ginger pecan biscotti
page 263

## Vegetarian Menu

### Nibbles

Spicy nuts page 21

Mushroom pâté page 41

### Main

Your choice of

Chargrilled vegetable terrine
page 122

Ratatouille tarte tatin page 125

Couscous vegetable loaf
page 127

### Accompaniments

Honey-roasted vegetables,
duchess potatoes page 155

Broccoli with almonds 147

Chickpea and roast vegetable salad
page 167

### Dessert

Your choice of

Chocolate hazelnut torte
page 218

Cranberry kisel page 281

### With coffee

Cardamom lime crescents page 263

Creamy coconut ice
page 260

Cinnamon stars page 288

Panforte page 274

Florentines page 255

# CHRISTMAS DAY COUNTDOWN

The key to success is organization, so to help you plan ahead and save time and worry here's a schedule to guide you through the days and months leading up to Christmas Day.

### ONE YEAR AHEAD

❖ Of course, it sounds ridiculous to start planning this early, but it's worth having a look at the post-Christmas sales. This is an ideal time to stock up on budget-priced wrapping paper and decorations and start gathering ideas for your next Christmas bash.

### SIX TO THREE MONTHS AHEAD

❖ Work out your budget, a rough guest list and plan your menu.
❖ If you need to hire equipment—anything from a marquee to cutlery—do so.
❖ Christmas cakes and puddings can be made well ahead of time if stored properly. Wrap securely in greaseproof paper, then in plastic wrap and store in an airtight container in the refrigerator or a cool, dark place. Indeed, a long storage time is actually beneficial as it allows the flavours to develop. As a general rule, Christmas cake can be stored for up to 3 months and puddings for up to 6 weeks. Both can also be frozen for up to 12 months.
❖ Make your liqueur fruits so they are ready for Christmas Day or for giving as gifts. If you can, buy fruits in season when they are cheaper and full of flavour. Bottled liqueur fruits will keep for up to 6 months.

### ONE MONTH AHEAD

❖ If you have storage space, purchase wine, beer and soft drinks now. Or, if you have planned a large party, order drinks now and arrange to have them delivered a few days ahead.
❖ Order turkeys and hams. As a general guide a 7 kg ham will serve around 20 people and a 4.5 kg turkey will feed 6–8 people when served as a main course with vegetables and all the trimmings.
❖ Make your mincemeat for mince pies as it takes a month to mature.
❖ Start thinking about table decorations and making some yourself.
❖ Think about and plan your table settings.
❖ Make jams, pickles and chutneys for stocking your pantry and for gifts.

## ONE WEEK AHEAD

❖ Ensure you have a carving knife and fork on hand—it is a good idea to have your knives professionally sharpened. Some sturdy chopping boards will come in handy too! Make sure your baking dish is large enough for your ham or turkey. If not, you could always buy disposable ones.

❖ Prepare your shopping list and buy most of your non-perishable ingredients. Pick up items like napkins, tablecloths, candles and toothpicks while you are shopping.

❖ Ice the Christmas cake, if required (see page 234).

❖ Make your jams, curds, chocolates and fudges.

❖ Make your gingerbread house, mince pies, shortbread, biscotti, panettone, panforte, stollen, etc. and keep them well sealed in an airtight container.

❖ Freeze ahead—the great thing about many Christmas goodies is that they can be made ahead and either frozen or left, well sealed, at either room temperature or in the refrigerator until ready to use.

## TWO DAYS AHEAD

❖ When planning the menu, try to choose a dessert, starter or side dish that can be made, at least partially, a couple of days ahead and then kept in the refrigerator.

❖ If you are having a buffet, wrap the cutlery in napkins and place in an attractive, decorated basket.

❖ Think about the food you are serving and select your serving dishes, platters and utensils. Make sure they are all clean, polished and a suitable size.

❖ Fill up your salt and pepper shakers, sugar bowls, etc.

❖ Defrost anything that needs defrosting. A large turkey can take up to 3 days—take it out of the original packaging and sit it on a rack in a baking tray in the refrigerator. Make sure it is not sitting in the liquid while thawing. Cover with plastic wrap.

## ONE DAY AHEAD

❖ Set your table—iron the tablecloth, put the candles in holders, fold the napkins and lay out any decorations.

❖ Polish glasses and cutlery, and then put a light cloth over the whole setting to ensure no dust or greasy fingers spoil your hard work.

❖ Buy all your last-minute fresh produce, seafood and fresh flowers.

❖ Make stuffings and refrigerate them in a covered bowl.

❖ Make your pavlova, or any dessert sauces or custards that will keep overnight.

❖ Prepare the glaze for your ham and score and stud the ham with cloves.

❖ Refrigerate all your drinks now unless you are purchasing ice tomorrow.

❖ Don't forget the little things like butter, coffee, milk and garbage bags.

❖ Calculate how long things will take to cook and plan what to cook when.

## CHRISTMAS DAY

❖ Preheat your oven. Just prior to cooking, prepare your roast by trimming, trussing, tying or stuffing as required. Do not stuff a turkey ahead of time as bacteria can develop in the cavity even when refrigerated and no-one wants to be responsible for giving their entire family food poisoning—especially on Christmas Day!

❖ Put the ham, turkey or other roast on to cook.

❖ Vegetables to be roasted should go on an hour before the meat is cooked.

❖ Other vegetables should be peeled and chopped when you first put your roast on and finished off just toward the end of cooking. Vegetables that don't take long to cook, such as peas, beans or asparagus, should be cooked while your roast is resting.

❖ Gravy can also be made while the meat is resting.

❖ If you are having pudding, remember it will take 2 hours to reheat so allow plenty of time.

❖ Chill the drinks, warm the plates, put on some music, fill your glass and, above all, enjoy yourself!

PS Don't forget the presents and the tree!!

# FESTIVE PARTY HINTS

❖ Write a checklist in order of things to do and cross them off as you do them. Not only will you feel blissfully organized, you will also feel a sense of achievement with every item you cross off the list.

❖ Plan ahead. Prepare as much as possible in advance (see our Christmas countdown on the previous page for some planning ideas). Many things can be made ahead, then refrigerated and even frozen. Bases for dressings and glazes can be made several days ahead, adding herbs etc. close to serving to prevent discolouration. Puddings and cakes can be made (and some decorated) several months ahead. In fact, in some cases, this will actually improve the flavour. Many frozen desserts can also be prepared in advance.

❖ It is worth paying extra for good-quality dried and glacé fruits for your cake or pudding. Look for plump, moist and glossy fruit to improve the overall flavour and final result. Soaking the chopped fruits for 2–4 days before baking also enhances both flavour and moistness. For those who like their cake a little on the tipsy side, make the cake at least a few weeks ahead, and then once a week prick the top of the cake with a very thin cake skewer and carefully spoon or brush over a little alcohol of your choice (usually brandy), letting it soak in. Make sure you re-wrap the cake well each time so it stays moist.

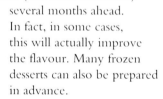

❖ If you are planning to make a boiled pudding, don't forget to buy some calico and string (or the correct-sized steamer basin) and make sure you have a pot large enough to boil the pudding in.

❖ Christmas is a time for people dropping in. To avoid potential embarrassment, make sure you have plenty of goodies on hand, such as slices, biscuits, nuts, cake or chocolates. If you are making gifts of jams or vinegars, make a

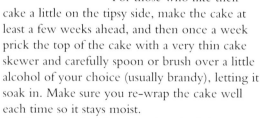

couple of extra jars for those unexpected guests who arrive with a present.

❖ Order turkeys and hams and other unusual food items well ahead so you don't miss out.

❖ Buy non-perishable foods early on to avoid frustrating delays at the supermarket. Make detailed shopping lists and delegate if possible. Perhaps most importantly, don't turn down offers of help!

❖ Buy wine, sparkling wine and soft drinks well ahead, keeping an eye out for specials in the days and weeks leading up to Christmas.

❖ Check that you have enough crockery, glassware, cutlery etc. for the number of people you are expecting, allowing a few spares. Hiring can be inexpensive if you shop around to get the

most competitive rate. Alternatively, borrow from friends or family—mix and match crockery can look wonderful!

❖ Make sure you have an esky handy. Because they are well insulated, they're terrific for keeping food hot or cold. Place the cooked ham, turkey or other large joint in the esky loosely covered while finishing the vegetables and gravy.

❖ Make ice cubes from fruit juices for additional festive colour and flavour in your drinks and punches.

❖ Make your own tablecloths. Hem long lengths of Christmas fabric and trim with tassels or fringing for a festive look. While you're at it, make some matching napkins.

❖ Put together your own Christmas hampers. Small packets of biscuits, jams and chocolate make lovely personal gifts, especially when you have taken care to choose your friends' particular favourites. Wrap them in clear or coloured cellophane and tie with ribbons.

❖ Christmas cakes and puddings make great gifts too, and look wonderful when packaged either with colourful wrappings or simply some brown paper, straw and a couple of holly leaves.

❖ If your attempts to roast a turkey or bake a ham are a one-off and your budget is tight, buy disposable foil baking dishes from supermarkets. Be careful though, they can bend with too much weight which can be hazardous when hot. Use two foil dishes together (one inside the other) to give a stronger base under the weight of your turkey or ham.

❖ You will need plenty of fridge space for a large turkey or ham. This may require removing a shelf and some organisation to fit everything and obviously you want to have this worked out before the kitchen frenzy on Christmas Day. If you are really pushed for space for storing food, think about hiring a fridge or freezer for the festive season.

❖ Don't leave foods unrefrigerated for too long in warmer climates or heated rooms. Room temperature is the perfect environment for bacteria to breed, and this can cause food poisoning, especially in chicken, duck and turkey. *Not* the effect you're after!

❖ Think about what else you need to be cooking in the oven at the same time as your roast. For example, how are you going to fit the roast vegetables in the oven if they are being served alongside the ham? A covered kettle barbecue is ideal for cooking hams, allowing you a lot more space in your oven on the day. And bear in mind that the ham and turkey will keep hot for quite a while once removed from the oven.

❖ Don't worry if you have leftovers—you don't have to eat ham sandwiches for a week. Turkey, ham and salmon leftovers can easily be turned into a variety of tasty dishes, as you will see in our chapter on leftovers.

❖ Freeze your leftover ham bone and cooked or uncooked (after boning) turkey bones for later in the year. Make split pea and ham soup with the ham bone and make delicious stock from the turkey bones.

❖ Freeze suitable leftovers in quantities for 1–2 people. Smaller portions obviously defrost more quickly than if frozen in large blocks. They are also welcome when it's time to relax.

# HOW TO CARVE

Carving a roast can be tricky, so follow these instructions and even the most inexperienced carver will be able to serve a perfect Christmas roast in a quick and fuss-free manner.

Turkey and ham are the most popular Christmas roasts—and the most daunting. They are rarely eaten at other times of the year and can easily confound even the most confident of cooks when it comes to carving and presenting them. Before carving any roast, it is important to let the meat 'rest' for 15 minutes or so. Remove the roast from the oven and cover it with foil so the heat does not escape too quickly and the juices can settle and distribute evenly, moistening and tenderizing the flesh.

Make sure your carving knife is sharp and try to slice rather than saw—the more you hack into the meat, tearing the flesh, the more juices are lost, making the meat dry. Electric knives can make life much easier. A carving fork is also important for holding the meat steady. Do not pierce the meat—try to use the back of the fork to get a good hold. When carving a bird, however, a sharp-pronged fork is needed to dig deep into the carcass (not the flesh) to keep it still.

Always carve on a carving board, not a serving platter. China and metal surfaces can scratch easily and can be quite slippery, causing you to lose control of the knife. It is preferable to use a carving board with a rim around the edges to catch any excess juices—this not only stops the juices from spilling over onto the table but it also means they can be strained off and used in your gravy for an extra boost of flavour. It is also a good idea to place a damp cloth underneath your board to keep it steady while carving.

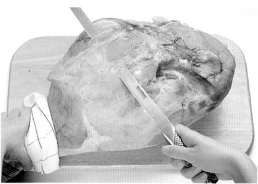

*Cut a slice from the underside of the ham to steady it while carving.*

*Remove a wedge of ham from the knuckle end before you carve.*

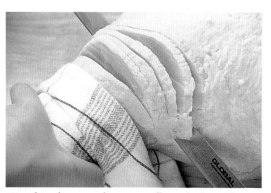

*Cut thin slices, working away from the knuckle.*

*Cut the slices away from the bone and serve.*

## HAM

**1** After it has rested, place the ham on a cutting board with the bone to the left. Use a clean tea towel to hold the bone firmly while carving. Remember to keep your fingers away from the blade! Slice a piece from the underside of the leg so that it sits flat on the board. Remove this slice and set aside.

**2** Slice into the meat about 10 cm (4 inches) from the knuckle. Make another cut at an angle to the first so that it forms a wedge, then remove. Continue cutting to the right, cutting several thin slices right down to the bone. The meat will still be attached to the bone so to release the pieces you must run the knife along the bone, under the meat. Lift off the slices with the flat of the knife. Cut enough slices for serving, covering the slices with foil as you go if the ham is to be served warm.

## TURKEY

**1** After it has rested, place the turkey on a cutting board, breast-side-up and with the legs facing you.

**2** Use a carving fork to steady the bird and cut downward into the skin and meat where the leg meets the breast. Bend the leg outwards with the carving knife until you can see the joint where the thighbone and the backbone connect.

Keep cutting at a slight angle towards the joint, then cut down and through it until the leg section (the thigh and drumstick) can be easily removed. Depending on the size of the turkey, you can also cut through the leg at the joint to remove the thigh and have two separate pieces. Set the meat aside on a warm serving dish and keep covered with foil while you are carving the rest of the turkey. This will keep it warm and stop it from drying out.

**3** On the same side of the bird, find where the wing meets the body and cut down, again until you meet the joint. You may need to pull the wing out with your left hand while you are cutting with your right hand to loosen the wing from the bird. Set aside and cover to keep warm.

**4** Continuing on the same side, begin to carve the breast. Start at the top of the breast where it attaches to the ridge of bone and carve downwards in even slices, at a slight angle, towards the cutting board. Add to the rest of the meat and cover. Now repeat this process on the other side of the turkey. To remove the wishbone, snip the sinews on either side.

**5** Remove the stuffing from the opening of the carcass with a spoon and, depending on the texture of the stuffing, serve it either in slices or in spoonfuls.

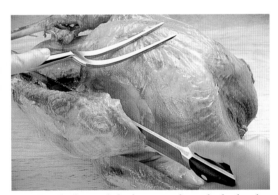

*Remove the leg and thigh section from the body of the turkey.*

*With larger birds it is possible to separate the leg and thigh.*

*Similarly, remove the turkey wing by cutting through the joint.*

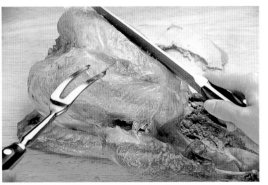

*Carve the turkey breast, using the fork to keep the bird steady.*

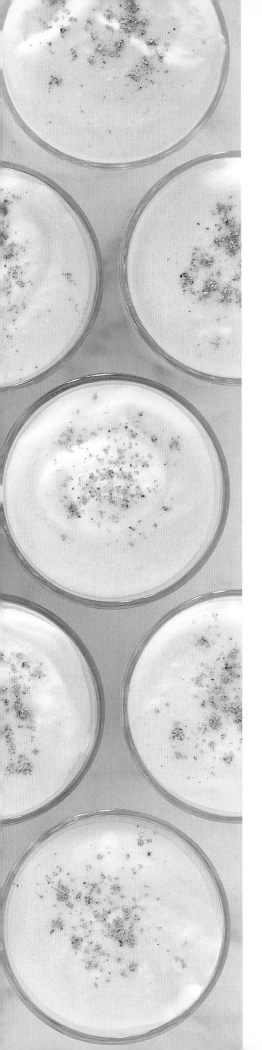

# PARTY TIME

Christmas provides us with the perfect excuse to eat, drink and be merry. High spirits prevail as we throw ourselves enthusiastically into the party season, but these feelings of excitement can quickly turn to panic when it's time to play host. By far the best (and least frenzied) way of preparing for a party is to choose just a handful of the following recipes and increase the quantity to suit your needs. Many of them can be made ahead of time, which is always a blessing when there are a thousand things to do. To add an extra festive touch, whip up some refreshing punches and cocktails and serve them with an extravagant garnish. Cheers!!

1 Put the chicken livers in a bowl, add the milk and stir to combine. Cover and refrigerate for 1 hour. Drain the livers and discard the milk. Rinse in cold water, drain and pat dry with paper towels.

2 Melt a third of the butter in a frying pan, add the spring onion and cook for 2–3 minutes, or until tender, but not brown. Add the livers and cook, stirring, over medium heat for 4–5 minutes, or until just cooked. Remove from the heat and cool a little.

3 Transfer the livers to a food processor and process until very smooth. Chop the remaining butter, add to the processor with the Grand Marnier and orange juice concentrate and process until creamy. Season, to taste, with salt and freshly ground black pepper. Transfer to a 1.25 litre (40 fl oz) serving dish, cover the surface with plastic wrap and chill for 1½ hours, or until firm.

4 For the jellied layer, whisk together the orange juice concentrate, Grand Marnier and ½ cup (125 ml/4 fl oz) of the consommé in a jug. Sprinkle the gelatine over the liquid in an even layer and leave until the gelatine is spongy— do not stir. Heat the remaining consommé in a pan, remove from the heat and add the gelatine mixture. Stir to dissolve the gelatine, then leave to cool and thicken to the consistency of uncooked egg white, but not set.

5 Press the orange slices lightly into the surface of the pâté and spoon the thickened jelly evenly over the top. Refrigerate until set. Serve at room temperature with toast or crackers.

**NOTE:** Grand Marnier is a cognac-based liqueur with an orange flavour.

## CHICKEN LIVER AND GRAND MARNIER PATE

**Preparation time:** 20 minutes + 2 hours 30 minutes refrigeration
**Total cooking time:** 10 minutes
**Serves** 8

★ ★

750 g (1½ lb) chicken livers, well trimmed
1 cup (250 ml/8 fl oz) milk
200 g (6½ oz) butter, softened
4 spring onions, finely chopped
1 tablespoon Grand Marnier
1 tablespoon frozen orange juice concentrate, thawed
½ orange, very thinly sliced

**Jellied layer**

1 tablespoon orange juice concentrate
1 tablespoon Grand Marnier
1¼ cups (315 ml/10 fl oz) canned chicken consommé, undiluted
2½ teaspoons powdered gelatine

*ABOVE: Chicken liver and Grand Marnier pâté*

## CHEESE BISCUITS

**Preparation time:** 15 minutes + 1 hour refrigeration
**Total cooking time:** 15 minutes
**Makes** about 40

★

1 cup (125 g/4 oz) plain flour
2 tablespoons self-raising flour
1 teaspoon curry powder
125 g (4 oz) butter
¾ cup (75 g/2½ oz) grated Parmesan
⅔ cup (85 g/3 oz) grated Cheddar
20 g (¾ oz) blue cheese, crumbled
1 tablespoon lemon juice

1 Preheat the oven to moderately hot 200°C (400°F/Gas 6). Sift the flours and curry powder into a bowl, add the butter and rub into the flour until the mixture resembles fine breadcrumbs. Stir in 1/2 cup (50 g/13/4 oz) of the Parmesan with the other cheeses and stir in the lemon juice with a flat-bladed knife, using a cutting action until the mixture comes together in beads. Gather the dough together into a ball.

2 Roll into a 30 cm (12 inch) log. Wrap in plastic and refrigerate for 1 hour.

3 Remove from the plastic and cut the log into 5 mm (1/4 inch) slices, reshaping into rounds if necessary. Place the rounds on a baking tray covered with baking paper, allowing a little room for spreading. Sprinkle with the remaining Parmesan and bake for about 15 minutes, or until golden. Cool on the trays. Store in an airtight container.

NOTE: These simple cheese biscuits are great for handing round with drinks at gatherings. They can be made ahead to the log stage and the log can be wrapped and kept in the refrigerator for up to 1 month, or in the freezer for up to 3 months. Having them stored away can be very handy when people arrive unexpectedly. Simply cut off as many slices from the roll as required and place on baking trays covered with baking paper, allowing room for spreading. Sprinkle with the grated Parmesan and bake as in the recipe.

# BLUE CHEESE AND PORT PATE

**Preparation time:** 10 minutes
  + 3–4 hours refrigeration
**Total cooking time:** Nil
**Serves** 8

350 g (11 oz) cream cheese, at room
  temperature
60 g (2 oz) unsalted butter, softened
1/3 cup (80 ml/23/4 fl oz) port
300 g (10 oz) blue cheese, at room
  temperature, mashed
1 tablespoon chopped fresh chives
1/2 cup (50 g/13/4 oz) walnut halves

1 Beat the cream cheese and butter in a small bowl with electric beaters until smooth, then stir in the port. Add the blue cheese and chives and stir until just combined. Season, to taste. Spoon into a serving dish and smooth the surface. Cover with plastic wrap and refrigerate for 3–4 hours, or until firm.

2 Arrange the walnuts over the top and press in lightly. Serve at room temperature. Delicious with crusty bread, crackers, celery sticks or wedges of firm fruit such as apple and pear.

**PATE**
Although traditional pâtés consist of a cooked, seasoned smooth meat paste made into a mould and served cold, vegetarian pastes with a similar texture are a popular party piece, especially with guests who prefer not to eat meat. They have the added advantage of being simple and quick to make.

*LEFT: Blue cheese and port pâté*

## HERB CHEESE LOG

Spread the cream cheese evenly with a palette knife, then sprinkle the herbs over the top.

Lift the foil from the tin, place on a work surface and roll into a log, starting from the longest edge.

# HERB CHEESE LOG

**Preparation time:** 25 minutes
+ 3 hours refrigeration
**Total cooking time:** Nil
Serves 12

★ ★

500 g (1 lb) cream cheese, at room
  temperature
1 tablespoon lemon juice
1 clove garlic, crushed
2 teaspoons chopped fresh thyme
2 teaspoons chopped fresh tarragon
1 tablespoon chopped fresh flat-leaf parsley
1 cup (50 g/1¾ oz) snipped fresh chives

1 Beat the cream cheese in a large bowl with electric beaters until soft and creamy. Mix in the lemon juice and garlic. In a separate bowl, combine the thyme, tarragon and parsley.
2 Line a 20 x 30 cm (8 x 12 inch) shallow tin with foil. Spread the chives over the base, then dollop the cream cheese over the chives. Using a palette knife, gently join the dollops, spreading the mixture and pushing it into any gaps. Sprinkle the herbs over the cheese. Lift the foil from the tin and place on a work surface. Roll into a log, starting from the longest edge, then cover and place on a baking tray.
3 Refrigerate for at least 3 hours, or preferably overnight. Serve with crackers or crusty bread.

## CHRISTMAS CHEESE SNACKS

**Preparation time:** 25 minutes + refrigeration
**Total cooking time:** 8 minutes
Makes about 30

★

1 cup (125 g/4 oz) plain flour
pinch of cayenne pepper
pinch of powdered mustard
80 g (2¾ oz) butter, chopped
125 g (4 oz) Cheddar, finely grated
1 egg yolk
1–2 teaspoons lemon juice
paprika, for dusting

*RIGHT: Herb cheese log*

1 Preheat the oven to hot 210°C (415°F/Gas 6–7). Lightly grease two baking trays.
2 Sift the flour, cayenne pepper and mustard into a large bowl. Rub in the butter with your fingertips until the mixture resembles fine breadcrumbs. Stir in the cheese. Make a well in the centre, add the egg yolk and lemon juice and mix with a flat-bladed knife, using a cutting action, until the mixture comes together in beads. Alternatively, this can be done in a food processor. Gently gather the dough together and lift out onto a lightly floured work surface. Gather into a ball, wrap in plastic wrap and refrigerate for 20 minutes.
3 Roll out the pastry on a lightly floured surface to about 5 mm (¼ inch) thick. Cut out biscuits with a floured Christmas-tree cutter. Gather the leftover dough together and re-roll. Place on the trays and bake for 6–8 minutes, or until golden brown. Lightly dust with paprika.

## SPICY NUTS

**Preparation time:** 10 minutes + cooling
**Total cooking time:** 20 minutes
**Serves** 6

2 tablespoons olive oil
½ teaspoon ground cumin
½ teaspoon ground coriander
½ teaspoon garlic powder
¼ teaspoon chilli powder
¼ teaspoon ground ginger
¼ teaspoon ground cinnamon
⅔ cup (65 g/2¼ oz) pecans
⅔ cup (100 g/3½ oz) raw cashews
1½ cups (240 g/7½ oz) raw almonds

1 Preheat the oven to slow 150°C (300°F/Gas 2). Heat the oil over low heat in a pan and stir in the spices for 2 minutes, or until fragrant. Remove from the heat, add the nuts and stir with a wooden spoon until the nuts are well coated. Spread over a baking tray and bake for 15 minutes, or until golden. Sprinkle with salt and cool.

## CHRISTMAS CAROLS

It has long been customary for people on Christmas Eve to gather around a Christmas tree and sing joyous songs with religious or festive themes, or serenade in the local neighbourhood. Lighter than hymns, most carols belong in the category of folk songs. Carols may have been sung as early as the thirteenth century when St Francis of Assisi arranged a manger scene in Italy and visitors to the scene sang carols that told the Nativity story. In England, in the fifteenth century, people sang carols to raise money for the needy. Eventually, carollers sang in the streets simply for entertainment.

*ABOVE: Spicy nuts*

# DEVILS AND ANGELS ON HORSEBACK

**Preparation time:** 10 minutes
 + 30 minutes soaking
**Total cooking time:** 6 minutes
**Makes** 24

4–6 bacon rashers
12 pitted prunes
12 oysters, fresh or bottled
2 tablespoons Worcestershire sauce
Tabasco sauce, to taste

1 Soak 24 toothpicks in cold water for
30 minutes to prevent them burning. Cut
each bacon rasher into thin strips.
2 Wrap a piece of bacon around each prune and
secure with a skewer.
3 Remove the oysters from their shells, or drain
from the bottling liquid. Sprinkle lightly with
Worcestershire sauce and ground black pepper,
to taste. Wrap each oyster in bacon, securing
with a toothpick. Preheat a lightly greased grill
or barbecue flatplate. Cook the savouries,
turning occasionally, until the bacon is crisp.
Serve sprinkled with a dash of Tabasco sauce.

# STEAMED PRAWN NORI ROLLS

**Preparation time:** 30 minutes
 + 1 hour refrigeration
**Total cooking time:** 5 minutes
**Makes** 24

500 g (1 lb) peeled raw prawns
1½ tablespoons fish sauce
1 tablespoon sake (rice wine)
2 tablespoons chopped fresh coriander
1 large kaffir lime leaf, shredded
1 tablespoon lime juice
2 teaspoons sweet chilli sauce
1 egg white, lightly beaten
5 sheets nori (dried seaweed)

**Dipping sauce**

⅓ cup (80 ml/2¾ fl oz) sweet chilli sauce
1 tablespoon lime juice

1 Put the prawns, fish sauce, sake, coriander,
kaffir lime leaf, lime juice and sweet chilli sauce
into a food processor or blender and process
until smooth. Add the egg white and pulse for
a few seconds, or until just combined.
2 Lay the nori sheets on a work surface and
spread prawn mixture over each, leaving a
2 cm (¾ inch) border at one end. Roll up
tightly, cover and refrigerate for 1 hour. Trim
the ends and with a very sharp knife cut into
2 cm (¾ inch) lengths.
3 Place the nori rolls in a paper-lined bamboo
steamer, cover the steamer and place over a wok
of simmering water. Steam for 5 minutes. Serve
with the dipping sauce.
4 Make the dipping sauce by combining the
sweet chilli sauce and lime juice in a bowl.

# MINI EGGS FLORENTINE

**Preparation time:** 20 minutes
**Total cooking time:** 25 minutes
**Makes** 24

8 slices white bread
1–2 tablespoons olive oil
12 quail eggs
2 teaspoons lemon juice
85 g (3 oz) butter, melted, cooled
2 teaspoons finely chopped fresh basil
20 g (¾ oz) butter, extra
50 g (1¾ oz) baby English spinach leaves

1 Preheat the oven to moderate 180°C (350°F/
Gas 4). Cut 24 rounds from the bread with a
4 cm (1½ inch) cutter. Brush both sides of the
rounds with the oil and bake for 10–15 minutes,
or until golden brown.
2 Add the quail eggs to a small pan of cold
water, bring to the boil, stirring gently (to
centre the yolk) and simmer for 4 minutes.
Drain, then soak in cold water until cool.
Peel, then cut in half, remove the yolks
and reserve the whites.
3 Process the quail egg yolks and lemon juice
together in a food processor for 10 seconds.
With the motor running, add the cooled melted
butter in a thin stream. Add the chopped basil
and process until combined.
4 Melt the extra butter in a pan, add the spinach
leaves and toss until just wilted. Place a little on
each bread round, top each with half a quail egg
white and fill the cavity with basil mixture.

**DEVILS OR ANGELS?**
There are two versions of
this popular party piece.
They consist of either a
prune (devil) or an oyster
(angel) wrapped in bacon
before being cooked.
However, in some parts of
the world both versions
are *angels* and are turned
into *devils* when enlivened
by the addition of a hot
sauce such as Tabasco. Just
to add to the confusion,
some people use scallops
instead of oysters, while
others cook the prunes in
wine and stuff them with
chicken livers, mango
chutney or an almond.

*OPPOSITE PAGE,
CLOCKWISE FROM
TOP LEFT: Devils and
angels on horseback;
Steamed prawn nori rolls;
Mini eggs florentine*

# PRAWN TOASTS

**Preparation time:** 50 minutes
**Total cooking time:** 8 minutes
Makes 25

★ ★ ★

**Mayonnaise**

$^1/_2$ cup (125 g/4 oz) whole-egg mayonnaise
1 teaspoon wasabi paste
2 teaspoons Japanese soy sauce

25 small raw prawns
1 loaf stale unsliced white bread
3 sheets nori (dried seaweed)
$^1/_2$ cup (80 g/2$^3/_4$ oz) sesame seeds
3 eggs, lightly beaten
oil, for deep-frying

**1** Mix the mayonnaise, wasabi paste and soy in a small bowl, then cover and refrigerate until ready to use.
**2** Peel the prawns leaving the tails intact. Gently pull out the dark vein from each prawn back starting at the head end.
**3** Cut the crust off the bread and cut the bread into twenty-five 3 cm (1$^1/_4$ inch) cubes. With a sharp knife, make an incision in the top of the bread three-quarters of the way through. Gently ease a prawn into the cut in each bread cube, leaving the tail sticking out. Cut 25 strips from the nori measuring 1 cm ($^1/_2$ inch) x 15 cm (6 inch). Wrap a strip around the outside of each bread cube and secure with a toothpick.
**4** Measure the sesame seeds into a bowl. Put the eggs in a small bowl and dip the bread in, draining off the excess. Coat the bread in the sesame seeds.
**5** Fill a wok or a deep heavy-based saucepan one third full of oil and heat until a cube of bread browns in 15 seconds. Cook the prepared cubes in batches for 1–2 minutes, or until the bread is golden and the prawns cooked through. Drain on crumpled paper towels, remove the toothpicks and season with salt. Serve topped with a teaspoon of the mayonnaise.
**NOTE:** Cook this recipe close to serving time to ensure the bread cubes stay crisp. The wasabi mayonnaise can be made several hours ahead, then covered and refrigerated until you are ready to use it.

# PUFF PASTRY TWISTS

**Preparation time:** 10 minutes
**Total cooking time:** 10 minutes per batch
Makes 96

★

2 sheets ready-rolled puff pastry, thawed
1 egg, lightly beaten
$^1/_2$ cup (80 g/2$^3/_4$ oz) sesame seeds, poppy seeds or caraway seeds

**1** Preheat the oven to moderately hot 200°C (400°F/Gas 6). Lightly grease two baking trays. Brush the pastry with the egg and sprinkle with the sesame seeds.
**2** Cut in half crossways and then into 1 cm ($^1/_2$ inch) wide strips. Twist the strips and place on greased baking trays. Bake for about 10 minutes, or until golden brown. Store in an airtight container for up to 1 week. Refresh in a moderate 180°C (350°F/Gas 4) oven for 2–3 minutes, then cool.

*ABOVE: Prawn toasts*

## LEMON PRAWN PATE

**Preparation time:** 20 minutes
+ 1 hour refrigeration
**Total cooking time:** 5 minutes
Serves 8

750 g (1 1/2 lb) raw prawns

100 g (3 1/2 oz) butter

3 cloves garlic, crushed

1 teaspoon grated lemon rind

3 tablespoons lemon juice

1/4 teaspoon freshly grated nutmeg

2 tablespoons whole-egg mayonnaise

2 tablespoons finely chopped
   fresh chives

bread or crackers, for serving

**1** Peel the prawns and gently pull out the dark vein from each prawn back, starting at the head end.

**2** Melt the butter in a frying pan. When it sizzles, add the garlic and prawns and stir for 3–4 minutes, or until the prawns are pink and cooked through. Allow to cool.

**3** Transfer to a food processor, add the lemon rind, lemon juice and nutmeg and process for 20 seconds, or until roughly puréed. Season, to taste, add the mayonnaise and chives, then process for 20 seconds, or until combined. Spoon into a dish and chill for at least 1 hour, or until firm.

**4** Remove from the refrigerator about 15 minutes before serving to soften the pâté slightly. Serve with slices of crusty bread or some cracker biscuits.

**NOTE:** This recipe can also be made successfully using yabbies, scampi or lobster meat instead of the prawns.

*ABOVE: Lemon
prawn pâté*

# COCKTAILS
This is a selection of simple cocktail drinks with quantities suitable for one person. Use glassware appropriate for the style of drink and remember to have plenty of ice in the freezer.

### CRANBERRY AND VODKA SPARKLE
Combine 1/2 cup (125 ml/4 fl oz) each of chilled cranberry juice and lemonade or mineral water in a jug with 2 teaspoons lime juice, 30 ml (1 fl oz) vodka and a few ice cubes. Mix well, pour into a tall glass and serve immediately.

### BLOODY MARY
Half fill a tall glass with crushed ice. Pour in 1/4 cup (60 ml/2 fl oz) vodka, then top up with tomato juice and stir. Stir in a dash of Tabasco sauce, Worcestershire sauce, lemon juice and a little salt and pepper. Traditionally, this drink is served with a celery stick, including leaves, as an edible swizzle stick. For Virgin Mary, a non-alcoholic version, delete the vodka.

### BUCK'S FIZZ
Pour 1/2 cup (125 ml/4 fl oz) fresh orange juice and a dash of Grenadine into a champagne flute. Top slowly with chilled good-quality sparkling white wine.

## SPARKLING WINE AND BRANDY COCKTAIL

Place 1–2 sugar cubes in a champagne flute. Add a dash of Angostura bitters over the sugar, then pour in 15 ml (¹/₂ fl oz) brandy. Slowly top up the glass with chilled good-quality sparkling white wine.

## PINA COLADA

Combine about 6 ice cubes in a drink shaker or jug with 45 ml (1¹/₂ fl oz) white rum, 30 ml (1 fl oz) coconut cream, 15 ml (¹/₂ fl oz) cream and about ¹/₂ cup (125 ml/4 fl oz) pineapple juice and mix well (or blend in a blender). Pour into a tall glass. You can garnish the glass with pineapple leaves and a maraschino cherry. Serve immediately.

## BRANDY ALEXANDER

Combine 6 ice cubes in a drink shaker or jug with 30 ml (1 fl oz) each of brandy and crème de cacao and ¹/₄ cup (60 ml/ 2 fl oz) cream. Shake or stir well, then strain into a champagne saucer and serve sprinkled lightly with some grated fresh nutmeg.

## MANGO DAIQUIRI

Combine about 6 ice cubes in a blender with 45 ml (1¹/₂ fl oz) white rum, 15 ml (¹/₂ fl oz) mango liqueur and 30 ml (1 fl oz) each of lemon juice and either Cointreau or Grand Marnier. Add the roughly chopped pulp of 1 mango, or a 400 g (13 oz) can mango slices, drained, and blend until smooth. Pour into a goblet-shaped glass.

## STRAWBERRY MARGARITA

Frost the rim of a martini glass by lightly beating an egg white until just frothy, then dipping the rim of the martini glass into the egg, then in salt. Place about 6 ice cubes in a blender with 30 ml (1 fl oz) each of tequila, strawberry liqueur, lime juice cordial and lemon juice and 15 ml (¹/₂ fl oz) Cointreau. Blend well, then pour into the martini glass, taking care to avoid touching the rim of the glass.

*FROM LEFT: Cranberry and vodka sparkle; Bloody Mary; Buck's fizz; Sparkling wine and brandy cocktail; Pina colada; Brandy Alexander; Mango daiquiri; Strawberry Margarita*

# PARTY PUNCHES

Here you will find a refreshing idea for a delicious punch whether you want one with or without alcohol. They will delight your guests and add colour to the table.

### PINEAPPLE AND PAWPAW JUICE

Roughly chop the flesh from a 2 kg (4 lb) pineapple. Juice the flesh in a juicer, then pour into a punch bowl. Blend a 1.2 kg (2 lb 6½ oz) peeled pawpaw in a blender until smooth. Add 2 cups (500 ml/16 fl oz) chilled ginger ale. Serve immediately in tall chilled

glasses. Garnish the glasses with pineapple slices and fronds. Serves 8.

### BERRY AND CHERRY PUNCH

Peel the skin from a lemon with a vegetable peeler, avoiding the bitter white pith. Cut into long thin strips. Drain a 425 g (14 oz) can pitted black cherries and place in a large jug. Add

125 g (4 oz) halved strawberries, 600 g (1¼ lb) assorted fresh or frozen berries, 2 cups (500 ml/16 fl oz) lemonade, 3 cups (750 ml/24 fl oz) ginger ale, 1 cup (250 ml/8 fl oz) cold black tea, 10 torn mint leaves and the lemon rind. Cover and chill for at least 3 hours. Add ice cubes when serving. Can be garnished with berries on a toothpick. Serves 10.

## SANGRIA

Mix 2 tablespoons caster sugar with 1 tablespoon each of lemon and orange juice in a large jug until the sugar has dissolved. Thinly slice an unpeeled orange, a lemon and a lime, discard any pips, and add to the jug with a 750 ml (24 fl oz) bottle of chilled red wine and plenty of ice. Stir well until very cold. Serve in large wine glasses. (Do not strain.) This traditional Spanish drink can be made in large quantities, and its flavour will improve over several hours—it can be made up to a day in advance. Chopped seasonal fruits, such as peaches, pears and pineapples, can be added to this basic recipe. Good-quality wine is not essential in Sangria, so use a table wine or even a cask wine. Serves 6.

## BRANDY ALEXANDER PUNCH

Pour 3 cups (750 ml/24 fl oz) brandy, 1½ cups (375 ml/12 fl oz) crème de cacao and six 300 ml (10 fl oz) cartons of cream into a large bowl. Whisk to just combine. Add ice cubes to a 3.5 litre (104 fl oz) punch bowl and pour in the brandy mixture. Sprinkle with grated nutmeg, then serve in cocktail glasses garnished with strawberry halves. Serves 16.

## PINEAPPLE DELIGHT

Roughly chop the flesh from a 1.5 kg (3 lb) pineapple, then blend in a blender until as smooth as possible. Pour 4 cups (1 litre/32 fl oz) lemonade into a jug and gently stir in the pineapple. Add ⅓ cup (80 ml/2¾ fl oz) lime juice and mix well. Pour into serving glasses and garnish with mint leaves. Serves 8.

## SPARKLING PUNCH

Pour 1 cup (250 ml/8 fl oz) chilled pineapple juice and 2 cups (500 ml/ 16 fl oz) each of chilled orange juice, apple cider and ginger ale into a large jug. Stir them all together, then stir in the flesh from 2 passionfruit. Garnish with halved orange and lemon slices. Ice cubes can be added to the jug or to each individual glass. Serves 6.

*FROM LEFT: Pineapple and pawpaw juice; Berry and cherry punch; Brandy Alexander punch; Sangria; Pineapple delight; Sparkling punch*

## CHRISTMAS TINSEL

Decorating the Christmas tree with shimmering tinsel to brighten it and create a magical quality is an old tradition. According to one legend, an old woman couldn't afford to decorate her tree. During the night, spiders lodged in the tree and covered it with webs. The Christ Child saw the webs, realised the woman would be sad and turned the spider webs into silver. The next morning the family was dazzled by the brilliant 'tinsel' that shone on the tree.

*ABOVE: Spinach dip*

## SPINACH DIP

**Preparation time:** 10 minutes
  + 3 hours refrigeration
**Total cooking time:** Nil
**Serves** 6–8

250 g (8 oz) frozen chopped spinach
300 g (10 oz) ricotta
3/4 cup (185 g/6 oz) sour cream
30 g (1 oz) packet spring vegetable soup mix
4 spring onions, finely chopped

**1** Thaw the spinach and squeeze out as much liquid as possible with your hands.
**2** Process the spinach, ricotta, sour cream, soup mix and spring onions in a food processor or blender until smooth. Cover and refrigerate for 2–3 hours. Serve with crisp lavash bread, biscuits or assorted crisp vegetables such as blanched snow peas (mangetout), cauliflower and carrots.
**NOTE:** Can be made a week in advance.

## PRAWN AND CHILLI PATE

**Preparation time:** 30 minutes
  + 1 hour refrigeration
**Total cooking time:** 10 minutes
**Serves** 6–8

750 g (1 1/2 lb) raw medium prawns
100 g (3 1/2 oz) butter
2 cloves garlic, crushed
1 small green chilli, seeded and chopped
1 teaspoon finely grated lime rind
1 tablespoon lime juice
2 tablespoons whole-egg mayonnaise
2 tablespoons chopped fresh coriander
Tabasco sauce, to taste, optional

**1** Peel the prawns and gently pull out the dark vein from each prawn back, starting at the head end. Melt the butter in a large frying pan and add the garlic, chilli and prawns. Cook over medium heat for 10 minutes, or until tender.

Put the smoked trout on a work surface and carefully peel away the skin.

Lift the flesh away from the bones, keeping the trout as intact as possible. Remove any stray bones.

**2** Transfer the prawns to a food processor, add the lime rind and juice and process until the prawns are roughly chopped. Add the mayonnaise and coriander and stir through. Season with Tabasco sauce and salt and pepper, to taste. Spoon into a serving dish.

**3** Chill for at least 1 hour or until firm. Return to room temperature half an hour before serving. Serve with grissini, plain biscuits or sweet chilli chips (see below).

**NOTE:** Can be made a couple of days ahead.

## SWEET CHILLI CHIPS

Preheat the oven to moderate 180°C (350°F/Gas 4). Cut 4 Lebanese pitta breads in half, then into small triangles. Line three baking trays with baking paper, arrange the pitta triangles on the trays and brush each side generously with sweet chilli sauce (you will need about 1 cup/250 ml/8 fl oz altogether). Bake, turning over once, for 5–10 minutes, or until the chips are golden brown. Makes about 64 triangles.

## SMOKED TROUT DIP

**Preparation time:** 25 minutes
**Total cooking time:** Nil
**Serves** 4–6

250 g (8 oz) smoked rainbow trout
1 1/2 teaspoons olive oil
1/2 cup (125 ml/4 fl oz) cream
1 tablespoon lemon juice
pinch of cayenne pepper

**1** Remove the skin and bones from the smoked trout. Put the flesh in a food processor or blender with the olive oil, 2 teaspoons of the cream and the lemon juice. Blend to a thick paste, then slowly add the remaining cream until well mixed. Season, to taste, with salt and the cayenne pepper. Serve with grissini or water crackers and baby radishes or other vegetables, for dipping.

**NOTE:** This dip can be made a few days ahead and kept, covered, in the refrigerator.

*ABOVE: Smoked trout dip*

# MUSHROOMS WITH TWO SAUCES

**Preparation time:** 30 minutes
+ 1 hour refrigeration
**Total cooking time:** 2 minutes per batch
Serves 8

 ✷ ✷

750 g (1¹/₂ lb) button mushrooms
¹/₃ cup (40 g/1¹/₄ oz) plain flour
1 cup (100 g/3¹/₂ oz) dry breadcrumbs
3 eggs
olive oil, for deep-frying

**Sauces**

1 small red pepper (capsicum)
2 egg yolks
1 teaspoon Dijon mustard
1 tablespoon lemon juice
1 cup (250 ml/8 fl oz) olive oil
1 small clove garlic, crushed
2 tablespoons natural yoghurt
2 teaspoons finely chopped fresh parsley

1 Wipe the mushrooms with paper towel and remove the stems. Measure the flour into a large plastic bag and the breadcrumbs into a separate bag. Lightly beat the eggs in a bowl.
2 Put the mushrooms in with the flour and shake until evenly coated. Shake off any excess flour, then dip half the mushrooms in egg to coat well. Transfer to the bag with the breadcrumbs and shake to cover thoroughly. Place on a tray covered with baking paper. Repeat with the rest of the mushrooms, then refrigerate them all for 1 hour.
3 Cut the red pepper into large flattish pieces, discarding the membranes and seeds. Cook, skin-side-up, under a hot grill until the skin blackens and blisters. Cool in a plastic bag, then peel. Process in a food processor or blender to a smooth paste.
4 Place the egg yolks, mustard and half the lemon juice in a bowl. Beat together for 1 minute with electric beaters. Add the oil, a teaspoon at a time, beating constantly until thick and creamy. Continue beating until all the oil is added, then add the remaining lemon juice. (If you prefer, you can make the mayonnaise in a blender.) Divide the mayonnaise between two bowls. Into one, stir the garlic, yoghurt and parsley and into the other, the red pepper mixture.

5 Fill a heavy-based saucepan one third full of oil and heat the oil to 180°C (350°F), or until a cube of bread dropped into the oil browns in 15 seconds. Gently lower batches of the mushrooms into the oil and cook for 1–2 minutes, or until golden brown. Remove with a slotted spoon and drain on paper towels.
6 To serve, arrange the mushrooms on serving plates and spoon a little of each sauce into each mushroom. If you prefer, you can keep the sauces separate, filling each mushroom with either one or the other.
NOTE: Cook the mushrooms just before serving. The sauces can be made up to 1 day ahead and refrigerated, covered.

# NOODLE NESTS WITH SMOKED SALMON TARTARE

**Preparation time:** 25 minutes
**Total cooking time:** 20 minutes
Makes 30

 ✷

200 g (6¹/₂ oz) fresh flat egg noodles
olive oil, for brushing
200 g (6¹/₂ oz) smoked salmon, diced
1 tablespoon extra virgin olive oil
3 teaspoons white wine vinegar
¹/₂ cup (125 g/4 oz) whole-egg mayonnaise
1 clove garlic, crushed
1 tablespoon finely chopped fresh dill

1 Preheat the oven to moderately hot 200°C (400°F/Gas 6). Lightly grease three 12-hole mini-muffin tins. (You can use two 12-hole mini-muffin tins and cook the remaining 6 after the first batch is finished.) Use scissors or a sharp knife to cut the noodles into 10 cm (4 inch) lengths. Put the egg noodles in a heatproof bowl and pour boiling water over to cover. Soak for 5 minutes, then drain and pat dry with paper towels. Divide the noodles among 30 holes of the mini-muffin tins, pressing down to form 'nests'. Brush lightly with olive oil and bake for 15 minutes.
2 Turn the noodles out onto a wire rack, then put the rack in the oven for 5 minutes, or until the noodles are crisp.
3 Stir together the salmon, extra virgin olive oil, vinegar, mayonnaise, garlic and fresh dill in a bowl. Spoon 1 heaped teaspoon into each noodle nest and garnish with fresh dill.

**DILL**
Fresh dill is best added to a cooked dish just before serving because much of the flavour is lost if dill is heated. The soft, feathery leaves have a subtle taste and aroma particularly suited to using with fish dishes. Dill has been used since ancient times for its flavour and also for its medicinal properties.

*OPPOSITE PAGE:*
*Mushrooms with two sauces (top); Noodle nests with smoked salmon tartare*

33

12 slices crusty Italian bread
2 cloves garlic, halved
1/3 cup (80 ml/2³/4 fl oz) extra virgin olive oil
1 tablespoon chopped fresh flat-leaf parsley

**1** For the pepper topping, cut all the peppers into large flattish pieces and cook, skin-side-up, under a hot grill until the skin blackens and blisters. Place in a plastic bag until cool, then peel. Slice the flesh into strips.
**2** For the tomato and basil topping, finely chop the tomatoes and combine in a bowl with the basil and olive oil. Season with black pepper.
**3** Toast the bread and, while still hot, rub with the cut side of a garlic clove. Drizzle olive oil over each slice and sprinkle with salt and plenty of freshly ground black pepper.
**4** Arrange the pepper topping on half the bread slices, then sprinkle with parsley. Arrange the tomato and basil topping on the remaining bread slices. Serve immediately.
**NOTE:** To speed up the preparation for this recipe, buy marinated roasted peppers (capsicums), available at delicatessens and some supermarkets.

## GRISSINI WRAPPED IN SMOKED SALMON

**Preparation time:** 20 minutes
**Total cooking time:** Nil
**Makes** 24

125 g (4 oz) cream cheese, at room
    temperature
1–2 tablespoons chopped fresh dill
1/4 teaspoon finely grated lemon rind
24 ready-made grissini
8–10 slices smoked salmon, cut into
    thin strips

**1** Mix the cream cheese, fresh dill and lemon rind in a bowl until the dill is well distributed. Season, to taste, with salt. Spread some of the cream cheese mixture onto three-quarters of each length of grissini. Wrap the salmon around the stick, over the cheese, securing it with more cheese. Repeat with the remaining grissini.
**NOTE:** Prepare these grissini close to serving (up to about 30 minutes before) as the biscuits will start to soften once the cheese is spread on them.

## BRUSCHETTA WITH MEDITERRANEAN TOPPINGS

**Preparation time:** 20 minutes
**Total cooking time:** 15 minutes
**Makes** 12

**Pepper (capsicum) topping**
1 yellow pepper (capsicum)
1 red pepper (capsicum)
1 green pepper (capsicum)

**Tomato and basil topping**
2 ripe tomatoes
3 tablespoons shredded fresh basil
1 tablespoon extra virgin olive oil

*ABOVE: Bruschetta with Mediterranean toppings*

# TOMATO AND BASIL CROUSTADES

Preparation time: 30 minutes
Total cooking time: 20 minutes
Serves 4

1 day-old unsliced white bread loaf
3 tablespoons olive oil
2 cloves garlic, crushed
3 tomatoes, diced
250 g (8 oz) bocconcini, cut into small chunks
1 tablespoon tiny capers, rinsed and dried
1 tablespoon extra virgin olive oil
2 teaspoons balsamic vinegar
4 tablespoons shredded fresh basil

1 Preheat the oven to moderate 180°C (350°F/Gas 4). Remove the crusts from the bread and cut the loaf into 4 even pieces. Using a small serrated knife, cut a square from the centre of each cube of bread, leaving a border of about 1.5 cm (⅝ inch) on each side. You should be left with 4 'boxes'. Combine the oil and garlic and brush all over the croustades. Place them on a baking tray and bake for about 20 minutes, or until golden and crisp. Check them occasionally to make sure they don't burn.

2 Meanwhile, combine the tomato and bocconcini with the tiny capers in a bowl. In a jug, stir together the oil and balsamic vinegar, then gently toss with the tomato mixture. Season with salt and freshly ground black pepper, then stir in the basil. Spoon into the croustades, allowing any excess to tumble over the sides.

NOTE: This recipe is a delicious first course for serving in summer. Choose very ripe tomatoes for maximum flavour. You can substitute diced feta for the bocconcini.

### CANDY CANES
Candy canes are often seen adorning Christmas trees. This tradition is believed to have begun after a clever choirmaster in Cologne came up with an idea to quieten restless children during mass. He devised a miniature shepherd's crook by putting a hook on one end of a straight white candy stick. Soon after, the canes were found hooked over the branches of Christmas trees and eventually stripes were added.

*LEFT: Tomato and basil croustades*

1 Preheat the oven to hot 210°C (415°F/ Gas 6–7). Line two large baking trays with baking paper. Mix the cream cheese, mustards, lemon juice and dill in a bowl, then cover and refrigerate.

2 Cut four 9.5 cm (3¾ inch) rounds from each sheet of puff pastry, using a fluted cutter, and place on the baking trays. Prick the pastries all over. Cover and refrigerate for 10 minutes.

3 Bake the pastries in batches for 7 minutes, then remove from the oven and use a spoon to flatten the centre of each pastry. Return to the oven and bake for another 5 minutes, or until the pastry is golden. Cool, then spread some of the cream cheese mixture over each pastry, leaving a 1 cm (½ inch) border. Arrange the salmon over the top. Decorate with a few capers and a sprig of fresh dill. Serve immediately.

## TURKEY MEATBALLS WITH MINT YOGHURT

**Preparation time:** 15 minutes
**Total cooking time:** 10 minutes
**Makes** 30

600 g (1¼ lb) turkey mince
2 cloves garlic, crushed
2 tablespoons finely chopped fresh mint
2 teaspoons finely chopped fresh rosemary
2 tablespoons mango-lime chutney
2 tablespoons oil

**Mint yoghurt**

200 g (6½ oz) natural yoghurt
2 tablespoons finely chopped fresh mint
2 teaspoons mango and lime chutney

1 Mix the mince, garlic, mint, rosemary and chutney in a bowl. With wet hands, roll tablespoons of the mixture into balls. Heat half the oil in a large frying pan over medium heat and cook the balls, turning often, for 5 minutes or until cooked through. Drain on crumpled paper towels. Repeat with the remaining oil and meatballs.

2 Put the mint yoghurt ingredients together in a small bowl and stir until well combined. Serve with the turkey balls.

NOTE: You may need to order the turkey mince from a poultry specialist or you can use chicken mince instead.

## SMOKED SALMON TARTLETS

**Preparation time:** 30 minutes
   + 10 minutes refrigeration
**Total cooking time:** 30 minutes
**Makes** 24

250 g (8 oz) cream cheese, at room temperature
1½ tablespoons wholegrain mustard
2 teaspoons Dijon mustard
2 tablespoons lemon juice
2 tablespoons chopped fresh dill
6 sheets ready-rolled puff pastry
300 g (10 oz) smoked salmon, cut into
   thin strips
2 tablespoons bottled tiny capers, drained
fresh dill sprigs, to garnish

*ABOVE: Smoked salmon tartlets*

# BLACK SESAME SEED TARTS WITH MARINATED FETA

**Preparation time:** 25 minutes
  + 10 minutes refrigeration
**Total cooking time:** 20 minutes
**Makes** 30

300 g (10 oz) tomatoes
200 g (6¹/₂ oz) feta, diced
¹/₂ cup (75 g/2¹/₂ oz) black olives, pitted
  and diced
1 teaspoon finely chopped
  fresh thyme
2 cloves garlic, crushed
1 tablespoon extra virgin olive oil
2 cups (250 g/8 oz) plain flour
125 g (4 oz) butter, chopped
60 g (2 oz) Parmesan, finely grated
1 tablespoon black sesame seeds
1 egg
fresh thyme, optional, to garnish

1 Preheat the oven to moderately hot 200°C (400°F/Gas 6). Lightly grease two 12-hole mini-muffin tins. Score a cross in the base of each tomato, place in a heatproof bowl and cover with boiling water. Leave for 30 seconds, then plunge in cold water. Peel away from the cross. Cut in half and scoop out the seeds with a teaspoon. Dice the flesh and combine in a bowl with the feta, black olives, thyme, garlic and oil. Set aside.

2 Sift the flour into a large bowl and add the butter. Rub together with your fingertips until the mixture resembles fine breadcrumbs. Stir in the Parmesan and black sesame seeds. Make a well, add the egg and mix with a flat-bladed knife, using a cutting action until the mixture comes together in beads (add a little cold water if too dry). On a lightly floured surface, press together into a ball, then wrap in plastic wrap and refrigerate for 10 minutes. Roll out to 2 mm (¹/₈ inch) thick between two sheets of baking paper. Remove the paper and cut out 30 rounds with a 6 cm (2¹/₂ inch) cutter. Gently press into the tins and bake for 10 minutes, or until dry and golden. Repeat with the remaining pastry rounds. Cool and place 1 heaped teaspoon feta filling into each pastry shell. Garnish and serve.

*ABOVE: Black sesame seed tarts with marinated feta*

**CORIANDER**
All parts of this plant, the leaves, stems, roots and dried seeds (whole or ground) can be used in cookery. The leaves are usually added at the end of cooking, either as a flavouring or a garnish. The stems are added if a strong flavour is required and the roots are chopped and used in curry pastes. Coriander is used quite extensively in Middle Eastern, Asian, South American, Mediterranean, Mexican and Chinese cookery. The herb is also known as cilantro.

## THAI CHICKEN BALLS

**Preparation time:** 20 minutes
**Total cooking time:** 40 minutes
**Makes** about 50 balls

 ✷ ✷

1 kg (2 lb) chicken mince
1 cup (80 g/2¾ oz) fresh breadcrumbs
4 spring onions, sliced
1 tablespoon ground coriander
1 cup (50 g/1¾ oz) chopped fresh coriander
¼ cup (60 ml/2 fl oz) sweet chilli sauce
1–2 tablespoons lemon juice
oil, for shallow-frying

1 Mix the mince and breadcrumbs in a large bowl. Add the spring onion, ground and fresh coriander, chilli sauce and lemon juice, to taste, and mix well. With wet hands, form into evenly shaped walnut-sized balls. Preheat the oven to moderately hot 200°C (400°F/Gas 6).
2 Heat 3 cm (1¼ in) oil in a deep frying pan to 180°C (350°F), or until a cube of bread browns in 15 seconds, and shallow-fry the balls in batches over high heat until golden. Bake on a baking tray for 5 minutes, or until cooked through.

## SEAFOOD PYRAMIDS

**Preparation time:** 30 minutes
**Total cooking time:** 15 minutes
**Makes** 24

✷ ✷

200 g scallops, without roe, chopped
8 spring onions, finely chopped
⅓ cup (35 g/1¼ oz) Japanese breadcrumbs
4 tablespoons finely chopped fresh coriander
2 cloves garlic, crushed
1 kaffir lime leaf, finely chopped
½ teaspoon sesame oil
24 won ton wrappers
oil, for deep-frying

**Dipping sauce**

2 tablespoons lime juice
1 tablespoon sake
2 teaspoons soy sauce
¼ teaspoon sesame oil
1 teaspoon grated fresh ginger

1 Combine the scallops, spring onion, Japanese breadcrumbs, coriander, garlic, kaffir lime leaf

*ABOVE: Thai chicken balls*

and sesame oil. Place 2 teaspoons of the mixture in the centre of each won ton wrapper. Brush the edges with water and bring the corners up to meet, pushing the edges together to form a pyramid shape.

**2** Fill a heavy-based saucepan one third full of oil and heat the oil to 180°C (350°F), or until a cube of bread browns in 15 seconds. Deep-fry the pyramids in batches, until crisp and golden. Drain on crumpled paper towels.

**3** Stir together all the dipping sauce ingredients and serve with the pyramids.

NOTE: Japanese breadcrumbs are readily available in Asian food speciality stores. They are white, quite big and crisp.

# STEAMED PRAWN WON TONS

Preparation time: 30 minutes
Total cooking time: 15 minutes
Makes 24

³/₄ cup (15 g/¹/₂ oz) dried Chinese
    mushrooms, sliced
24 raw prawns
1 tablespoon sake
1 tablespoon grated fresh ginger
1 teaspoon sesame oil
2 teaspoons sweet chilli sauce
24 gow gee wrappers

**Dipping sauce**

¹/₄ cup (60 ml/2 fl oz) soy sauce
1 tablespoon fish sauce
1 tablespoon lime juice
¹/₄ cup (60 ml/2 fl oz) sweet
    chilli sauce

**1** Put the Chinese mushrooms in a heatproof bowl, cover with boiling water and soak for 10 minutes. Drain well and finely chop. Meanwhile, peel the prawns, leaving the tails intact. Gently pull out the dark vein from each prawn back, starting at the head end. Cut the prawns in half and set aside the ends with the tails. Finely chop the remaining prawns.

**2** Combine the mushrooms and chopped prawns with the sake, ginger, sesame oil and chilli sauce. Put a heaped teaspoon of the mixture in the centre of each gow gee wrapper. Place a reserved prawn tail in the centre of each, standing up. Brush the edges of the wrappers with water and gather up to form parcels, leaving the prawn tails exposed. Steam in batches, in a bamboo steamer for 5 minutes, or until the prawns turn pink.

**3** Stir together all the dipping sauce ingredients in a bowl and serve with the pyramids.

NOTE: As an alternative, you can make coriander dipping sauce. Combine ¹/₄ cup (60 ml/2 fl oz) fish sauce, 1 tablespoon white vinegar, 1–2 finely chopped, seeded red chillies, 1 teaspoon sugar and 3 teaspoons chopped fresh coriander in a small bowl. Add 1–2 teaspoons of lime juice, to taste, and mix well. This sauce can also be served with fresh cooked peeled prawns, or drizzled on fresh oysters.

*ABOVE: Steamed
prawn won tons*

## CHEESE FRUIT LOG

When the cream cheese is smooth, add the apricots, spring onion, sun-dried tomatoes and pepper, to taste, and fold through.

Sprinkle the nuts and parsley on a sheet of baking paper and roll the cream cheese log in the mixture.

## CHEESE FRUIT LOG

**Preparation time:** 15 minutes + refrigeration
**Total cooking time:** 5 minutes
**Serves** 6

✮ ✮

1/4 cup (35 g/1 1/4 oz) shelled pistachio nuts
250 g (4 oz) cream cheese, at room
    temperature
50 g (1 3/4 oz) dried apricots,
    finely chopped
3 spring onions, finely chopped
1/4 cup (45 g/1 1/2 oz) sun-dried tomatoes,
    drained, finely chopped
3 tablespoons finely chopped fresh
    flat-leaf parsley

**1** Preheat the oven to moderately hot 200°C (400°F/Gas 6). Bake the pistachio nuts on a lined baking tray for 5 minutes, or until golden brown. Cool, then finely chop.
**2** Beat the cream cheese in a bowl until smooth. Fold in the dried apricots, spring onion and sun-dried tomatoes, and some pepper, to taste.

**3** Sprinkle the combined pistachio nuts and parsley over a sheet of baking paper, shaping into a 20 cm x 6 cm (8 x 2 1/2 inch) rectangle. Form the mixture into a 20 cm (8 inch) log and roll in the nut mixture. Wrap in plastic wrap and refrigerate for 2–3 hours, or until firm. Serve with plain savoury biscuits.

## TARAMASALATA

**Preparation time:** 25 minutes + 5 minutes soaking
**Total cooking time:** Nil
**Serves** 6

✮

4 slices white bread, crusts removed
1/4 cup (60 ml/2 fl oz) milk
100 g (3 1/2 oz) tarama or smoked cod's roe
1 egg yolk
1 clove garlic, crushed
1 tablespoon grated onion
1/4 cup (60 ml/2 fl oz) olive oil
1/3 cup (80 ml/2 3/4 fl oz) lemon juice

*ABOVE: Cheese fruit log*

**1** Soak the bread in the milk in a bowl for 5 minutes, then squeeze out the excess liquid.
**2** Process the roe and egg yolk in a food processor for 10 seconds. Add the bread, garlic and onion and process for 20 seconds.
**3** With the motor running, add the olive oil in a thin stream. Process until thick and creamy. Stir in the lemon juice before serving.
**NOTE:** Look for tarama and smoked cod's roe at delicatessens, fishmongers or Greek food stores.

## MUSHROOM PATE

**Preparation time:** 15 minutes
  + 2 hours refrigeration
**Total cooking time:** 5 minutes
Serves 8–10

40 g (1¼ oz) butter
1 tablespoon oil
400 g (13 oz) flat mushrooms, chopped
2 cloves garlic, crushed
3 spring onions, chopped
1 tablespoon lemon juice
100 g (3½ oz) ricotta
100 g (3½ oz) cream cheese, at room
  temperature
2 tablespoons chopped fresh coriander

**1** Heat the butter and oil in a large frying pan over medium heat. Add the mushrooms and garlic. Cook for 5 minutes, or until the mushrooms have softened and the mushroom liquid has evaporated. Stir in the spring onion, then allow to cool.
**2** Process the mushrooms with the lemon juice, ricotta, cream cheese and fresh coriander until smooth. Season, to taste, then spoon into a serving dish. Cover and refrigerate for 2 hours to firm.
**NOTE:** Large flat mushrooms have more flavour than the smaller button mushrooms. Choose firm undamaged dry ones and store in a paper bag in the refrigerator. Field (or wild) mushrooms, if available, can also be used, but, depending on how dirty they are, they may need peeling or washing before use.

### CHRISTMAS CARDS

Sending greeting cards at Christmas did not become popular until the 1870s. In the eighteenth century, in some places, Valentine and New Year cards were exchanged and in Britain children made cards at school with a Christmas greeting for their parents. In the early 1840s, Sir Henry Cole, an English businessman (interested in art) is said to have come up with the idea of producing a printed Christmas greeting card. An artist did a design and Sir Henry produced one thousand cards to sell. Although the idea didn't take off straight away, later in the century advances in the printing process and cheaper postage allowed the idea to gradually spread worldwide.

*LEFT: Mushroom pâté*

# REFRESHING JUICES

A colourful addition to the drinks menu, these fruity juices will be much appreciated

by those needing a lift but not wishing to indulge in alcohol.

### FRUIT SPARKLE

Pour 2 cups (500 ml/16 fl oz) chilled apricot nectar, 2 cups (500 ml/16 fl oz) chilled soda water, 1 cup (250 ml/8 fl oz) chilled apple juice and 1 cup (250 ml/8 fl oz) chilled orange juice into a large jug and stir well. Stir in about 8 ice cubes, then pour into tall glasses and serve. Serves 4–6.

### PASSIONFRUIT LIME CRUSH

Combine 1/2 cup (125 g/4 oz) passionfruit pulp (you will need about 6 passionfruit), 3/4 cup (185 ml/6 fl oz) lime juice cordial and 3 cups (750 ml/24 fl oz) ginger ale in a large jug and mix together well. Pour into large glasses that have been half filled with crushed ice. Serve immediately. Serves 4.

### RUBY GRAPEFRUIT AND LEMON SORBET FIZZ

Pour 2 cups (500 ml/16 fl oz) chilled ruby grapefruit juice and 1 cup (250 ml/8 fl oz) chilled soda water into a jug. Stir in 1 tablespoon caster sugar, then pour into chilled glasses. Top with a scoop of lemon sorbet. Mix the sorbet in or serve with a parfait spoon. Serves 4.

## BLUEBERRY CRUSH

Blend 150 g (5 oz) blueberries in a blender with 1 tablespoon caster sugar until smooth. Mix well with 3 cups (750 ml/24 fl oz) apple and blackcurrant juice and 2 cups (500 ml/16 fl oz) soda water. Serve immediately in chilled glasses half filled with ice cubes. If you have a good blender, you may wish to add the ice cubes when blending the blueberries, to make a slushy. Serves 4–6.

## HAWAIIAN SMOOTHIE

Put 2 cups (500 ml/16 fl oz) chilled apple juice in a blender with 200 g (7 oz) peeled and seeded papaya or pawpaw, 400 g (13 oz) peeled and seeded watermelon and about 20 ice cubes. Blend until smooth. Serves 4.

## VIRGIN MARY

Stir 3 cups (750 ml/24 fl oz) tomato juice in a large jug with 1 tablespoon Worcestershire sauce, 2 tablespoons lemon juice, 1/4 teaspoon ground nutmeg and a few drops of Tabasco sauce until well mixed. Place 12 ice cubes in a blender and blend for 30 seconds, or until the ice is crushed. Spoon the crushed ice into the tomato juice mixture, then carefully pour into tall glasses. Add a celery stick to each glass—this not only adds a delicious subtle flavour to the drink but also serves as an edible swizzle stick. Decorate each glass with some very thin lemon slices. Season with salt and freshly ground black pepper, to taste, before serving. Serves 4.

## MINT JULEP

Roughly chop 2 cups (40 g/1 1/4 oz) fresh mint leaves, place in a bowl and bruise with a wooden spoon to release the oils. Transfer to a heatproof jug and add 2 tablespoons sugar, 1 tablespoon lemon juice, 2 cups (500 ml/16 fl oz) pineapple juice and 1 cup (250 ml/8 fl oz) boiling water. Mix, cover with plastic wrap and set aside for 30 minutes. Strain, then cover and refrigerate until well chilled. Mix in 2 cups (500 ml/16 fl oz) chilled ginger ale. Put ice cubes in glasses and pour in the drink. Garnish each glass with a few fresh mint leaves. Serves 4–6.

*FROM LEFT: Fruit sparkle; Passionfruit lime crush; Ruby grapefruit and lemon sorbet fizz; Blueberry crush; Hawaiian smoothie; Virgin Mary; Mint julep*

# HOT CLASSICS

Whether it's hot or cold outside, warming drinks create a comforting welcome to any gathering, whether you are celebrating Christmas or just relaxing in holiday mode.

### BUTTERED RUM

Place 1 tablespoon sugar, 1 cup (250 ml/ 8 fl oz) rum and 2 cups (500 ml/16 fl oz) boiling water in a heatproof jug. Stir to dissolve the sugar, then divide among 4 mugs. Stir 1–2 teaspoons softened unsalted butter into each mug and serve. Serves 4.

### MULLED WINE

Push 12 cloves into 2 oranges and place in a saucepan with $1/4$ cup (60 g/2 oz) sugar, 1 whole nutmeg, grated, 4 cinnamon sticks and 2 thinly sliced lemons. Pour in 2 cups (500 ml/16 fl oz) water and bring to the boil, then reduce the heat, cover the pan and simmer for

20 minutes. Allow to cool, then strain and discard the fruit and spices. Pour the mixture into a saucepan, add 3 cups (750 ml/24 fl oz) full-bodied red wine and heat until almost boiling—do not allow to boil or the alcohol will evaporate off. Serve in heatproof glasses. Serves 6.

## EGGNOG

Separate 4 eggs and beat the yolks and
1/3 cup (90 g/3 oz) caster sugar in a
heatproof bowl until light and fluffy. Add
1 1/4 cups (315 ml/10 fl oz) hot milk and
stir to combine. Bring a saucepan of
water to the boil and reduce the heat to
simmer. Place the bowl over simmering
water and stir with a wooden spoon for
about 5–10 minutes until the mixture
thickens and lightly coats the back of the
spoon. Remove from the heat and allow
to cool. Stir in 1/2 cup (125 ml/4 fl oz)
bourbon. Beat 1/2 cup (125 ml/4 fl oz)
cream and the 4 egg whites separately
until soft peaks form. Fold the cream,
then egg whites into the bourbon in two
batches. Pour into glasses and sprinkle
with grated nutmeg. Serves 6–8.

## HOT TODDY

Put 1 tablespoon soft brown sugar,
4 slices of lemon, 4 cinnamon sticks,
12 whole cloves, 1/2 cup (125 ml/4 fl oz)
whisky and 4 cups (1 litre/32 fl oz)
boiling water in a heatproof jug. Stir to
combine and leave to infuse for a few
minutes, then strain. Add more sugar, to
taste. Serve in heatproof glasses. Serves 4.

## BRANDIED APPLE CIDER

Thinly slice 2 apples into discs, discarding
the ends—do not core. Place the apple in
a large heavy-based saucepan and add
2 x 375 ml (12 fl oz) bottles alcoholic
cider and 1 cup (250 ml/8 fl oz) brandy
or Calvados. Heat until almost boiling—
do not boil. Serve in heatproof glasses.
Serves 4.

## CARAMEL AND VANILLA
## MILKSHAKE

Slowly heat 1 litre (32 fl oz) milk
in a saucepan—be careful not to boil.
Add 100 g (3 1/2 oz) hard caramels
and heat over low heat until melted,
stirring occasionally. Place in a blender
with 2–3 scoops vanilla ice cream and
blend briefly until smooth. Pour into
4 tall heatproof glasses. Serves 4.

*FROM LEFT: Buttered rum; Mulled wine;
Eggnog; Hot toddy; Brandied apple cider;
Caramel and vanilla milkshake*

## RAISED PORK PIE

Cover the outside of the tin with the rolled pastry, working quickly so the pastry does not have time to set.

Tie the greased paper collar to fit snugly around the outside of the pastry.

Cut a small hole in the top of the pie so you can fit a funnel into it to pour in the gelatine.

Let the cooked pie cool, then gradually pour the gelatine in through the hole until the pie is full.

*RIGHT: Raised pork pie*

# RAISED PORK PIE

**Preparation time:** 20 minutes + 2 hours
15 minutes refrigeration + overnight setting
**Total cooking time:** 1 hour 5 minutes
Serves 6

★ ★ ★

1.2 kg (2 lb 6½ oz) minced pork
⅔ cup (90 g/3 oz) pistachio nuts, chopped
2 green apples, peeled and finely chopped
6 fresh sage leaves, finely chopped
4 cups (500 g/1 lb) plain flour
150 g (5 oz) butter
2 eggs, lightly beaten
1 egg yolk
1 cup (250 ml/8 fl oz) vegetable stock
⅔ cup (170 ml/5½ fl oz) unsweetened
apple juice
2 teaspoons powdered gelatine

**1** Preheat the oven to moderately hot 200°C (400°F/Gas 6). Put the pork, pistachio nuts, apple and sage leaves in a bowl, mix well and season. Fry a small piece of the mixture, taste and adjust the seasoning, to taste. Cover the mixture and refrigerate.

**2** Wrap a piece of plastic wrap around a 6 cm (2½ inch) high, 20 cm (8 inch) diameter straight-sided tin, then turn the tin over and grease the plastic on the outside base and side of the tin.

**3** Put the flour and 1 teaspoon salt in a bowl and make a well in the centre. Put the butter in a saucepan with ¾ cup (185 ml/6 fl oz) water. Bring to the boil and add to the flour, with the beaten eggs. Mix with a wooden spoon until combined, then turn out onto a lightly floured work surface and bring the mixture together, adding another 1–2 tablespoons boiling water if necessary to form a smooth dough. Wrap in plastic wrap and refrigerate for 10 minutes.

**4** Wrap a third of the pastry in plastic wrap—do not refrigerate. Roll the remaining pastry into

a circle large enough to just cover the outside of the tin. Lift onto a rolling pin and place over the tin, pressing to the shape of the tin and working quickly before the pastry sets. Refrigerate for about 2 hours, until the pastry hardens, then carefully pull out the tin and remove the plastic wrap. Put the pastry on a lightly greased baking tray. Attach a paper collar made of 2 layers of greased baking paper around the outside of the pastry so it fits snugly and supports the pastry. Secure it with a paper clip at the top and bottom. Fill the pastry with the pork mixture, then roll out the remaining pastry to form a lid. Brush the rim of the base with a little water and press the lid on to attach. Pinch to seal. Cut a small hole in the top of the pie to fit a funnel.

**5** Bake for 40 minutes and check the pastry top. If it is still pale, bake for another 10 minutes, then remove the paper. Brush with egg yolk mixed with 1 tablespoon water and bake for another 15 minutes, or until the sides are brown. Cool completely.

**6** Bring the vegetable stock and half the apple juice to the boil in a saucepan, then remove from the heat. Sprinkle the gelatine over the surface of the remaining apple juice in a jug, leave to go spongy, then pour into the stock and mix well until the gelatine dissolves. Place a small funnel (large icing nozzles work well) in the hole of the pie, pour in a little of the gelatine mixture, leave to settle and then pour in a little more until the pie is full. It is important to fill the pie completely to ensure there are no gaps when the gelatine mixture sets. You may not need to use all the liquid. Refrigerate for several hours, or overnight, until the gelatine has set completely. Serve cold.

## CAMEMBERT AND POTATO TERRINE

**Preparation time:** 1 hour
+ overnight refrigeration
**Total cooking time:** 55 minutes
**Serves** 8–10

✹ ✹ ✹

6 new potatoes, unpeeled

3 green apples

125 g (4 oz) butter

3 tablespoons olive oil

200 g (6¹/² oz) Camembert, chilled and very
    thinly sliced

2 tablespoons chopped fresh parsley

**1** Par-boil the potatoes in lightly salted water for about 15 minutes. Drain and cool, then peel and cut into slices 1 cm (¹/² inch) thick.

**2** Core and slice the apples into 5 mm (¹/⁴ inch) thick rounds.

**3** Heat half the butter and half the oil in a large frying pan and cook the potato until just golden. Drain on crumpled paper towels. Heat the remaining butter and oil. Lightly fry the sliced apple until golden, then remove and drain on crumpled paper towels. Preheat the oven to moderate 180°C (350°F/Gas 4).

**4** Line a 25 x 11 cm (10 x 4¹/² inch) terrine with baking paper. Arrange a layer of potato in the base of the terrine. Add a layer of apple, then Camembert. Sprinkle with parsley and season with salt and pepper, to taste. Build up the layers, finishing with potato.

**5** Oil a piece of foil and cover the terrine, sealing well. Place the terrine in a baking dish and half fill the dish with boiling water. Bake for 20 minutes. Remove from the water-filled baking dish. Cover with foil, then put a piece of heavy cardboard, cut to fit, on top of the terrine. Put weights or food cans on top of the cardboard to compress the terrine. Refrigerate overnight. Turn out and slice, to serve.

*ABOVE: Camembert and potato terrine*

## SALMON AND FENNEL FRITTATA

Pour the wine over the onion and fennel and cook, stirring frequently, until the vegetables are tender.

Pour half the egg mixture into the tin and sprinkle with some smoked salmon.

*ABOVE: Salmon and fennel frittata*

# SALMON AND FENNEL FRITTATA

**Preparation time:** 35 minutes
**Total cooking time:** 1 hour 15 minutes
**Serves** 8

★

1½ tablespoons olive oil

1 onion, finely chopped

1 fennel bulb (about 280 g/9 oz),
  finely chopped

¼ cup (60 ml/2 fl oz) white wine

2 cups (60 g/2 oz) watercress sprigs

12 eggs

1¾ cups (440 ml/14 fl oz) cream

3 tablespoons chopped fresh dill

½ cup (50 g/1¾ oz) grated Parmesan

300 g (10 oz) smoked salmon, cut into strips

1 Preheat the oven to moderate 180°C (350°F/ Gas 4). Lightly grease a 22 cm (9 inch) springform tin and line the base and side with baking paper, making sure you have a tight seal all the way around the tin. Place the tin on a baking tray in case it leaks.

2 Heat the olive oil in a heavy-based saucepan and add the onion, fennel and a pinch of salt. Cook over low heat for 5 minutes, stirring occasionally. Add the white wine and cook for another 5 minutes, or until the vegetables are tender. Remove from the heat and leave to cool.

3 Finely chop half the watercress and divide the remainder into small sprigs. Beat the eggs lightly in a bowl, then add the cream, dill, grated Parmesan, chopped watercress, and onion and fennel mixture. Season, to taste, with salt and black pepper.

4 Pour half the egg mixture into the prepared tin, sprinkle with 200 g (6½ oz) smoked salmon and pour in the remaining egg mixture. Bake for

1 hour, or until the frittata is set in the centre and golden on the surface. Remove from the pan and peel off the baking paper from the side. Flip over onto a plate and remove the paper from the base. Flip over again onto a serving dish and arrange the remaining salmon and watercress on top. Cut into wedges and serve warm.

## PRAWN COCKTAILS

**Preparation time:** 20 minutes
**Total cooking time:** Nil
**Serves** 4

1/4 cup (60 g/2 oz) whole-egg mayonnaise
2 teaspoons tomato sauce
dash of Tabasco sauce
1/4 teaspoon Worcestershire sauce
2 teaspoons thick (double) cream
1/4 teaspoon lemon juice
24 cooked large prawns
4 lettuce leaves, shredded
lemon wedges, for serving

**1** Mix the mayonnaise, sauces, cream and juice together in a small bowl.
**2** Peel the prawns, leaving the tails intact on eight of them. Gently pull out the dark vein from the back of each prawn, starting at the head end.
**3** Divide the lettuce among 4 glasses. Arrange the prawns without the tails in the glasses and drizzle with the sauce. Hang 2 of the remaining prawns over the edge of each glass and serve with lemon wedges.

### CHEESY PROSCIUTTO TWISTS

Brush a thawed sheet of puff pastry with a little beaten egg and cut into 1.5 cm (5/8 inch) wide strips. Holding both ends, twist the strips in opposite directions to create twists. Place the twists on lightly greased baking trays and bake in a hot 210°C (415°F/Gas 6–7) oven for 10 minutes or until lightly browned and puffed. Remove from the trays and cool on a wire rack. Cut about 8 slices prosciutto into half lengthways, twist the prosciutto around the puff twists and serve. Makes 16.

**PRAWNS**
Dishes using prawns are a delicious addition to the table at parties. Fresh prawns should look shiny and have a pleasant sea smell. Don't buy prawns if they show any signs of dark discolouration around the head and legs or if they smell like ammonia. Prawns come in a variety of sizes so choose the size that best suits your dish.

*LEFT: Prawn cocktails*

## PORK AND VEAL TERRINE

Stir together the onion mixture, pork and veal mince, breadcrumbs, egg, brandy and herbs.

Press the mixture firmly into the terrine dish and neatly fold the bacon over the top.

# PORK AND VEAL TERRINE

**Preparation time:** 20 minutes
  + overnight refrigeration
**Total cooking time:** 1 hour 20 minutes
**Serves** 6

8–10 thin bacon rashers
1 tablespoon olive oil
1 onion, chopped
2 cloves garlic, crushed
1 kg (2 lb) pork and veal mince
1 cup (80 g/2¾ oz) fresh breadcrumbs
1 egg, beaten
¼ cup (60 ml/2 fl oz) brandy
3 teaspoons chopped fresh thyme
3 tablespoons chopped fresh parsley

**1** Preheat the oven to moderate 180°C (350°F/ Gas 4). Lightly grease a 25 x 11 cm (10 x 4½ inch) terrine. Line the terrine with the bacon so that it overlaps slightly and hangs over the sides.
**2** Heat the oil in a frying pan, add the onion and garlic and cook for 2–3 minutes, or until the onion is soft. Cool, then mix with the mince, breadcrumbs, egg, brandy, thyme and parsley in a large bowl. Season with salt and pepper. Fry a small piece of the mixture to check the seasoning, and adjust if necessary.
**3** Spoon the mixture into the bacon-lined terrine, pressing down firmly to avoid any air bubbles. Fold the bacon over the top of the terrine, cover with lightly greased foil and place in a baking dish.
**4** Place enough boiling water in the baking dish to come halfway up the side of the terrine. Bake for 1–1¼ hours, or until the juices run clear when the terrine is pierced with a skewer. Remove the terrine from the water-filled baking dish and pour off the excess juices. Cover with foil, then put a piece of heavy cardboard, cut to fit, on top of the terrine. Put weights or food cans on top of the cardboard to compress the terrine. Refrigerate overnight, then cut into slices to serve.
**NOTE:** The terrine can be made ahead of time and stored, covered, in the refrigerator for up to 5 days.

# MINI FRITTATAS

**Preparation time:** 30 minutes
**Total cooking time:** 45 minutes
**Makes** 12

1 kg (2 lb) orange sweet potato (kumera), cut into small cubes
1 tablespoon oil
30 g (1 oz) butter
4 leeks, white part only, finely sliced
2 cloves garlic, crushed
250 g (8 oz) feta, crumbled
8 eggs
½ cup (125 ml/4 fl oz) cream

**1** Preheat the oven to moderate 180°C (350°F/Gas 4). Grease 2 trays of six 1-cup (250 ml/8 fl oz) muffin holes. Cut small rounds of baking paper and place one into each hole.
**2** Boil, steam or microwave the sweet potato until tender. Drain well and set aside.
**3** Heat the oil and butter in a frying pan over low heat and cook the leek for 10 minutes, stirring occasionally, or until very soft and lightly golden. Add the garlic and cook for another minute. Allow to cool, then stir in the feta and sweet potato. Divide the mixture among the muffin holes.
**4** Whisk the eggs and cream together in a bowl and season with salt and cracked black pepper. Pour the egg mixture into each hole until three-quarters filled. Bake for 25–30 minutes, or until golden and set. Leave in the tins for 5 minutes, then ease out with a knife. Delicious served warm or at room temperature. Suitable for serving as a light meal with salad or as part of a buffet.

*OPPOSITE PAGE:*
*Pork and veal terrine*

1 Line a 25 x 11 cm (10 x 4½ inch) loaf tin with foil, then line with the prosciutto slices so that the prosciutto hangs over the sides, making sure each slice overlaps slightly. Trim the chicken livers of any fat and veins.

2 Heat the butter and oil in a frying pan and cook the bacon, onion and garlic for 5 minutes, or until the onion is soft but not brown.

3 Add the chicken livers to the frying pan with the bay leaves. Increase the heat to hot and cook for 3–4 minutes, or until the livers are brown on the outside, but still slightly pink on the inside.

4 Add the sherry or brandy to the frying pan and simmer, stirring constantly, for 3 minutes, or until the liquid has almost all evaporated. Remove the bay leaves. Put the mixture in a food processor and blend to a very fine texture. Gradually add the butter to the food processor and blend until the mixture is smooth. Season, to taste, then stir in the nuts.

5 Spoon the mixture into the loaf tin and fold the prosciutto over the top. Cover with plastic wrap and refrigerate for at least 3 hours, or overnight. Cut into slices for serving.

NOTE: The flavour of the pâté will improve after a couple of days. It can be kept in the refrigerator for 3–4 days.

## CHICKEN LIVER PATE WITH PISTACHIOS AND PROSCIUTTO

**Preparation time:** 20 minutes
   + 3 hours refrigeration
**Total cooking time:** 15 minutes
**Serves** 10

8–10 very thin slices prosciutto
500 g (1 lb) chicken livers
30 g (1 oz) butter
¼ cup (60 ml/2 fl oz) olive oil
2 rashers bacon, finely diced
1 onion, finely chopped
2 cloves garlic, crushed
3 bay leaves
⅓ cup (80 ml/2¾ fl oz) sherry or brandy
125 g (4 oz) butter, softened
⅓ cup (50 g/1¾ oz) pistachio nuts, toasted

*ABOVE: Chicken liver pâté with pistachios and prosciutto*

## RED PEPPER (CAPSICUM) AND FETA BITES

Slice 2 red peppers (capsicums) into large, flattish pieces and remove the membranes and seeds. Place the pepper pieces skin-side-up under a hot grill until the skin blackens and blisters. Remove and cool under a tea towel or in a sealed plastic bag. While the peppers are cooling, cut a 250 g (8 oz) block of Greek feta into 2 cm (¾ inch) cubes. Peel the cooled peppers and slice into 1.5 cm (⅝ inch) strips. Whisk together 2 tablespoons extra virgin olive oil, 1 tablespoon balsamic vinegar and some salt and pepper and pour over the pepper slices. Toss to coat. Wrap the pepper slices around the feta cubes and secure with a toothpick. Serve on a platter. Makes about 30.

## POTATO AND SAGE CHIPS

**Preparation time:** 15 minutes
**Total cooking time:** 30 minutes
**Makes** 25

2 large all-purpose potatoes, such
as pontiac, desiree or sebago
2 tablespoons olive oil
25 sage leaves

1 Preheat the oven to moderately hot 200°C
(400°F/Gas 6). Carefully cut the potatoes
lengthways into paper-thin slices. Toss the
slices in the oil.
2 Line two baking trays with baking paper.
Sandwich a sage leaf between two slices of
potato. Sprinkle with salt. Repeat to use all
the potato. Bake for about 25–30 minutes,
or until browned and crisp, turning once
during cooking.
**NOTE:** Some chips may take longer to cook
than others. Watch them carefully to prevent
them from burning.

## CUCUMBER ROUNDS WITH AVOCADO AND TURKEY

**Preparation time:** 20 minutes
**Total cooking time:** Nil
**Makes** 30

3 Lebanese cucumbers
100 g (3¹/₂ oz) sliced smoked turkey
¹/₂ avocado, mashed
1 clove garlic, crushed
2 tablespoons cranberry sauce
2 tablespoons sour cream
cranberry sauce, extra, to garnish
alfalfa sprouts or mustard cress, to garnish

1 Slice the cucumbers into 1.5 cm (⁵/₈ inch)
rounds to make 30 pieces. Cut 30 rounds from
the turkey using a 3 cm (1¹/₄ inch) cutter.
2 Combine the avocado with the garlic,
cranberry sauce and sour cream. Spoon
1 teaspoon onto each cucumber round and top
with a round of turkey. Spoon a little cranberry
sauce on top and garnish with alfalfa sprouts.

*ABOVE: Potato and sage chips (left); Cucumber rounds with avocado and turkey*

# TOMATO AND HALOUMI SKEWERS

**Preparation time:** 30 minutes
**Total cooking time:** 10 minutes
**Makes** 22

500 g (8 oz) haloumi cheese
5 cups (250 g/8 oz) fresh basil leaves
150 g (5 oz) semi-dried tomatoes
2 tablespoons balsamic vinegar
2 tablespoons extra virgin olive oil
1 teaspoon sea salt

**1** Cut the cheese into 1.5 cm (⅝ inch) pieces. Thread a basil leaf onto a small skewer, followed by a piece of haloumi, a semi-dried tomato, another piece of haloumi and another basil leaf. Repeat to use all the ingredients.
**2** Place the skewers on a preheated barbecue hotplate and cook, turning occasionally until the cheese is golden brown, brushing with the combined vinegar and oil while cooking. Sprinkle with the salt and serve hot or warm.

*BELOW: Tomato and haloumi skewers*

NOTES: To make your own semi-dried tomatoes, preheat the oven to warm 160°C (315°/Gas 2–3) and cut ripe Roma (egg) tomatoes into quarters. Place on a wire cake rack and sit the rack on a baking tray. Sprinkle lightly with salt and pepper and a pinch of sugar. Bake for about 3–4 hours, until dry but still soft. The drying time will depend on the amount of moisture and the size of the tomatoes. Keep in a container in the refrigerator for 4–5 days. Drizzle with olive oil if you wish.

Haloumi, a white cheese, has a rubbery texture and a milky, slightly minty, salty taste. When cooked, it will hold its shape, the outside will brown and the inside will melt. Originally made using the milk from sheep or goats, it is now often made with the milk from cows. It is available in small rectangular blocks in vacuum-sealed packets, or in bulk in brine, from delicatessens and some supermarkets.

# PESTO PALMIERS

**Preparation time:** *20 minutes*
**Total cooking time:** *15–20 minutes per batch*
**Makes** *60*

1 cup (50 g/1¾ oz) fresh basil leaves
1 clove garlic, crushed
¼ cup (25 g/¾ oz) grated Parmesan
1 tablespoon pine nuts, toasted
2 tablespoons olive oil
4 sheets ready-rolled puff pastry, thawed

**1** Preheat the oven to hot 220°C (425°F/Gas 7). Roughly chop the basil leaves in a food processor with the garlic, Parmesan and pine nuts. With the motor running, gradually add the oil in a thin stream and process until smooth.
**2** Spread each pastry sheet with a quarter of the basil mixture. Roll up one side until you reach the middle then repeat with the other side. Place on a baking tray. Repeat with the remaining pastry and basil mixture. Freeze for 30 minutes.
**3** Slice each roll into 1.5 cm (⅝ inch) slices. Curl each slice into a semi-circle and place on a lightly greased baking tray. Allow room for the palmiers to expand during cooking. Bake in batches for 15–20 minutes, or until golden brown.
**NOTE:** Palmiers are delicious bite-sized specially shaped pastry snacks which traditionally were sweet. They were made by sprinkling sugar between the pastry folds and then cutting into slices before baking until crisp and golden. Sometimes they were dusted with icing sugar and served as a petit four with coffee. Other savoury variations include spreading with a prepared tapenade paste made with olives, capers, anchovies, oil and garlic, or with tahini, a sesame seed paste. Another simple version is to sprinkle just the grated Parmesan between the pastry layers.

## PINE NUTS

These small, elongated, creamy kernels are sold shelled and blanched. The kernels are taken from the nuts of umbrella-shaped pine trees, sometimes called parasol pines, which are native to the Mediterranean. Recipes often suggest toasting or roasting them before use because this enhances their flavour. The easiest way to do this is to bake on a tray in a moderate 180°C (350°F/Gas 4) oven for 5 minutes, watching carefully that they don't burn. They can also be toasted in a dry frying pan over low heat, tossing constantly until golden.

*LEFT: Pesto palmiers*

# ROASTS

It's the moment everyone's been waiting for. The tantalising aroma of a sizzling roast has wafted through the house for long enough. It's time to carve! Whether it be traditional roast turkey with cranberry sauce, succulent loin of pork with apple and prune stuffing or a wonderfully indulgent whole glazed ham, this is the focal point of the Christmas festivities. Mouths water and stomachs grumble in anticipation as the accompaniments make their way to the table — for what would a roast be without flavoursome sauces and gravies and richly herbed stuffings? To share such a meal with your loved ones is a gift in its own right.

# ROAST TURKEY WITH STUFFING

**Preparation time:** 45 minutes + making stuffing
**Total cooking time:** 2 hours
**Serves** 6–8

3 kg (6 lb) turkey
1 quantity stuffing (see recipes on right)
2 tablespoons oil
2 cups (500 ml/16 fl oz) chicken stock
2 tablespoons plain flour

**1** Remove the neck and giblets from inside the turkey. Wash the turkey well and pat dry inside and out with paper towels. Preheat the oven to moderate 180°C (350°F/Gas 4).
**2** Make the stuffing you prefer and loosely stuff into the turkey cavity. Tuck the wings underneath and join the cavity with a skewer. Tie the legs together. Place on a rack in a baking dish. Roast for 2 hours, basting with the combined oil and 1/2 cup (125 ml/4 fl oz) of the stock. Cover the breast and legs with foil after 1 hour if the turkey is overbrowning. Remove from the oven, cover and leave to rest for 15 minutes.
**3** To make the gravy, drain off all except 2 tablespoons of pan juices from the baking dish. Place the dish on the stove over low heat, add the flour and stir well. Stir over medium heat until browned. Gradually add the remaining stock, stirring until the gravy boils and thickens. Serve the turkey with gravy and roast vegetables.
**NOTE:** Do not stuff the turkey until you are ready to cook it. Stuffing can be made ahead of time and frozen for up to a month in an airtight container. If you prefer to cook the stuffing separately, press it lightly into a lightly greased ovenproof dish and bake for about 30 minutes, or until golden brown. Small greased muffin tins can also be used (bake for 15–20 minutes). Alternatively, you can form the mixture into balls and fry in a little melted butter or oil, over medium heat, until golden brown all over.

# CITRUS STUFFING

Heat 1 tablespoon oil in a small frying pan and cook 1 finely chopped onion until soft. Transfer to a large bowl and cool. Add 200 g (6 1/2 oz) sausage mince, 2 crushed cloves of garlic, 2 cups (160 g/5 1/2 oz) fresh white breadcrumbs, 2 teaspoons each of grated lemon and orange rinds and 1/2 cup (60 g/2 oz) finely chopped pecans and mix well. Season, to taste, with salt and pepper and mix.

# COUNTRY SAGE STUFFING

Melt 45 g (1 1/2 oz) butter in a small saucepan and cook 1 finely chopped onion and 1 sliced celery stick over medium heat for 3 minutes, or until the onion has softened. Transfer to a bowl and add 10 shredded large fresh sage leaves, 2 cups (160 g/5 1/2 oz) fresh white breadcrumbs, 1 1/2 teaspoons dried sage, 4 tablespoons finely chopped fresh parsley, 2 lightly beaten egg whites, 1 teaspoon salt and 1/2 teaspoon white pepper.

# CASHEW STUFFING

Melt 60 g (2 oz) butter in a frying pan and cook 1 chopped onion until golden. Cool, then mix thoroughly with 2 cups (370 g/12 oz) cooked long-grain brown rice, 1 cup (185 g/6 oz) chopped dried apricots, 1/2 cup (80 g/2 3/4 oz) unsalted cashews, 3 tablespoons chopped fresh parsley, 2 tablespoons chopped fresh mint and 1 tablespoon lemon juice. Season, to taste, with salt and pepper. (You will need to cook 1 cup/200 g/6 1/2 oz brown rice for this recipe.)

# SPINACH AND RICOTTA STUFFING

Heat 2 tablespoons oil in a small saucepan, add 1 finely chopped onion and 2 crushed cloves of garlic and cook, stirring over medium heat for 5 minutes, or until soft. Squeeze as much liquid as possible from 2 thawed 250 g (8 oz) packets of frozen spinach and add the spinach to the pan. Cook, stirring for 2–3 minutes, or until as dry as possible. Remove from the heat and place in a large bowl to cool. Add 1/2 cup (80 g/2 oz) pine nuts, 1 cup (80 g/2 3/4 oz) stale white breadcrumbs, 400 g (13 oz) ricotta and 200 g (7 1/2 oz) finely chopped semi-dried tomatoes. Season, to taste, with salt and pepper.

**TURKEY**
For centuries in England, the main course enjoyed for Christmas dinner consisted of boar's head and fattened goose. The turkey was imported from America to Europe, then to the United Kingdom in the early sixteenth century. Because of its succulent meat, it soon became an established part of the traditional English Christmas dinner and its popularity has spread to many other countries.

*OPPOSITE PAGE: Roast turkey with stuffing. Stuffings: In cavity, citrus; In bowls, Cashew (top left), Spinach and ricotta; Balls of stuffing, clockwise from top, Country sage, Spinach and ricotta (2), Country sage, Spinach and ricotta*

# GLAZED HAM

The size of ham we have used is enough for about 20 people. Choose your favourite glaze and follow the directions below. Carving is easier if you hold onto the unglazed shank end.

### PREPARING, GLAZING AND HEATING LEG HAM

Preheat the oven to moderate 180°C (350°F/Gas 4). Cut a line through the thick rind of a 7 kg (14 lb) smoked, cooked leg ham, 6 cm (2½ inches) from the shank end so you can easily lift the rind. (For an uncooked leg of ham, refer to the note further on.) To remove the rind, run your thumb around the edge, under the rind and carefully pull back, easing your hand under the rind between the fat and the rind. With a sharp knife, lightly score the fat to form a diamond pattern. Do not cut all the way through to the ham or the fat will fall off during cooking. Spread half the glaze of your choice over the ham with a palette knife or the back of a spoon and press a clove into the centre of each diamond. Put the ham on a rack in a deep baking dish and pour 2 cups (500 ml/16 fl oz) water into the dish. Cover the ham and dish securely with greased foil and cook for

45 minutes. Remove from the oven and brush or spread the remaining glaze over the ham. Increase the heat to hot 210°C (415°F/Gas 6–7) and bake, uncovered, for 20 minutes, or until the surface is lightly caramelized. Set aside for 15 minutes before carving.

**NOTE:** If you are using an uncooked leg ham, for a 7 kg (14 lb) leg ham, soak the ham overnight in a large clean bucket or container of cold water, changing the water a couple of times. Preheat the oven to warm 160°C (315°F/Gas 2–3). Tip out the soaking water and rinse the ham thoroughly under cold running water. Pat dry with paper towels and place in a deep baking dish large enough to hold the ham (the end may stick out slightly). Chop an onion, carrot and stick of celery and place around the baking dish with a couple of bay leaves and a few peppercorns. Pour 2 cups (500 ml/ 16 fl oz) cold water into the dish and cover the dish completely with foil. Bake for 2 hours 40 minutes (20 minutes per kilo, plus 20 minutes). When cooked, remove the ham from the liquid and discard the liquid and vegetables. Allow the ham to cool (this can be done several days ahead if you wish). When ready to use, prepare, glaze and heat as described for the cooked leg of ham above.

## HONEY GLAZE

Mix ²/₃ cup (125 g/4 oz) soft brown sugar, 3 tablespoons honey and 1 tablespoon hot English mustard together in a bowl.

## ORANGE GLAZE

Stir together 1 cup (250 ml/8 fl oz) orange juice, ³/₄ cup (140 g/4¹/₂ oz) soft brown sugar, 1 tablespoon French mustard, ¹/₂ cup (175 g/6 oz) honey, 2 teaspoons soy sauce and 2 tablespoons Grand Marnier in a bowl.

## MUSTARD AND REDCURRANT GLAZE

Put ¹/₃ cup (90 g/3 oz) Dijon mustard, 1 cup (315 g/10 oz) redcurrant jelly, 4 crushed cloves of garlic and 2 tablespoons each of oil and soy sauce into a small saucepan. Stir and gently warm over medium heat for 2–3 minutes, or until the jelly has melted. Take care the glaze doesn't catch on the base of the pan.

## PORK WITH APPLE AND PRUNE STUFFING

Use a spoon to spread the stuffing over the meat side of the pork loin.

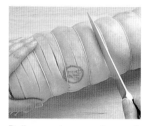

Roll up and secure the pork with string, then score the rind at regular intervals.

## PORK WITH APPLE AND PRUNE STUFFING

**Preparation time:** 35 minutes
**Total cooking time:** 2 hours
**Serves** 8

✶ ✶

1 green apple, chopped
1/3 cup (90 g/3 oz) pitted prunes, chopped
2 tablespoons port
1 tablespoon chopped fresh parsley
2 kg (4 lb) piece boned pork loin
olive oil and salt, to rub on pork
gravy with wine (see page 68), for serving

1 Preheat the oven to very hot 240°C (475°F/ Gas 9). To make the stuffing, combine the apple, prunes, port and parsley. Lay the pork loin on a board with the rind underneath. Spread the stuffing over the meat side of the loin, roll up and secure with skewers or string at regular intervals. If some of the filling falls out while tying, carefully push it back in. Score the pork rind with a sharp knife at 1 cm (1/2 inch) intervals (if the butcher hasn't already done so) and rub generously with oil and salt.

2 Place on a rack in a baking dish. Bake for 15 minutes, then reduce the heat to moderate 180°C (350°F/Gas 4) and bake for 1 1/2–2 hours, or until the pork is cooked through. The juices will run clear when a skewer is inserted into the thickest part of the meat. Cover and stand for 15 minutes before removing the skewers or string and carving. Reserve any pan juices for making the gravy.

**NOTE:** If the rind fails to crackle, carefully remove it from the meat, cutting between the fat layer and the meat. Scrape off any excess fat and put the rind on a piece of foil. Place under a moderate grill, and grill until the rind has crackled. Alternatively, place between several sheets of paper towel and microwave on high in 1 minute bursts, for about 2–3 minutes altogether (depending on the thickness of the rind).

*ABOVE: Pork with apple and prune stuffing*

# ROAST GOOSE

**Preparation time:** 15 minutes
**Total cooking time:** 1 hour 30 minutes
**Serves** 6

3 kg (6 lb) fresh or frozen goose
1 tablespoon plain flour
2 tablespoons brandy
1½ cups (375 ml/12 fl oz) chicken stock
bread sauce (see page 69), for serving

**1** If using a frozen goose, thaw in the refrigerator—it may take 1–2 days. Preheat the oven to moderate 180°C (350°F/Gas 4). Remove any excess fat from inside the cavity of the goose. Place the goose in a large pan, cover with boiling water, then drain. Dry thoroughly with paper towels.

**2** Place the goose breast-side-down on a rack in a very large baking dish. (Make sure the goose doesn't sit directly on the dish or it will be very greasy.) Using a fine skewer, prick the skin of the goose all over, being careful to pierce only the skin, not the flesh.

**3** Bake the goose for 1 hour, then remove from the oven and drain off any excess fat. Turn the goose over and bake for another 30 minutes, or until the outside is golden and crisp. Remove from the baking dish, cover loosely with foil and leave for 5–10 minutes.

**4** For gravy, drain all except 2 tablespoons of fat from the baking dish and place the dish on the stove over low heat. Add the flour and stir to incorporate all the sediment. Stir constantly over medium heat until well browned, without burning. Remove from the heat and gradually stir in the brandy and chicken stock. Return to the heat and stir constantly, until the gravy boils and thickens. Season with salt and pepper, and serve with bread sauce.

**NOTE:** This cooking time will produce a well-done goose. If you prefer it a little less cooked, reduce the initial cooking time by 20 minutes. You may need to order the goose in advance from a poultry store or butcher as fresh geese are very hard to find.

*BELOW: Roast goose*

# ROAST RACK OF VENISON

**Preparation time:** 30 minutes
+ overnight marinating
**Total cooking time:** 35 minutes
Serves 6–8

 ✷ ✷

### Marinade

1 cup (250 ml/8 fl oz) red wine
1/4 cup (60 ml/2 fl oz) olive oil
2 tablespoons brandy
1 spring onion or brown onion, finely chopped
2 cloves garlic, crushed
2 bay leaves
6 juniper berries, crushed
1 tablespoon fresh thyme leaves
8 whole black peppercorns

2 racks of venison (10 chops per rack)
1 cup (250 ml/8 fl oz) beef stock
1 tablespoon redcurrant jelly
2 tablespoons port
40 g (1 1/4 oz) butter, cut into small cubes
20 whole canned chestnuts (about 150 g/5 oz)

1 Stir the marinade ingredients together in a large bowl. Put the venison racks in the bowl and turn them over a few times until coated in the marinade. Cover and marinate in the refrigerator overnight, turning occasionally.
2 Preheat the oven to hot 220°C (425°F/Gas 7). Remove the venison racks from the marinade, reserving the marinade. Roast the racks for 30 minutes for medium, or slightly longer if you prefer well-done meat. Remove from the oven, cover with foil and leave to rest for 10 minutes while you make the sauce.
3 Put the reserved marinade in a small saucepan with the beef stock and bring to the boil over medium heat. Boil until reduced to 1 cup (250 ml/8 fl oz). Reduce the heat, stir in the redcurrant jelly and port and simmer gently. Whisk 30 g (1 oz) butter into the sauce until amalgamated. Remove from the heat.
4 Drain the chestnuts and heat in a small saucepan with the remaining butter. Season with freshly ground black pepper.
5 Carve the racks into chops and serve with the hot chestnuts. Strain the warm sauce through a sieve and serve over the meat. Serve immediately. Bread sauce (see page 69) is often served with the venison.

# ROAST CHICKEN WITH BACON AND SAGE STUFFING

**Preparation time:** 15 minutes
**Total cooking time:** 1 hour 10 minutes
Serves 6

✷

2 x 1.2 kg (2 lb 7 oz) chickens
4 rashers bacon
2 tablespoons oil
1 small onion, finely chopped
1 tablespoon chopped fresh sage
1 1/2 cups (125 g/4 oz) fresh breadcrumbs
1 egg, lightly beaten

1 Preheat the oven to moderate 180°C (350°F/Gas 4). Remove the giblets and any large fat deposits from the chickens. Wipe over and pat dry inside and out with paper towels.
2 Finely chop two of the bacon rashers. Heat half the oil in a small frying pan. Add the onion and the finely chopped bacon and cook until the onion is soft and the bacon is starting to brown. Transfer to a bowl and cool. Add the sage, breadcrumbs and egg to the onion, season, to taste, and mix lightly. Spoon some stuffing into each chicken cavity.
3 Fold the wings back and tuck under the chickens. Tie the legs of each chicken together with string. Place the chickens on a rack in a large baking dish, making sure they are not touching, and brush with some of the remaining oil. Pour 1 cup (250 ml/8 fl oz) water into the baking dish.
4 Cut the remaining bacon into long, thin strips and lay across the chicken breasts. Brush the bacon with oil. Bake for 45–60 minutes, or until the juices run clear when a thigh is pierced with a skewer.
**NOTE:** This chicken dish is delicious served with the Gravy with wine (see page 68) and roast vegetables.

ROAST CHICKEN WITH BACON AND SAGE STUFFING

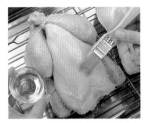

Put the stuffed chicken on a rack in a baking dish and brush with oil.

Lay strips of bacon across the chicken breasts and brush the bacon with oil.

*OPPOSITE PAGE:*
*Roast chicken with bacon and sage stuffing (top); Roast rack of venison*

## ROAST DUCK

**Preparation time:** 40 minutes
**Total cooking time:** 2 hours 15 minutes
**Serves** 4

★ ★

2 kg (4 lb) duck, with neck
2 chicken wings, chopped
1/2 cup (125 ml/4 fl oz) white wine
1 onion, chopped
1 carrot, sliced
1 ripe tomato, chopped
bouquet garni (a bay leaf and small sprigs of
    parsley, thyme and marjoram, tied together)

**Orange sauce**

2 tablespoons shredded orange rind
2/3 cup (170 ml/5 1/2 fl oz) orange juice
1/3 cup (80 ml/2 3/4 fl oz) Cointreau
2 teaspoons cornflour

**1** Place the duck neck, chicken wings and wine in a pan. Boil over high heat for 5 minutes, or until the wine has reduced by half. Add the onion, carrot, tomato, bouquet garni and 2 cups (500 ml/16 fl oz) water. Bring to the boil and simmer gently for 40 minutes. Strain and set aside 1 cup (250 ml/8 fl oz) of the stock.
**2** Preheat the oven to moderate 180°C (350°F/ Gas 4). Place the duck in a large saucepan, cover with boiling water, then drain. Dry with paper towels. With a fine skewer, prick all over the outside of the duck, piercing only the skin, not the flesh. Place the duck breast-side-down on a rack in a baking dish and bake for 50 minutes.
**3** Drain off any fat, turn the duck over and pour the reserved stock into the pan. Bake for 40 minutes, or until the breast is golden brown. Remove the duck from the pan and leave in a warm place for 15 minutes before carving. Reserve any pan juices for making gravy or orange sauce.
**4** For the orange sauce, skim any fat off the reserved pan juices. Place in a saucepan with the rind, juice and Cointreau and bring to the boil. Reduce the heat and simmer for 5 minutes. Blend the cornflour with 1 tablespoon water, add to the sauce and stir over heat until the mixture boils and thickens.
**NOTE:** You may need to order your duck in advance from a game specialist or poulterer. Some large supermarkets have them.

*ABOVE: Roast duck*

# ROAST PHEASANT

**Preparation time:** 20 minutes
**Total cooking time:** 1 hour
**Serves** 4–6

2 x 1 kg (2 lb) pheasants
6 thin rashers bacon
8 sprigs fresh thyme
2 large pieces of muslin
80 g (2³/4 oz) butter, melted
2 apples, cored and cut into thick wedges
1/4 cup (60 ml/2 fl oz) apple cider
1/2 cup (125 ml/4 fl oz) cream
2 teaspoons fresh thyme leaves
2–4 teaspoons apple cider vinegar

1 Preheat the oven to very hot 230°C (450°C/ Gas 8). Rinse the pheasants and pat dry. Tie the legs together with string and tuck the wings under. Wrap bacon around each pheasant and secure with toothpicks. Thread the thyme sprigs through the bacon. Dip the pieces of muslin into the melted butter and wrap one around each pheasant. Place on a rack in a baking dish and bake for 10 minutes. Reduce the oven to moderately hot 200°C (400°C/Gas 6) and bake for another 35 minutes. About 20 minutes before the end of the cooking, add the apple wedges to the base of the dish. The pheasants are cooked when the juices run clear when the pheasants are pricked with a fine skewer. Remove the pheasants and apple wedges, discard the muslin and toothpicks, then cover and keep warm while making the sauce.

2 Place the baking dish with the juices on the stovetop. Pour the apple cider into the pan and bring to the boil. Cook for 3 minutes, or until reduced by half. Scrape the base of the pan to lift any sticky pan juices. Strain into a clean saucepan. Add the cream to the saucepan and boil for 5 minutes, or until the sauce thickens slightly. Stir in the thyme leaves and season well with salt and freshly cracked black pepper. Add the apple cider vinegar, to taste. Serve with the pheasant and apple.

**NOTE:** Muslin is available at drapery stores. The buttered muslin and bacon help protect the delicate breast meat from drying out. Do not overcook pheasant as it may dry out. Traditionally it was served while still pink but most people today prefer it to be cooked through for safety.

*ABOVE: Roast pheasant*

# SAUCES

These delicious classic sauces and gravies can be quickly made while the roast is cooking or resting. Mint sauce will develop in flavour if made a day in advance.

### APPLE SAUCE

Peel and core 4 green apples, then roughly chop the flesh. Place the flesh in a pan with 1 tablespoon caster sugar, $1/2$ cup (125 ml/4 fl oz) water, 2 whole cloves and 1 cinnamon stick. Cover and simmer for 10 minutes, or until soft. Remove from the heat and discard the cloves and cinnamon stick. Mash or, for a finer sauce, press through a sieve. Stir in 1–2 teaspoons lemon juice, or to taste. Serve with roast pork or ham. Makes 1 cup (250 ml/8 fl oz).

### GRAVY WITH WINE

Discard all but 2 tablespoons of the pan juices from the baking dish you cooked the roast in. Heat the dish on the stovetop over moderate heat, stir in 2 tablespoons plain flour and cook, stirring, until well browned. Remove from the heat and gradually add 2 teaspoons Worcestershire sauce, 2 tablespoons red or white wine and $21/4$ cups (560 ml/18 fl oz) beef or chicken stock. Return to the heat, stir until the mixture boils and thickens, then simmer for 2 minutes. Season with salt and pepper, to taste. Suitable for all roast meats. Makes $11/2$ cups (375 ml/12 fl oz).

## MINT SAUCE

Sprinkle 1 tablespoon caster sugar over ½ cup (10 g/¼ oz) fresh mint leaves on a chopping board, then finely chop the mint. Transfer to a bowl and add 2 tablespoons caster sugar. Cover with ¼ cup (60 ml/2 fl oz) boiling water and stir until the sugar has dissolved. Stir in ¾ cup (185 ml/6 fl oz) malt vinegar, cover and chill overnight. Traditionally served with roast lamb.
Makes 1½ cups (375 ml/12 fl oz).

## CREAMY HORSERADISH

Combine 175 g (6 oz) horseradish cream, 1 finely chopped spring onion and ¼ cup (60 g/2 oz) sour cream in a bowl. Fold in ½ cup (125 ml/4 fl oz) whipped cream. Season. Serve with roast beef or veal.
Makes 1½ cups (375 ml/12 oz).

## BREAD SAUCE

Slice 1 small onion and combine in a small pan with 1¼ cups (315 ml/10 fl oz) milk, 1 bay leaf, 4 black peppercorns and 2 whole cloves. Bring to the boil over medium heat, then lower the heat and simmer for 10 minutes. Strain into a large heatproof bowl and discard the onion and flavourings. Add 1¼ cups (100 g/3½ oz) fresh breadcrumbs to the bowl with a pinch of ground nutmeg and 20 g (¾ oz) butter. Stir until smooth, then season with salt and pepper, to taste. Bread sauce is traditionally served with roast goose, turkey or chicken.
Makes 1¼ cups (315 ml/10 fl oz).

## RASPBERRY AND CRANBERRY SAUCE

Purée 150 g (5 oz) fresh or frozen raspberries, then press through a sieve to remove the seeds. Combine the purée in a small pan with ¼ cup (60 ml/2 fl oz) orange juice, ½ cup (160 g/5½ oz) cranberry sauce, 2 teaspoons Dijon mustard and 1 teaspoon finely grated orange rind. Stir over heat until smooth. Add ¼ cup (60 ml/2 fl oz) port and simmer for 5 minutes. Remove and allow to cool—the sauce will thicken slightly. Serve with roast turkey, goose, ham or duck.
Makes 1 cup (250 ml/8 fl oz).

*FROM LEFT: Apple sauce; Gravy with wine; Mint sauce; Creamy horseradish; Bread sauce; Raspberry and cranberry sauce*

# ACCOMPANIMENTS

Apart from the old favourites on the previous page, the flavour of roasts and cold

cuts can be transformed by serving with one of these imaginative concoctions.

### BEETROOT RELISH

Put 750 g (1½ lb) peeled and coarsely grated fresh beetroot in a large saucepan with 1 chopped onion, 400 g (13 oz) peeled, cored and chopped green apples, 1⅔ cups (410 ml/13 fl oz) white wine vinegar, ½ cup (95 g/3 oz) soft brown sugar, ½ cup (125 g/4 oz) sugar, 2 tablespoons lemon juice and 2 teaspoons salt and stir over low heat, without boiling, until all the sugar has dissolved. Bring to the boil and simmer, stirring

often, for 20–30 minutes, or until the beetroot and onion are tender and the relish is reduced and thickened. Spoon into clean, warm jars and seal. Turn upside down for 2 minutes, invert and leave to cool. Label and date. Leave for a month before using. Store in a cool, dark place up to 12 months. Refrigerate after opening, for up to 6 weeks. Serve with ham, beef, turkey, duck or goose.
Makes 1 litre (32 fl oz).

### MOSTARDA DI FRUTTA

Blend 1 teaspoon of cornflour with 1 tablespoon water in a small bowl. Pour ¾ cup (185 ml/6 fl oz) water into a saucepan and pour in 1¼ cups (315 ml/ 10 fl oz) white wine. Add 1 tablespoon honey, 3 cloves, 1 tablespoon yellow mustard seeds, ¼ teaspoon ground nutmeg, ½ teaspoon grated nutmeg and 2 broken cinnamon sticks. Bring to the boil, then stir in the cornflour mixture, lower the heat and cook, stirring, for

5 minutes or until the mixture boils and thickens. Add 175 g (6 oz) chopped assorted glacé fruits and 1 tablespoon lemon juice and simmer for 15 minutes, or until the fruit is soft and the mixture is thick. Spoon into a warm clean jar and seal immediately. Delicious served with cold meats, especially ham, and poultry and game. Makes 1 cup (250 ml/8 fl oz).

## GRAINY SWEET MUSTARD

Combine 30 g (1 oz) brown or black mustard seeds with 70 g (2¼ oz) yellow mustard seeds in a bowl. Add ½ cup (125 ml/4 fl oz) white wine vinegar, cover and leave overnight. Process three-quarters of the seeds, 2 teaspoons lemon juice, 1 teaspoon salt and 1 tablespoon honey in a food processor until roughly crushed. Transfer to a bowl and stir in the remaining seeds. Spoon into clean jars. Seal. Refrigerate after opening. Keeps for 2 months. Makes 1 cup (250 g/8 oz).

## WASABI MAYONNAISE

Combine ½ cup (125 g/4 oz) each of whole-egg mayonnaise and thick natural yoghurt in a small bowl with 2 teaspoons wasabi paste and 1 tablespoon each of freshly squeezed lime juice and chopped fresh coriander. Stir thoroughly until combined, then allow to stand for at least 20 minutes before serving. This mayonnaise is particularly suitable for serving with cold seafood such as oysters, prawns and fish.
Makes 1 cup (250 g/8 oz).

## RED PEPPER (CAPSICUM) AND CORIANDER AIOLI

Drain the oil from 150 g (5 oz) char-grilled peppers (capsicums). Process the peppers in a food processor with 1 cup (250 g/8 oz) whole-egg mayonnaise for 2 minutes, or until smooth. Add 1 crushed clove of garlic and 1 tablespoon each of lemon juice and chopped fresh coriander. Process until combined. Serve with hot and cold cuts of meat, or seafood such as prawns, fish and scallops. Makes 1½ cups (375 ml/12 fl oz).

## HONEY MUSTARD

Combine 8 tablespoons honey, 4 tablespoons each of yellow mustard and cider vinegar, and 2 tablespoons olive oil in a small pan. Stir constantly over medium heat for 5 minutes, or until thickened. Allow the mixture to cool completely, then spoon into clean jars. Seal the jars, then label and date them. Honey mustard is delicious served with beef, ham or veal. Makes ⅔ cup (170 g/5½ oz).

*FROM LEFT: Beetroot relish; Mostarda di frutta; Grainy sweet mustard; Wasabi mayonnaise; Red pepper and coriander aïoli; Honey mustard*

71

## ROAST LEG OF PORK

**Preparation time:** 30 minutes
**Total cooking time:** 3 hours 25 minutes
**Serves** 6–8

4 kg (8 lb) leg of pork
oil and salt, to rub on pork

### Gravy

1 tablespoon brandy or Calvados
2 tablespoons plain flour
1 1/2 cups (375 ml/12 fl oz) chicken stock
1/2 cup (125 ml/4 fl oz) unsweetened apple juice

1 Preheat the oven to very hot 250°C (500°F/ Gas 10). Score the pork rind with a sharp knife at 2 cm (3/4 inch) intervals. Rub in oil and salt to ensure a crisp crackling. Place the pork, with the rind uppermost, on a rack in a large baking dish.
2 Add a little water to the dish. Bake for 30 minutes, or until the rind begins to crackle and bubble. Reduce the heat to moderate 180°C (350°F/Gas 4) and continue to bake for 2 hours 40 minutes (20 minutes per 500 g/1 lb). The pork is cooked if the juices run clear when the flesh is pierced with a fork. Do not cover or the crackling will soften. Leave in a warm place for 10 minutes before carving.
3 For the gravy, drain off all but 2 tablespoons of the juices from the baking dish. Place the dish on top of the stove over moderate heat, add the brandy and stir quickly to lift the sticky juices from the bottom of the pan. Cook for 1 minute. Remove from the heat, stir in the flour and mix well. Return the pan to the heat and cook for 2 minutes, stirring constantly. Remove from the heat, gradually stir in the stock and apple juice, then return to the heat and cook, stirring constantly, until the gravy boils and thickens. Season, to taste, with salt and pepper. Slice the pork and serve with the crackling, gravy and apple sauce (see page 68).
**NOTE:** Cook the pork just before serving. Cover and refrigerate leftover pork for up to 3–4 days.

*ABOVE: Roast leg of pork*

Put the turkey breast-side-
down and cut the meat
away along the contours of
the bone.

Scrape the flesh from the
wing knuckle and carefully
cut around the joint to
remove the bone.

Spread the stuffing evenly
along the centre of the
turkey meat.

Fold the turkey breast
inwards and sew the turkey
together with a trussing
needle and kitchen string.

# TURKEY BUFFE WITH
# AND FRUIT STUFFING

**Preparation time:** 1 hour
**Total cooking time:** 2 hours 10 minutes
**Serves** 6–8

★★★

2.8 kg (5 lb 10 oz) turkey buffe

## Stuffing

1 1/2 cups (280 g/9 oz) cooked long-grain rice
1/4 cup (40 g/1 1/4 oz) pine nuts, toasted
180 g (6 oz) dried apricots, chopped
250 g (8 oz) chopped pitted prunes
4 spring onions, sliced
1 tablespoon finely grated orange rind
1/3 cup (80 ml/2 3/4 fl oz) orange juice
1 egg, lightly beaten

## Glaze

1/2 cup (125 ml/4 fl oz) orange juice
15 g (1/2 oz) butter
2 teaspoons soft brown sugar

**1** Bone the turkey breast and remove the bone from the wings.
**2** To make the stuffing, combine the rice, pine nuts, apricots, prunes, spring onion, orange rind, juice, 1/2 teaspoon salt and some white pepper. Mix well and stir in the egg.
**3** Lay the turkey flat and spread the stuffing along the centre. Fold the breast inwards and sew the turkey together using a trussing needle and kitchen string. Tuck in the skin at the neck and press the wings in towards the breast. Sew or tie securely with string, or secure well with skewers. Preheat the oven to moderate 180°C (350°F/Gas 4).
**4** To make the glaze, stir the orange juice, butter and sugar together in a small pan. Bring to the boil and stir until the sugar is dissolved. Allow to cool.
**5** Put the turkey on a rack in a baking dish. Bake for 1 3/4–2 hours, basting with the glaze. (If the turkey is overbrowning, loosely cover it with foil.) When cooked, remove from the oven and cover and set aside for 20 minutes before removing the string or skewers. Slice and serve with the remaining glaze.
**NOTE:** For this recipe, you will need to cook about 1/2 cup (100 g/3 1/2 oz) raw rice.

*ABOVE: Turkey buffe with
rice and fruit stuffing*

# ROAST BEEF WITH YORKSHIRE PUDDINGS

**Preparation time:** 15 minutes + 1 hour refrigeration
**Total cooking time:** 1 hour 40 minutes
Serves 6

★ ★

2 kg (4 lb) piece roasting beef
   (Scotch fillet, rump or sirloin)
2 cloves garlic, crushed

**Yorkshire puddings**

3/4 cup (90 g/3 oz) plain flour
1/2 cup (125 ml/4 fl oz) milk
2 eggs

**Red wine gravy**

2 tablespoons plain flour
1/3 cup (80 ml/2 3/4 fl oz) red wine
2 1/2 cups (600 ml/20 fl oz) beef stock

*BELOW: Roast beef with Yorkshire puddings*

**1** Preheat the oven to very hot 240°C (475°F/ Gas 9). Rub the piece of beef with the crushed garlic and some freshly cracked black pepper and drizzle with oil. Bake on a rack in a baking dish for 20 minutes.

**2** Meanwhile, for the Yorkshire puddings, sift the flour and 1/2 teaspoon salt into a large bowl, then make a well in the centre and whisk in the milk. In a separate bowl, whisk the eggs together until fluffy, then add to the batter and mix well. Add 1/2 cup (125 ml/4 fl oz) water and whisk until large bubbles form on the surface. Cover the bowl with plastic wrap and refrigerate for 1 hour.

**3** Reduce the oven to moderate 180°C (350°F/ Gas 4) and continue to roast the meat for 1 hour for a rare result, or longer for well done. Cover loosely with foil and leave in a warm place while making the Yorkshire puddings.

**4** Increase the oven to hot 220°C (425°F/Gas 7). Pour off all the pan juices into a jug and spoon 1/2 teaspoon of the juices into twelve 1/3 cup (80 ml/2 3/4 fl oz) patty or muffin tins. (Reserve the remaining juice for the gravy.) Heat the muffin tins in the oven until the fat is almost

smoking. Whisk the batter again until bubbles form on the surface. Pour into each muffin tin to three-quarters full. Bake for 20 minutes, or until puffed and lightly golden. Make the gravy while the Yorkshire puddings are baking.

**5** To make the gravy, heat 2 tablespoons of the reserved pan juices in the baking dish on the stove over low heat. Add the flour and stir well, scraping the dish to incorporate all the sediment. Cook over medium heat for 1–2 minutes, stirring constantly, until the flour is well browned. Remove from the heat and gradually stir in the wine and stock. Return to the heat, stirring constantly, until the gravy boils and thickens. Simmer for 3 minutes, then season, to taste, with salt and freshly ground black pepper. Strain, if desired.

**6** Serve the beef with the hot Yorkshire puddings and red wine gravy.

**NOTE:** Cooking times vary, but generally, for every 500 g (1 lb) beef, allow 20 minutes for rare, 30 minutes for medium, and 35 minutes for well done.

# ROAST LEG OF LAMB WITH GARLIC AND ROSEMARY

**Preparation time:** 20 minutes
**Total cooking time:** 1 hour 30 minutes
**Serves** 6

2 kg (4 lb) leg of lamb
2 cloves garlic, cut into thin slivers
2 tablespoons fresh rosemary sprigs
2 teaspoons oil

**1** Preheat the oven to moderate 180°C (350°F/ Gas 4). Using a small sharp knife, cut small slits all over the lamb. Insert the slivers of garlic and sprigs of rosemary into the slits.

**2** Brush the lamb with the oil and sprinkle with salt and black pepper. Place on a rack in a baking dish. Add ½ cup (125 ml/4 fl oz) water to the dish. Bake for about 1 hour 30 minutes for medium, or until cooked as desired, basting often with the pan juices. Keep warm and leave for 10–15 minutes before carving. Serve with mint sauce (see page 69).

*ABOVE: Roast leg of lamb with garlic and rosemary*

## CHICKEN BALLOTTINE

Cut through the skin of the chicken down the centre back with a sharp knife.

Separate the flesh from the bone down one side to the breast.

Gradually ease the meat away from the thigh, drumstick and wing.

Roll the chicken up to enclose the filling, then secure with toothpicks.

*ABOVE: Chicken ballottine*

# CHICKEN BALLOTTINE

**Preparation time:** 40 minutes
**Total cooking time:** 1 hour 45 minutes
  + refrigeration
**Serves** 8

✳ ✳ ✳

1.6 kg (3 1/4 lb) chicken
2 red peppers (capsicums)
1 kg (2 lb) silverbeet
30 g (1 oz) butter
1 onion, finely chopped
1 clove garlic, crushed
1/2 cup (50 g/1 3/4 oz) grated Parmesan
1 cup (80 g/2 3/4 oz) fresh breadcrumbs
1 tablespoon chopped fresh oregano
200 g (6 1/2 oz) ricotta

1 To bone the chicken, cut through the skin on the centre back with a sharp knife. Separate the flesh from the bone down one side to the breast, being careful not to pierce the skin. Follow along the bones closely with the knife, gradually easing the meat from the thigh, drumstick and wing. Cut through the thigh bone where it meets the drumstick and cut off the wing tip.

Repeat on the other side, then lift the rib cage away, leaving the flesh in one piece and the drumsticks still attached to the flesh. Scrape all the meat from the drumstick and wings, discarding the bones. Turn the wing and drumstick flesh inside the chicken and lay the chicken out flat, skin-side-down. Refrigerate.
2 Preheat the oven to moderate 180°C (350°F/ Gas 4). Cut the peppers into large flattish pieces, discarding the membranes and seeds. Cook skin-side-up under a hot grill until the skins blister and blacken. Cool in a plastic bag, then peel.
3 Discard the stalks from the silverbeet and finely shred the leaves. Melt the butter in a large frying pan and cook the onion and garlic over medium heat for 5 minutes, or until soft. Add the silverbeet and stir until wilted and all the moisture has evaporated. Cool. In a food processor, process the silverbeet and onion mixture with the Parmesan, breadcrumbs, oregano and half the ricotta. Season with salt and cracked pepper.
4 Spread the silverbeet mixture over the chicken and lay the pepper pieces over the top. Form the remaining ricotta into a roll and place across the width of the chicken. Fold the sides of the chicken in over the filling so they overlap slightly. Tuck the ends in neatly. Secure with toothpicks, then tie with string at 3 cm (1 1/4 inch) intervals.
5 Grease a large piece of foil and place the

chicken in the centre. Roll the chicken up securely in the foil, sealing the ends well. Bake on a baking tray for 1¼–1½ hours, or until the juices run clear when a skewer is inserted in the centre of the meat. Cool, then refrigerate until cold before removing the foil, toothpicks and string. Cut into 1 cm (½ inch) slices to serve.
NOTE: You can ask the butcher or chicken specialist to bone the chicken.

# ROAST TURKEY BREAST WITH PARSLEY CRUST

**Preparation time:** 10 minutes
**Total cooking itme:** 45 minutes
Serves 8

**Parsley crust**
60 g (2 oz) butter
4 spring onions, finely chopped
2 garlic cloves, crushed
2 cups (160 g/5½ oz) fresh white breadcrumbs

2 tablespoons finely chopped fresh parsley
1 kg (2 lb) turkey breast supreme
1 egg, lightly beaten
raspberry and redcurrant sauce (see page 69) or beetroot relish (see page 70), for serving

1 To make the parsley crust, melt the butter in a small frying pan over medium heat. Add the spring onion and garlic and stir until softened. Add the breadcrumbs and parsley and stir until combined. Cool.
2 Preheat the oven to moderate 180°C (350°F/ Gas 4). Place the turkey in a deep baking dish and pat the turkey dry with paper towels. Brush with egg.
3 Press the parsley crust firmly onto the turkey. Bake for 45 minutes, or until the crust is lightly golden. Serve sliced, with raspberry and redcurrant sauce, or beetroot relish, or your favourite accompaniment.
NOTE: The parsley crust can be made a day in advance. Turkey breast supreme is a boneless breast of the turkey with the skin on. It is available from chicken shops and supermarkets.

CHRISTMAS LEGENDS
Most people believe that the white, deep green and red colours we associate with Christmas come from the snowy fields in the northern hemisphere winter contrasting with the brilliant evergreens and crimson berries on the holly plant. However, there is a legend that tells of a lamb making its way to Bethlehem to see the Christ Child. Along the way, its fluffy white fleece was caught on a thorny holly plant and in the struggle to get free, the lamb pricked its skin and tiny droplets of blood oozed out and were frozen onto the branches.

*LEFT: Roast turkey breast with parsley crust (served with beetroot relish)*

## TURKEY ROLL WITH MANDARIN SAUCE

Follow along the rib cage closely with the knife, gradually easing the meat from the bones as you go.

Repeat cutting on the other side and lift the rib cage away, leaving the flesh in one piece and the drumsticks still attached.

Carefully scrape all the meat from the drumsticks and wings, discarding the bones.

Fold the turkey over to enclose the stuffing, then secure with toothpicks or skewers. Truss with kitchen string at regular intervals.

*OPPOSITE PAGE: Turkey roll with mandarin sauce*

# TURKEY ROLL WITH MANDARIN SAUCE

**Preparation time:** 1 hour
+ 30 minutes soaking
**Total cooking time:** 2 hours
**Serves** 8

★★★

No. 34 (3.4 kg) turkey
90 g (3 oz) dried apricots, chopped
30 g (1 oz) butter
1 onion, finely chopped
1 clove garlic, crushed
400 g (13 oz) chicken mince
1 1/2 cups (120 g/4 oz) fresh breadcrumbs
1/2 cup (35 g/1 1/4 oz) currants
1/2 cup (35 g/1 1/4 oz) pistachio nuts, toasted and chopped
3 tablespoons chopped fresh parsley

**Mandarin sauce**

2 mandarins
1 tablespoon long thin strips of mandarin rind
2 tablespoons sugar
1 tablespoon brandy
1 cup (250 ml/8 fl oz) mandarin juice
1/3 cup (80 ml/2 3/4 fl oz) chicken stock
3 teaspoons cornflour
1 spring onion, finely sliced

**1** To bone the turkey, cut through the skin on the centre back with a sharp knife or pair of scissors. Separate the flesh from the bone down one side to the breast, being careful not to pierce the skin. Follow along the ribcage closely with the knife, gradually easing the meat from the bones. Repeat on the other side, then lift the rib cage away, leaving the flesh in one piece and the drumsticks still attached to the flesh. Cut off the wing tips and scrape all the meat from the drumsticks and wings, discarding the bones. Turn the wing and drumstick flesh inside the turkey and lay the turkey out flat, skin-side-down. Refrigerate.

**2** Place the apricots in a small bowl, cover with boiling water and soak for 30 minutes. Preheat the oven to moderate 180°C (350°F/Gas 4).

**3** Meanwhile, melt the butter in a frying pan, add the onion and garlic and cook, stirring, for about 5 minutes, or until the onion is soft. Remove from the heat. Combine the mince, onion mixture, breadcrumbs, currants, nuts, parsley and drained apricots in a large bowl and mix well. Season with salt and pepper and fry a little of the mixture to taste for seasoning. Adjust the seasoning if necessary. Place the turkey on the work surface skin-side-down and form the stuffing mixture into a large sausage shape about the same length as the turkey. Fold the turkey over to enclose the stuffing. Secure with toothpicks or skewers and truss with kitchen string at 3 cm (1 1/4 inch) intervals.

**4** Place in a large lightly greased baking tray. Rub with a little extra oil and some salt and pepper. Roast the turkey roll for 1 1/2–2 hours, or until the juices run clear. Cover and set aside for 10 minutes while preparing the sauce. Carefully remove the string and toothpicks. Cut into slices and serve with the mandarin sauce. If you wish, make a gravy out of the pan juices (see page 68).

**5** For the mandarin sauce, firstly segment the mandarins. Use a sharp knife to remove the rind and white pith, then cut between the membranes to release the segments. Place the strips of mandarin rind in a small pan, cover with water and bring to the boil. Drain and repeat (this removes the bitterness from the rind). Sprinkle the sugar over the base of a saucepan over medium heat and stir gently until all the sugar has dissolved and turned caramel. Remove from the heat, cool slightly, then carefully stir in the brandy, stirring until combined. Return to the heat, stir to dissolve any toffee, then add the combined mandarin juice and chicken stock and stir until heated through. Add the combined cornflour and 1 tablespoon water and stir over heat until the mixture boils and thickens. Add the mandarin segments and rind, stirring until heated through. Stir in the spring onion, then season, to taste.

NOTE: You can ask your butcher or poulterer to bone the turkey. You may have to shop or ring around so leave yourself plenty of time. If time is short, buy a boned and rolled frozen turkey from the supermarket. Defrost according to the instructions, then follow the recipe.

1 Preheat the oven to hot 210°C (415°F/ Gas 6–7). Trim the meat of any excess fat and sinew. Fold the thinner part of the tail end under and tie the meat securely with kitchen string at regular intervals to form an even shape.

2 Rub the meat with freshly ground black pepper. Heat the oil over high heat in a large frying pan. Add the meat and brown well all over. Remove from the heat and allow to cool. Remove the string.

3 Spread the pâté over the top and sides of the beef. Cover with the mushrooms, pressing them onto the pâté. Roll the block pastry out on a lightly floured surface to a rectangle large enough to completely enclose the beef.

4 Place the beef on the pastry, brush the edges with egg, and fold over to enclose the meat completely, brushing the edges of the pastry with the beaten egg to seal, and folding in the ends. Invert onto a greased baking tray so the seam is underneath. Cut leaf shapes from the sheet of puff pastry and use to decorate the Wellington. Use the egg to stick the shapes on. Cut a few slits in the top to allow the steam to escape. Brush the top and sides of the pastry with egg, and cook for 45 minutes for rare, 1 hour for medium or 1½ hours for well done. Leave in a warm place for 10 minutes before cutting into slices for serving.

NOTE: Use a firm pâté, discarding any jelly. Cover the pastry loosely with foil if it begins to darken too much.

## BEEF WELLINGTON

Preparation time: 25 minutes
Total cooking time: 1 hour 30 minutes
Serves 6–8

★ ★

1.2 kg (2 lb 6½ oz) beef fillet or
    rib-eye in 1 piece
1 tablespoon oil
125 g (4 oz) pâté
60 g (2 oz) button mushrooms, sliced
375 g (12 oz) block puff pastry, thawed
1 egg, lightly beaten
1 sheet ready-rolled puff pastry, thawed

*ABOVE: Beef Wellington*

## CHIPOLATAS WRAPPED IN BACON

Preheat the oven to moderate 180°C (350°/ Gas 4). Remove the rind from 6 thin bacon rashers, then halve the bacon widthways. Using 12 chipolatas, wrap a piece of the bacon around each one and secure with toothpicks. Line a baking tray with baking paper and place the chipolatas on the tray. Bake for 25–30 minutes, or until the chipolatas are thoroughly cooked through. Alternatively, the chipolatas can be placed around the base of a roast during the last 20–25 minutes of cooking time. Makes 12.

Spoon the pâté mixture into the meat pocket and press it in with the back of a teaspoon.

Tie thick kitchen string at regular intervals to hold the meat together.

# STANDING RIB ROAST WITH PATE

**Preparation time:** 30 minutes
**Total cooking time:** 2 hours 20 minutes
**Serves** 6

 ✷ ✷

1 rasher bacon, chopped

1 onion, finely chopped

125 g (4 oz) mushrooms, finely chopped

½ cup (50 g/1¾ oz) dry breadcrumbs

125 g (4 oz) pâté (see Note)

2 tablespoons chopped fresh parsley

1 teaspoon chopped fresh oregano

1 egg, lightly beaten

4 kg (8 lb) standing rib roast (6 chops)

1 Preheat the oven to very hot 240°C (475°F/ Gas 9). Place the bacon in a dry frying pan, and cook gently over medium heat until it begins to soften and release its fat. Add the onion and mushroom and cook, stirring, for

3 minutes. Transfer to a bowl and mix in the breadcrumbs, pâté, parsley, oregano and egg. Season, to taste, with salt and freshly ground black pepper.

2 Cut a slit in the meat, between the rib bones and the meat, to form a pocket. Spoon the pâté mixture into the pocket. Secure the meat firmly with string.

3 Place the meat in a baking dish fat-side-up (the bones form a natural rack). Bake for 15 minutes, then reduce the heat to moderate 180°C (350°F/Gas 4). Bake for another 1½ hours for rare, or up to 2 hours for medium, or until cooked according to taste. Work out the cooking time based on 15–20 minutes per 500 g (1 lb) of meat. This will achieve a roast that is well done on the outside and rare inside.

4 Allow the meat to rest for 15 minutes before carving. Remove the string and cut the meat into thick slices, allowing 1 bone per person. Delicious served with gravy (see page 68) and roast vegetables.

**NOTE:** You can use any firm-textured pâté, such as peppercorn or Grand Marnier. Discard the jelly from the top of the pâté.

*ABOVE: Standing rib roast with pâté*

## QUAILS WITH BACON AND ROSEMARY

Place the quails on top of the onion, bacon and rosemary, and brush with the melted butter.

Gradually stir the blended cream and cornflour into the port mixture.

## QUAILS WITH BACON AND ROSEMARY

**Preparation time:** 30 minutes
**Total cooking time:** 35 minutes
**Serves** 4

★ ★

8 quails
1 onion, chopped
3 rashers bacon, chopped
1 tablespoon fresh rosemary leaves
30 g (1 oz) butter, melted
1/2 cup (125 ml/4 fl oz) port
1/2 cup (125 ml/4 fl oz) cream
1 teaspoon cornflour

1 Preheat the oven to moderately hot 200°C (400°F/Gas 6). Wash the quails thoroughly under cold running water, then dry thoroughly inside and out with paper towels. Tuck the wings underneath the quails and tie the legs close to the body with kitchen string.

2 Spread the onion, bacon and rosemary over the base of a baking dish, and add the quails. Brush each quail with melted butter. Combine the port with 1/4 cup (60 ml/2 fl oz) of water, then pour 1/2 cup (125 ml/4 fl oz) of this mixture over the quails.

3 Bake for about 25 minutes, or until the juices run clear when the quails are pierced in the thigh with a skewer. Cover and leave for 10 minutes in a warm place.

4 Carefully strain any juices from the baking dish into a small saucepan, reserving the rosemary and bacon mixture. Add the remaining port and water mixture to the pan, and bring to the boil. Reduce the heat and gradually stir in the blended cream and cornflour, stirring until the mixture boils and is slightly thickened. Serve the quails with the sauce and the reserved rosemary and bacon mixture. Delicious with roast vegetables.

**NOTE:** This recipe can also be made with chicken thigh cutlets instead of the quails.

*ABOVE: Quails with bacon and rosemary*

# ROAST SIRLOIN WITH MUSTARD SAUCE

**Preparation time:** 15 minutes
**Total cooking time:** 1 hour 30 minutes
**Serves** 6

★ ★

1.5 kg (3 lb) beef sirloin
1/3 cup (90 g/3 oz) wholegrain mustard
1 tablespoon Dijon mustard
1 teaspoon honey
1 clove garlic, crushed
1 tablespoon oil

**Mustard sauce**

1 cup (250 ml/8 fl oz) white wine
1 tablespoon Dijon mustard
1/4 cup (60 g/2 oz) wholegrain mustard
2 tablespoons honey
200 g (6 1/2 oz) chilled butter, cubed

**1** Preheat the oven to hot 220°C (425°F/Gas 7). Cut most of the fat from the piece of beef sirloin, leaving a thin layer.
**2** Mix together the mustards and add the honey and garlic. Spread evenly over the sirloin in a thick layer.
**3** Place the oil in a baking dish and heat it in the oven for 2 minutes. Place the meat in the hot dish and roast for 15 minutes.
**4** Reduce the oven temperature to moderately hot 200°C (400°F/Gas 6) and cook for about 40 minutes for rare, 45–50 minutes for medium rare and 60–65 minutes for well done. Remove from the oven, cover the meat and set aside for 10–15 minutes before carving.
**5** For the mustard sauce, pour the wine into a pan and cook over high heat for 5 minutes, or until reduced by half. Add the mustards and honey. Reduce the heat to a simmer and slowly whisk in the butter, without boiling. Remove from the heat and season, to taste. Serve thin slices of the meat with the sauce and roast vegetables.

**MUSTARD**
Mustard seeds come from various species of mustard plant and have differing strengths, colours and sizes. The main types of mustard seeds are yellow, brown and black, the black ones being hotter. Dijon mustard is made from mustard flour mixed with grape must (unfermented juice pressed from the grape, also known as verjuice), vinegar, herbs and spices. Wholegrain mustard uses ground and half-ground seeds resulting in a grainy texture. In cookery, mustard is often added towards the end of the cooking process as it loses its aroma when subjected to heat.

*ABOVE: Roast sirloin with mustard sauce*

## BAKED VEAL WITH SPICY CHICKEN STUFFING

Process the stuffing ingredients until they are fairly smooth, then spread over the veal.

Roll the veal up to enclose the stuffing, then tie at regular intervals with kitchen string.

# BAKED VEAL WITH SPICY CHICKEN STUFFING

Preparation time: 15 minutes
Total cooking time: 1 hour 40 minutes
Serves 6

 ★ ★

1.8 kg (3 lb 10 oz) shoulder of veal, boned and butterflied (ask your butcher to do this)
1 tablespoon olive oil

**Spicy stuffing**

2 teaspoons olive oil
6 spring onions, finely chopped
500 g (1 lb) chicken mince
1 cup (80 g/2³/₄ oz) fresh wholemeal breadcrumbs
1 teaspoon grated fresh ginger
2 red chillies, seeded and chopped
2 eggs, lightly beaten
¹/₃ cup (40 g/1¹/₄ oz) chopped pecans
¹/₂ teaspoon ground black pepper
¹/₄ teaspoon paprika
¹/₂ teaspoon ground coriander

**1** Preheat the oven to moderate 180°C (350°F/ Gas 4). Trim the veal of excess fat and sinew. Place the veal flesh-side-up on a board.
**2** For the spicy stuffing, heat the oil in a large heavy-based frying pan, add the onion and chicken mince and cook over medium heat for 4 minutes, or until brown. Use a fork to break up any lumps.
**3** Remove from the heat and add the remaining stuffing ingredients. Stir to combine. Place in a food processor and process until fairly smooth. Spread the stuffing over the flattened veal, then roll up and tie securely with kitchen string. Brush well with the tablespoon of olive oil and season with salt and pepper. Place on a rack in a baking dish. Pour 1¹/₂ cups (375 ml/12 fl oz) water into the baking dish.
**4** Bake for 1¹/₂ hours for medium, or until cooked to your liking. Add extra water to the pan as necessary and skim fat from the surface. Remove the veal from the dish, cover and set aside for 10 minutes before removing the string and carving.
**5** Drain any excess fat from the pan juices and boil the juices on the stovetop for 2–5 minutes, or until reduced by about half. Strain, then season, to taste, and serve with the sliced veal.

# ROAST CHICKEN WITH RICE STUFFING

Preparation time: 20 minutes + 1 hour standing
Total cooking time: 1 hour 35 minutes
Serves 4

 ★

¹/₂ cup (95 g/3 oz) wild rice
15 pitted prunes, quartered
2 tablespoons port
¹/₃ cup (45 g/1¹/₂ oz) hazelnuts
60 g (2 oz) butter
4 spring onions, finely chopped
¹/₂ green apple, coarsely grated
¹/₂ teaspoon grated orange rind
¹/₂ teaspoon ground cardamom
1 egg, lightly beaten
1.5 kg (3 lb) chicken

**1** Measure the rice into a saucepan and add enough boiling water to come 2.5 cm (1 inch) above the rice. Bring to the boil, reduce the heat and simmer for 10 minutes. Remove from the heat, cover and leave for 1 hour, then drain well.
**2** Preheat the oven to moderate 180°C (350°F/ Gas 4). Combine the prunes and port in a bowl, cover and set aside.
**3** Bake the hazelnuts on a baking tray for 8 minutes. Wrap in a tea towel and rub off the skins. Coarsely chop the hazelnuts.
**4** Melt half the butter in a pan and add the spring onion. Cook over low heat, stirring, for 2 minutes or until soft. Remove from the heat and mix in the rice, prune and port mixture, hazelnuts, apple, orange rind, cardamom and beaten egg. Season with salt and pepper.
**5** Wipe the chicken and pat dry inside and out with paper towels. Spoon the stuffing into the cavity and close the cavity with a toothpick or skewer. Tuck the wings under the chicken and tie the drumsticks securely together with string. Place on a rack in a baking dish.
**6** Melt the remaining butter and brush over the chicken. Bake for 1 hour 15 minutes, or until brown and tender. Cover loosely with foil and leave in a warm place for 10 minutes. Remove the toothpicks and string before carving.

*OPPOSITE PAGE: Baked veal with spicy chicken stuffing (top); Roast chicken with rice stuffing*

## MINTED RACKS OF LAMB

Trim any excess fat from the lamb and clean away any meat or sinew from the bones.

Place the racks, overlapping, on a rack in a baking dish.

Brush the mint glaze all over the back of the racks of lamb.

*RIGHT: Minted racks of lamb*

## MINTED RACKS OF LAMB

**Preparation time:** 15 minutes
**Total cooking time:** 45 minutes
**Serves** 4

4 x 4-cutlet racks of lamb
1 cup (300 g/10 oz) mint jelly
2 tablespoons white wine
3 tablespoons finely chopped fresh chives

**1** Preheat the oven to moderately hot 200°C (400°F/Gas 6). Trim any excess fat from the lamb, leaving a thin layer of fat, and clean any meat or sinew from the ends of the bones using a small sharp knife. Cover the bones with foil. Place on a rack in a baking dish.
**2** Mix the mint jelly and white wine together in a small pan over high heat. Bring to the boil and boil for 4 minutes, or until the mixture is reduced and thickened. Cool slightly, add the chives, then brush over the racks of lamb. Bake for 15–20 minutes for rare, or 35 minutes if you prefer medium-rare, brushing with glaze every 10 minutes. Remove the foil and leave the lamb to stand for 5 minutes before serving with vegetables.

## HERBED BABY CHICKENS

**Preparation time:** 30 minutes
**Total cooking time:** 35 minutes
**Serves** 4

130 g (4¹/₂ oz) butter, softened
2 teaspoons chopped fresh lemon thyme
1 tablespoon chopped fresh parsley
2 spring onions, finely chopped
1 teaspoon finely grated lemon rind
1¹/₂ tablespoons lemon juice
4 x 500 g (1 lb) baby chickens
30 g (1 oz) butter, melted, extra
2 teaspoons lemon juice, extra

**1** Mix the softened butter with the herbs, spring onion, lemon rind, lemon juice, and plenty of salt and pepper.

**2** Preheat the oven to moderately hot 200°C (400°F/Gas 6). Cut the chickens down either side of the backbone. Discard the backbone, and gently flatten the chickens. Carefully lift the skin from the breastbone and the legs and push the butter underneath. Tuck the wings and neck in.

**3** Place the chickens on a rack in a baking dish. Brush with the combined extra butter and extra lemon juice. Bake for 30–35 minutes, or until the juices run clear.

# PEPPERED BEEF FILLET WITH BEARNAISE SAUCE

**Preparation time:** 30 minutes
**Total cooking time:** 45 minutes
**Serves** 6

1 kg (2 lb) beef eye fillet
1 tablespoon oil
2 cloves garlic, crushed
1 tablespoon cracked black peppercorns
2 teaspoons crushed coriander seeds

**Béarnaise sauce**

3 spring onions, chopped
1/2 cup (125 ml/4 fl oz) dry white wine
2 tablespoons tarragon vinegar
1 tablespoon chopped fresh tarragon
125 g (4 oz) butter
4 egg yolks
1 tablespoon lemon juice

**1** Preheat the oven to hot 210°C (415°F/ Gas 6–7). Trim the fillet, removing any excess fat. Tie at regular intervals with kitchen string. Combine the oil and garlic, brush over the fillet, then roll the fillet in the combined peppercorns and coriander seeds.

**2** Place the meat on a rack in a baking dish. Bake for 10 minutes, then reduce the oven to moderate 180°C (350°F/Gas 4) and cook for another 15–20 minutes for a rare result, or until cooked according to taste. Cover and leave for 10–15 minutes.

**3** For the béarnaise sauce, put the spring onion, wine, vinegar and tarragon in a small saucepan. Boil the mixture rapidly until only 2 tablespoons of the liquid is left. Strain and set aside. Melt the butter in a small pan.

**4** Place the wine mixture in a food processor with the egg yolks, and process for 30 seconds. With the motor running, add the hot butter in a thin stream, leaving the milky white sediment behind in the saucepan. Process until thickened. Add the lemon juice, to taste, and season with salt and white pepper.

**5** Serve the beef with the béarnaise sauce, and some broccoli and potatoes.

**NOTE:** Béarnaise sauce has a strong taste which is produced by quickly cooking the wine and vinegar with the spring onion and pungent fresh tarragon until the liquid reduces.

*ABOVE: Peppered beef fillet with béarnaise sauce*

## LEMONS

When squeezing juice from a lemon, do it as close as possible to the time you will be using it as the flavour deteriorates when exposed to air. To make the lemon easier to juice, roll it on the bench with the palm of your hand a few times or soak it in a bowl of hot water for 15–30 minutes. An average-sized lemon will yield 2–3 tablespoons of juice. Select lemons that are brightly coloured and feel heavy for their size.

*ABOVE: Herbed rack of veal*

# HERBED RACK OF VEAL

**Preparation time:** 45 minutes
**Total cooking time:** 1 hour 40 minutes
**Serves** 4–6

1.2 kg (2 lb 6$^1/_2$ oz) rack of veal
  (8 cutlets)
1 cup (80 g/2$^3/_4$ oz) fresh breadcrumbs
$^1/_2$ cup (50 g/1$^3/_4$ oz) dry breadcrumbs
1 tablespoon chopped fresh parsley
1 tablespoon chopped fresh basil
2 egg whites, lightly beaten
2 cloves garlic, crushed
1 tablespoon oil
30 g (1 oz) butter, melted

**Lemon sauce**
$^1/_3$ cup (80 ml/2$^3/_4$ fl oz) dry white wine
2 tablespoons lemon juice
2 teaspoons sugar
$^1/_2$ cup (125 ml/4 fl oz) cream
60 g (2 oz) chilled butter, cubed
1 tablespoon chopped fresh parsley

**1** Preheat the oven to warm 160°C (315°F/Gas 2–3). Trim the veal of excess fat. Combine all the breadcrumbs, parsley and basil in a bowl. Add the combined egg whites, garlic, oil and butter, and mix well. Add a little water if the mixture is too dry. Press the mixture firmly over the meat and place in a baking dish, crust-side-up. Bake for 1$^1/_4$ hours for a medium result, or 1$^1/_2$ hours for well done.
**2** Remove the meat from the pan and leave in a warm place for 10 minutes. Drain off all except 2 tablespoons of pan juices.

**3** For the lemon sauce, put the baking dish with the reserved pan juices on the stove. Add ½ cup (125 ml/4 fl oz) water with the wine, lemon juice, sugar and cream. Bring to the boil, then reduce the heat. Simmer for 5–7 minutes, or until the mixture is reduced by about ½ cup (125 ml/4 fl oz). Remove from the heat and whisk in the butter, 1 cube at a time, then strain and stir in the parsley. Cut the veal rack into cutlets and serve with the lemon sauce and some steamed baby squash.

## GAME PIE

**Preparation time:** 40 minutes + refrigeration
**Total cooking time:** 2 hours 30 minutes
**Serves** 4–6

★★★

1 kg (2 lb) rabbit, boned, cut into bite-sized
    pieces
1.25 kg (2½ lb) venison goulash or
    diced venison
¼ cup (30 g/1 oz) plain flour
2–3 tablespoons oil
2 rashers bacon, chopped
1 onion, sliced into thin wedges
2 cloves garlic, crushed
150 g (5 oz) button mushrooms, cut in halves
1 cup (250 ml/8 fl oz) red wine
1 cup (250 ml/8 fl oz) beef stock
3 sprigs fresh thyme
2 bay leaves
1½ x 375 g (12 oz) blocks puff pastry, thawed
1 egg yolk
2 tablespoons milk

**1** Lightly coat the rabbit and venison in seasoned flour. Heat the oil in a large saucepan and cook the bacon over medium heat until golden. Remove. Brown the meats well in batches, remove and set aside. Add the onion and garlic to the saucepan and cook until browned.
**2** Return the bacon and meat to the saucepan and add the mushrooms, wine, stock, thyme and bay leaves. Bring to the boil, then reduce the heat and simmer over low heat, stirring occasionally, for 1½ hours, or until the meat is tender. Transfer to a heatproof bowl. Remove the thyme and bay leaves. Refrigerate until cold.
**3** Preheat the oven to moderately hot 200°C (400°F/Gas 6). Spoon the mixture into a

2 litre (64 fl oz) ovenproof dish. Roll the half block of pastry on a lightly floured surface to about 5 mm (¼ inch) thick. Cut strips the width of the pie dish rim and secure to the dish with a little water. Reserve the leftover pastry. Roll the other block of pastry on a lightly floured surface until large enough to fit the top of the pie dish. Brush the edges of the pastry strips with a little combined egg yolk and milk. Drape the pastry over the rolling pin and lower it onto the top of the pie. Trim off any excess pastry using a sharp knife. Score the edges of the pastry with the back of a knife to seal. Use any leftover pastry to decorate the top. Cut two slits in the top of the pastry and brush all over with the remaining egg and milk mixture. Bake for 30–40 minutes, or until puffed and golden.
**NOTE:** Ask the butcher to bone the rabbit. Order the venison from the butcher or poultry shop.

*ABOVE: Game pie*

Remove from the heat and allow to cool.

**2** Place the veal in a baking dish and rub with salt and white pepper. Pour the onion and wine mixture into the baking dish with the veal.

**3** Mix the breadcrumbs and cheese, and press firmly on the veal to form a thick coating. (This will help stop the veal drying out.) Melt the remaining butter and pour over the cheese crust.

**4** Roast the veal for 1¼–1½ hours, checking every 30 minutes and being careful not to disturb the crust. If the crust is browning too quickly, cover lightly with foil. Leave for 10 minutes before carving into 1 cm (½ inch) slices. Spoon pan juices over the top.

**NOTE:** Nut of veal is a piece from the leg.

## LAMB CROWN ROAST WITH SAGE STUFFING

**Preparation time:** 30 minutes
**Total cooking time:** 50 minutes
**Serves** 4–6

1 crown roast of lamb (minimum 12 cutlets)
20 g (¾ oz) butter
2 onions, chopped
1 green apple, peeled and chopped
2 cups (160 g/5½ oz) fresh breadcrumbs
2 tablespoons chopped fresh sage
1 tablespoon chopped fresh parsley
¼ cup (60 ml/2 fl oz) unsweetened apple juice
2 eggs, separated

**1** Preheat the oven to hot 210°C (415°F/ Gas 6–7). Trim the meat of excess fat and sinew.

**2** Melt the butter in a small pan. Add the onion and apple and cook over medium heat until soft. Remove from the heat and stir into the combined breadcrumbs, sage and parsley. Whisk the apple juice and egg yolks together, then lightly stir into the breadcrumb mixture.

**3** Beat the egg whites in a small bowl with electric beaters until soft peaks form. Fold lightly into the stuffing mixture.

**4** Place the roast on a sheet of greased foil in a baking dish. Wrap some foil around the tops of the bones to prevent burning. Spoon the stuffing into the cavity. Roast for 45 minutes for medium, or until cooked to your liking. Leave for 10 minutes before cutting between the cutlets.

**NOTE:** Excess stuffing can be moistened with apple juice, rolled in greased foil and baked.

## VEAL FOYOT

**Preparation time:** 25 minutes
**Total cooking time:** 1 hour 35 minutes
**Serves** 6

50 g (1¾ oz) butter
1 onion, chopped
¾ cup (185 ml/6 fl oz) white wine
¾ cup (185 ml/6 fl oz) beef stock
1.4–1.5 kg (2 lb 13 oz–3 lb) nut of veal
1 cup (80 g/2¾ oz) fresh breadcrumbs
125 g (4 oz) Gruyère cheese, grated

**1** Preheat the oven to moderate 180°C (350°F/ Gas 4). Melt half the butter in a saucepan and fry the onion until soft. Add the wine and stock, bring to the boil and boil for 2 minutes. Add ¼ teaspoon each of salt and white pepper.

*ABOVE: Veal foyot*

## ROAST PORK FILLET WITH APPLE AND MUSTARD SAUCE AND GLAZED APPLES

**Preparation time:** 30 minutes
**Total cooking time:** 25 minutes
**Serves** 4

750 g (1 1/2 lb) pork fillet

30 g (1 oz) butter

1 tablespoon oil

1 clove garlic, crushed

1/2 teaspoon grated fresh ginger

1 tablespoon seeded mustard

1/4 cup (60 ml/2 fl oz) apple sauce

2 tablespoons chicken stock

1/2 cup (125 ml/4 fl oz) cream

1 teaspoon cornflour

**Glazed apples**

2 green apples

50 g (1 3/4 oz) butter

2 tablespoons soft brown sugar

**1** Trim the pork fillet, removing any fat or sinew from the outside. Tie the fillet with kitchen string at 3 cm (1 1/4 inch) intervals to keep in shape.

**2** Heat the butter and oil in a frying pan, add the pork fillet and cook until lightly browned all over. Remove and place on a rack in a baking dish. (Retain the cooking oils in the frying pan.) Add 1/2 cup (125 ml/4 fl oz) water to the baking dish and bake in a moderate 180°C (350°F/Gas 4) oven for 15–20 minutes. Leave in a warm place for 10 minutes before removing the string and slicing.

**3** For the sauce, reheat the oils in the frying pan, add the garlic and ginger and stir for 1 minute. Stir in the mustard, apple sauce and stock. Slowly stir in the combined cream and cornflour and stir until the mixture boils and thickens.

**4** For the glazed apples, cut the apples into 1 cm (1/2 inch) slices. Melt the butter in the pan and add the sugar. Stir until the sugar dissolves. Add the apple slices and pan-fry, turning occasionally, until the apples are glazed and lightly browned.

**5** Slice the pork and serve the apple and mustard sauce over it. Serve with the glazed apples.

**NOTE:** Pork fillets can be thick and short or long and thin and the time they take to cook will vary accordingly.

*ABOVE: Roast pork fillet with apple and mustard sauce and glazed apples*

# SEAFOOD

If you prefer a lighter Christmas meal or simply feel like a change, you can't go past lovely fresh seafood. This chapter offers some irresistible alternatives to roast turkey that are guaranteed to tempt even the most die-hard of traditionalists. Rosy pink salmon, whether baked or lightly poached, makes a magnificent celebration feast. Or, if you're feeling really indulgent, why not go all out and treat yourselves to lobster with a creamy parsley mayonnaise. For any lover of seafood, though, luxury begins and ends with the oyster. Served with a little lemon and cracked black pepper or with a robust sauce, these velvety morsels are true perfection.

POACHED OCEAN
TROUT

Strain the cooled liquid into a fish kettle that is big enough to hold the whole fish.

After 10 minutes cooking, test the fish with a fork. The thickest part should flake easily.

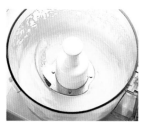

Blend the mixture in the food processor until thick and creamy.

*OPPOSITE PAGE:*
*Poached ocean trout*

# POACHED OCEAN TROUT

**Preparation time:** 50 minutes
**Total cooking time:** 50 minutes
**Serves** 8–10

★★

2 litres (64 fl oz) good-quality white wine
1/4 cup (60 ml/2 fl oz) white wine vinegar
2 onions
10 whole cloves
4 carrots, chopped
1 lemon, cut in quarters
2 bay leaves
4 stalks fresh parsley
1 teaspoon whole black peppercorns
2.5 kg (5 lb) ocean trout, cleaned, gutted
  and scaled

**Dill mayonnaise**

1 egg, at room temperature
1 egg yolk, at room temperature
1 tablespoon lemon juice
1 teaspoon white wine vinegar
1 1/2 cups (375 ml/12 fl oz) light olive oil
1–2 tablespoons chopped fresh dill

**1** Combine the wine and vinegar with 2.5 litres (80 fl oz) water in a large heavy-based pan.
**2** Stud the onions with the cloves. Add to the pan with the carrot, lemon, bay leaves, parsley and peppercorns. Bring to the boil, reduce the heat and simmer for 30–35 minutes. Cool. Strain into a fish kettle that will hold the trout.
**3** Place the whole fish in the fish kettle and add water if necessary, to just cover the fish. Bring to the boil, then reduce the heat to a low simmer, cover and poach gently for 10–15 minutes, until the fish flakes when tested in the thickest part. Remove the kettle from the heat and leave the fish to cool in the liquid.
**4** For the dill mayonnaise, process the egg, yolk, lemon juice and wine vinegar in a food processor for 10 seconds, or until blended. With the motor running, add the oil in a thin, steady stream, blending until all the oil is added and the mayonnaise is thick and creamy—it should be thick enough to form peaks. Transfer to a bowl and stir in the dill and salt and pepper, to taste.
**5** Remove the cold fish from the liquid, place on a serving platter and peel back the skin. Garnish with watercress and lemon slices. Serve with the dill mayonnaise.

NOTE: Atlantic salmon, snapper, sea bass or red emperor can also be used. If you don't have a fish kettle, use a baking dish big enough to hold the fish, cover and bake in a moderate 180°C (350°F/Gas 4) oven for 20–30 minutes.

# BAKED SALMON

**Preparation time:** 10 minutes
**Total cooking time:** 30 minutes + 45 minutes
  standing
**Serves** 8

★

2 kg (4 lb) Atlantic salmon, cleaned, gutted
  and scaled
2 spring onions, roughly chopped
3 sprigs fresh dill
1/2 lemon, thinly sliced
6 black peppercorns
1/4 cup (60 ml/2 fl oz) dry white wine
3 bay leaves

**1** Preheat the oven to moderate 180°C (350°F/ Gas 4). If the salmon is too long for your baking dish, remove the head. Rinse the salmon under cold running water and pat dry inside and out with paper towels. Stuff the cavity with the spring onion, dill, lemon slices and peppercorns.
**2** Brush a large double-layered piece of foil with oil and lay the salmon on the foil. Sprinkle the wine all over the salmon and arrange the bay leaves over the top. Fold the foil over and wrap up tightly.
**3** Bake in a shallow baking dish for 30 minutes. Turn the oven off and leave the salmon in the oven for 45 minutes with the door closed. Do not open or remove the foil during the cooking or standing time.
**4** Undo the foil and carefully peel away the skin of the salmon on the top side. Carefully flip the salmon onto the serving plate and remove the skin from the other side. Pull out the fins and any visible bones. Serve at room temperature with lemon slices.
NOTE: This is delicious served with tarragon mayonnaise. Place 2 egg yolks, 1 teaspoon Dijon mustard and 2 teaspoons lemon juice in a food processor and process for 10 seconds. With the motor running, add 1 cup (250 ml/8 fl oz) light olive oil in a slow, thin stream until combined. Stir in 2 teaspoons of lemon juice, 2 teaspoons of chopped French tarragon and season with salt and white pepper.

## MIXED SEAFOOD SALAD

After removing the heads from the yabbies, cut down either side of each undershell with scissors.

Pull back the shells and remove the yabby flesh in one piece.

When the fish is just tender, remove from the pan with a slotted spoon.

*ABOVE: Mixed seafood salad*

# MIXED SEAFOOD SALAD

**Preparation time:** 1 hour + 1 hour refrigeration
**Total cooking time:** 15 minutes
**Serves** 8

✷✷

20 (about 800 g/1 lb 10 oz) large cooked prawns
12 cooked yabbies or small crayfish
20 scallops (about 310 g/10 oz)
1/2 cup (125 ml/4 fl oz) white wine
pinch of dried thyme
pinch of dried tarragon or a bay leaf
400 g (13 oz) salmon or trout fillets
6 hard-boiled eggs
150 g (5 oz) mixed lettuce leaves
2 tablespoons chopped fresh flat-leaf parsley
2 ripe avocados, sliced
2 tablespoons lemon juice

**Dill dressing**

1/2 cup (125 ml/4 fl oz) extra virgin olive oil
2 tablespoons white wine vinegar
1 teaspoon sugar
2 teaspoons Dijon mustard
1 tablespoon chopped fresh dill

**Green goddess dressing**

2 egg yolks
2 teaspoons Dijon mustard
3 tablespoons lemon juice
1 cup (250 ml/8 fl oz) olive oil
4 anchovy fillets, finely chopped
1 clove garlic, crushed
1/4 cup (60 g/2 oz) sour cream
3 tablespoons chopped fresh mixed herbs
   (chives, parsley, dill)

**1** Peel the prawns and pull out the dark vein from each prawn back, starting at the head end.
**2** Place the yabbies on their backs. Cut through the base of the head of each yabby to remove and discard each head. With scissors, cut down either side of each soft undershell, pull back and remove the flesh in one piece.
**3** Slice or pull off any vein, membrane or hard white muscle from the scallops, leaving the roe attached.
**4** Put 1 cup (250 ml/8 fl oz) water with the wine, herbs, and a pinch each of salt and pepper, in a saucepan. Bring to the boil, then reduce the heat and simmer for 5 minutes. Add the scallops and poach for 1–2 minutes, or until they have just turned white, then remove with a slotted

spoon and drain on a wire rack. Add the fish fillets to the saucepan and poach for about 5 minutes, until cooked and just tender. Remove with a slotted spoon and drain on a wire rack. Break into large pieces.

**5** Combine the prawns, yabbies, scallops and fish in a bowl.

**6** For the dill dressing, combine the oil, wine vinegar, sugar, mustard and dill in a small jug. Whisk until blended, then season, to taste, with salt and freshly ground black pepper. Pour over the seafood, cover and refrigerate for 1 hour.

**7** For the green goddess dressing, process the egg yolks, mustard and 2 tablespoons lemon juice in a food processor or blender for 30 seconds, or until light and creamy. With the motor running, add the oil in a thin, steady stream, increasing the flow as the mayonnaise thickens. Add the remaining lemon juice, to taste, the anchovy fillets, garlic, sour cream and fresh herbs. Season with salt and pepper and pulse for 30 seconds to combine.

**8** Peel and slice the eggs, reserving 2 yolks. Put half the lettuce leaves in a deep serving bowl. Arrange half the seafood over the lettuce, reserving the dill dressing. Sprinkle with half the parsley, top with half the avocado, drizzle with half the lemon juice, then finish with half the sliced eggs, including the extra whites. Season with salt and pepper. Repeat the layers and season, to taste. Drizzle with the reserved dill dressing. Crumble the reserved egg yolks over the top. Serve with the green goddess dressing.

## PICKLED PRAWNS

**Preparation time:** 20 minutes
  + 48 hours refrigeration
**Total cooking time:** Nil
**Serves** 4–6

40 cooked large prawns

1 fennel bulb, or 2 baby bulbs (600 g/1 1/4 lb)

2 small red onions, thinly sliced

2 tablespoons thin strips of orange rind

2 tablespoons thin strips of lime rind

1/2 cup (125 ml/4 fl oz) lime juice

1/3 cup (80 ml/2 3/4 fl oz) orange juice

1 cup (250 ml/8 fl oz) olive oil

1/2 cup (125 ml/4 fl oz) tarragon vinegar

2 red birds-eye chillies, finely sliced

1 teaspoon sugar

**1** Peel the prawns, leaving the tails intact. Gently pull out the dark vein from each prawn back, starting at the head end. Slice the fennel thinly, removing any tough outer layers first and reserving some of the green fronds for garnish. Place the prawns, fennel, onion and orange and lime rind in a non-metallic bowl and mix well.

**2** Mix the remaining ingredients together, add 1 teaspoon salt and pour over the prawn mixture. Cover, either with a lid or plastic wrap, and refrigerate for 48 hours. Stir the mixture once or twice during this time to make sure every part of the prawns comes into contact with the marinade.

**3** Garnish the prawns with the reserved fennel fronds and serve with fresh crusty bread and a mixed salad.

**NOTE:** Pickled prawns can be combined with a mixture of cooked seafood such as calamari, baby octopus, mussels, scallops, and pieces of white-fleshed fish such as perch or ling.

*ABOVE: Pickled prawns*

# OYSTERS
There is probably nothing more delicious than a fresh oyster straight from the shell, but oysters are also superb when combined with other flavours. These recipes all use 24 oysters.

### OYSTERS WRAPPED IN CUCUMBER

Trim the ends from a Lebanese cucumber with a vegetable peeler, then carefully peel 24 long thin strips from the entire width of the cucumber. Cut 8–10 chives into lengths 1 cm (½ inch) longer than the width of the cucumber strip. Place an oyster and 3 lengths of chive on one end of each cucumber strip, so the chives stick out the top. Roll up to enclose. Place 24 chives in a small bowl, cover with boiling water, then drain. Tie a chive around each roll to secure. Stand upright and top each with a little sour cream and salmon roe.

### OYSTERS WITH PINE NUTS AND BACON

Remove 24 oysters from their shells. Clean and dry the shells. Finely chop 2 rindless rashers of bacon and fry in a frying pan for about 2 minutes, or until just soft. Remove from the pan. Melt 30 g (1 oz) butter in the same pan, add 1 finely chopped small onion and stir until soft. Add 125 g (4 oz) torn rocket leaves to the pan and stir until just wilted. Stir in 2 teaspoons Worcestershire sauce. Divide the rocket among the oyster shells, replace the oysters in the shells and top with the combined bacon and 2 tablespoons roughly chopped toasted pine nuts. Grill under a hot grill for 2–3 minutes, or until the bacon is crisp.

## OYSTERS IN POTATOES WITH CHEESE SAUCE

Cook 24 baby new potatoes in boiling water for 5 minutes, or until tender. Drain and cool. Slice a round from the top of each potato and with a melon baller, scoop a ball from the centre of each. Trim the bases to sit flat. Fill a saucepan one third full of oil and heat to 180°C (350°F), or until a cube of bread dropped in the oil turns brown in 15 seconds. Deep-fry the potatoes until golden, then drain on paper towels. Melt 15 g (½ oz) butter in a small saucepan, add 24 oysters and toss quickly to seal. Remove from the pan. Add half a small finely chopped onion to the pan and fry until soft. Add 1 tablespoon brandy and, keeping away from anything flammable, ignite with a match. Allow the flames to die down. Add ½ cup (125 ml/4 fl oz) cream, bring to the boil, then reduce the heat and simmer until slightly thickened. Remove from the heat, stir in ¼ cup (30 g/1 oz) grated Cheddar and 2 teaspoons chopped fresh dill. Season. Return the oysters to the sauce, then spoon into the potatoes. Grill until golden brown. Sprinkle with dill.

## CRUMBED OYSTERS WITH WASABI CREAM

Remove 24 oysters from their shells. Clean and dry the shells. Toss the oysters in plain flour, then in 1 beaten egg. Toss in ⅔ cup (55 g/2 oz) fresh breadcrumbs, combined with 1 tablespoon sesame seeds and 2 teaspoons black sesame seeds. Fill a saucepan one third full of oil and heat to 180°C (350°F), or until a cube of bread dropped in the oil browns in 15 seconds. Deep-fry the oysters until golden, then drain. Beat 1½ tablespoons cream until thick, then beat in 1 teaspoon wasabi paste and 2 tablespoons mayonnaise. Spoon a little into each dried shell. Top with an oyster and a piece of segmented lime. (Remove the rind and pith with a sharp knife, then cut between the membranes to release the segments.)

## OYSTERS WITH BLOODY MARY SAUCE

Remove 24 oysters from their shells. Clean and dry the shells. Combine ¼ cup (60 ml/2 fl oz) tomato juice, 2 teaspoons vodka, 1 teaspoon lemon juice, ½ teaspoon Worcestershire sauce and a few drops of Tabasco sauce in a small bowl. Cut 1 celery stick into very thin julienne strips and place in the bases of the oyster shells. Top with an oyster and drizzle with tomato mixture. Sprinkle with 1−2 teaspoons snipped chives.

*FROM LEFT: Oysters wrapped in cucumber; Oysters with pine nuts and bacon; Crumbed oysters with wasabi cream (top); Oysters in potatoes with cheese sauce; Oysters with bloody Mary sauce*

GRAVLAX

Rub the sugar mixture into the second salmon fillet.

Whisk all the ingredients of the mustard sauce together in a bowl.

The salmon can be served sliced thinly on an angle towards the tail.

# GRAVLAX

**Preparation time:** 20 minutes
+ 24 hours refrigeration
**Total cooking time:** Nil
**Serves** 20

★ ★ ★

1/4 cup (60 g/2 oz) sugar
2 tablespoons coarse sea salt
1 teaspoon crushed black peppercorns
2.5 kg (5 lb) salmon, filleted and deboned but with the skin left on (ask your fishmonger to do this)
1 tablespoon vodka or brandy
4 tablespoons very finely chopped fresh dill

## Mustard sauce

1 1/2 tablespoons cider vinegar
1 teaspoon caster sugar
1/2 cup (125 ml/4 fl oz) olive oil
2 teaspoons chopped fresh dill
2 tablespoons Dijon mustard

1 Combine the sugar, salt and peppercorns in a small dish. Remove any bones from the salmon fillets with tweezers. Pat dry with paper towels and lay one fillet skin-side-down in a shallow tray or baking dish. Sprinkle with half the vodka or brandy, rub half the sugar mixture into the flesh, then sprinkle with half the dill. Sprinkle the remaining vodka over the second salmon fillet and rub the remaining sugar mixture into the flesh. Lay it flesh-side-down on top of the dill-coated salmon. Cover with plastic wrap and place a heavy board on top—weigh this down with 3 heavy cans or a foil-covered brick. Refrigerate for 24 hours, turning the salmon over after 12 hours.

2 To make the mustard sauce, whisk together the ingredients, then cover until needed.

3 When the salmon is ready, take off the weights and remove the plastic wrap. Lift off the top fillet and lay both fillets on a wooden board. Brush off all the dill and any seasoning mixture with a stiff pastry brush. Sprinkle with the remaining fresh dill and press it onto the salmon flesh, shaking off any excess. Serve the salmon whole on the serving board and thinly slice (use a very sharp knife with a long flexible blade—a filleting knife is ideal), as required, on an angle towards the tail. Serve with the mustard sauce.

NOTE: Gravlax can be refrigerated, covered, for up to a week. It can also be frozen.

**CHRISTMAS CANDLES**
Candles are a traditional part of Christmas and are used extensively in churches, often lit for the service on Christmas Eve. They are said to symbolise Christ, 'The Light of the World'. The tradition may be related to the Jewish Hanukkah, the 'Annual Festival of Lights'. In some parts of the world, people light candles placed on their windowsills. This is supposed to go back as far as the Middle Ages when people lit the candles as a guide for the Christ child to their homes.

# SCALLOPS EN BROCHETTE

**Preparation time:** 15 minutes + 30 minutes soaking skewers
**Total cooking time:** 10 minutes
**Serves** 6

36 scallops
8–10 slices prosciutto
8–10 spring onions
60 g (2 oz) butter, melted
1 clove garlic, crushed
2 tablespoons lime juice
lime slices or wedges, for serving

**1** If using wooden skewers, soak them in cold water for 30 minutes to prevent them burning during cooking.
**2** Slice or pull off any vein, membrane or hard white muscle from the scallops, leaving the roe attached. Cut each slice of prosciutto into 3 pieces (this may depend on the size of the scallop) and gently wrap a piece of prosciutto around each scallop. Cut the spring onions into short lengths. Thread them onto skewers, alternating 3 scallops and 3 pieces of spring onion on each skewer.
**2** Place on a preheated grill or barbecue and cook for 3–5 minutes each side, or until the prosciutto is lightly browned and the scallops are just cooked through. Brush occasionally with the combined melted butter, garlic and lime juice. Serve with any remaining warm butter mixture and lime slices.

## SPICY COCKTAIL SAUCE

Stir together ¾ cup (185 g/6 oz) whole-egg mayonnaise, 3 tablespoons tomato sauce, 2 teaspoons Worcestershire sauce, 1 teaspoon each of lemon juice and sweet chilli sauce and 2 teaspoons chopped fresh parsley in a bowl. This spicy sauce is suitable for serving with cooked fish. Makes about ¾ cup (185 ml/6 fl oz).

*ABOVE: Scallops en brochette*

**Second layer**

250 g (8 oz) skinless, boneless salmon fillet

2 egg whites, chilled

2 tablespoons chopped fresh chives

1 cup (250 ml/8 fl oz) cream, chilled

**Tomato coulis**

2 tablespoons extra virgin olive oil

1 onion, very finely chopped

750 g (1 1/2 lb) ripe Roma (egg) tomatoes, peeled, seeded and diced

2 tablespoons Grand Marnier, optional

**1** Preheat the oven to moderate 180°C (350°F/Gas 4). Brush a 1.5 litre (22 x 12 cm/9 x 5 inch) loaf tin with oil and line the base with baking paper. To make the first layer, peel the prawns and gently pull out the dark vein from each prawn back, starting at the head end. Finely chop the prawns in a food processor. Add the egg whites to the processor one at a time, processing until smooth. Season to taste, with salt, pepper and grated nutmeg. Add the cream slowly, being careful not to overmix. Spoon into the tin, cover and refrigerate.

**2** Cook the beans in boiling water until tender, then drain and plunge into cold water. Drain again and dry with paper towels. Arrange lengthways over the prawn mixture.

**3** To make the second layer, process the salmon until finely chopped. Add the egg whites one at a time and process until smooth, then add the chives. Add the cream slowly, being careful not to overmix. Spread evenly over the beans.

**4** Cover the loaf tin tightly with lightly greased foil and place in a baking dish. Pour boiling water into the dish to come halfway up the sides of the tin. Bake for 25 minutes, or until lightly set in the centre. Leave to cool before removing the foil. Cover with plastic wrap and refrigerate until firm. Serve at room temperature. Before serving the terrine, pour off any excess liquid that has gathered in the terrine dish.

**5** For the tomato coulis, heat the oil in a pan, add the onion and cook over medium heat for 5 minutes, or until soft. Add the tomato and Grand Marnier and bring to the boil. Boil for 8 minutes, or until thickened slightly. Cool, then process until smooth. Season, to taste, and serve with slices of terrine.

NOTE: This terrine can be made a day or two in advance and kept, covered, in the refrigerator. To minimize the amount of excess liquid that appears in this dish, use fresh seafood as frozen seafood will create more liquid.

# SEAFOOD TERRINE

**Preparation time:** 1 hour + cooling and refrigeration

**Total cooking time:** 50 minutes

**Serves 8**

**First layer**

500 g (1 lb) raw prawns, chilled

2 egg whites, chilled

freshly grated nutmeg, to taste

1 cup (250 ml/8 fl oz) cream, chilled

150 g (5 oz) baby green beans

*ABOVE: Seafood terrine*

# FESTIVE PRAWN SALAD

Preparation time: 30 minutes
Total cooking time: 10 minutes
Serves 8

2 kg (4 lb) small cooked prawns
1 small baguette, very thinly sliced
2 tablespoons oil
1 clove garlic, halved
100 g (3¹/₂ oz) baby English spinach
100 g (3¹/₂ oz) baby rocket leaves
2 tablespoons extra virgin olive oil
1 tablespoon lemon juice
3 avocados, sliced

**Rouille**

1 small red pepper (capsicum)
1 red chilli
1 slice white bread, crusts removed
2 cloves garlic, halved
1 egg yolk
1 tablespoon lime juice
¹/₄ cup (60 ml/2 fl oz) olive oil

1 Peel the prawns and gently pull out the dark vein from each prawn back. Set aside. Preheat the oven to moderately hot 200°C (400°F/ Gas 7). Lightly brush both sides of the bread slices with oil. Place on baking trays and cook for 10 minutes, or until crisp and golden brown. Rub each slice with the cut garlic.

2 For the rouille, remove the seeds and membrane from the pepper and chilli, cut into flattish pieces and cook skin-side-up under a hot grill until the skins blacken and blister. Cool in a plastic bag, then peel. Soak the bread in 3 tablespoons water, then squeeze out any excess. Place the pepper, chilli, bread, garlic, egg yolk and lime juice in a food processor and process to combine. With the motor running, gradually add the olive oil in a thin stream, until the mixture is the texture of thick smooth mayonnaise.

3 Place the prawns and half the rouille in a bowl and mix to coat the prawns. Season.

4 Toss the spinach and rocket in a bowl with the oil and lemon juice until lightly coated. Place a mound in the centre of each plate and top each with 4 slices of avocado.

5 Spoon some of the prawn mixture on top of the avocado. Serve with a stack of toasts and extra rouille.

**PEPPERS** (CAPSICUMS)
Sweet peppers, or capsicums, became popular in cookery early in the twentieth century. Peppers come from a genus of plants which includes a wide range of species. Within this range, the size, shape, colour, hotness (chillies) and taste vary considerably. This is probably the reason there is often confusion about what each type is called. The extensive range includes those known as peppers, sweet peppers, bell peppers, pimento, chilli peppers and chillies. Red peppers are sweeter than the other colours and are especially good for roasting and grilling.

*LEFT: Festive prawn salad*

# LOBSTER WITH PARSLEY MAYONNAISE

**Preparation time:** 25 minutes
**Total cooking time:** Nil
**Serves** 4

2 cooked medium rock lobsters
mixed lettuce leaves, for serving
lemon wedges, for serving
fresh chives, chopped, for serving

## Parsley mayonnaise

2 cups (40 g/1¼ oz) firmly packed fresh
   parsley sprigs, stalks removed
3 teaspoons Dijon mustard
1 teaspoon honey
1 tablespoon lemon juice
¼ cup (60 ml/2 fl oz) cream
¼ cup (60 g/2 oz) whole-egg mayonnaise

**1** Using a sharp knife, cut each lobster in half lengthways through the shell. Lift the meat from the tail and body. Crack the legs and prise the meat from them. Remove the cream-coloured vein and soft body matter and discard. Cut the lobster meat into 2 cm (¾ inch) pieces, cover and refrigerate.
**2** For the parsley mayonnaise, finely chop the parsley sprigs and put in a food processor with the mustard, honey, lemon juice, cream and mayonnaise. Blend until well combined, then season, to taste, with salt and cracked black pepper. Spoon the mixture into a bowl or jug, cover and refrigerate until required.
**3** Place a bed of lettuce on each serving plate, top with slices of lobster and spoon parsley mayonnaise over the top. Serve with wedges of lemon and a sprinkle of chopped fresh chives.

# DRESSED CRAB

**Preparation time:** 40 minutes + freezing
**Total cooking time:** 15 minutes
**Serves** 1–2

★ ★ ★

1 kg (2 lb) live mud crab
2–3 teaspoons lemon juice
1½ tablespoons whole-egg mayonnaise
1 cup (80 g/2¾ oz) fresh breadcrumbs
1 teaspoon Worcestershire sauce
2 hard-boiled eggs
2 tablespoons chopped fresh parsley
1 tablespoon chopped fresh chives

**1** Freeze the crab for about 1 hour to immobilize it, then drop it into a large pan of boiling water. Reduce the heat and simmer for 10–15 minutes, or until bright orange all over— it should be cooked through by this stage. Drain and cool.
**2** Twist the claws off the crab. Pull back the small flap on the underside of the crab and prise off the top shell. Scrape out any creamy brown meat and set aside. Wash and dry the top shell and set aside. Remove the intestines and grey feathery gills from the main body and discard. Scrape out any remaining creamy brown meat and add to the rest. Cut the crab in half and remove the white meat. Crack the claws and remove any meat. Keep the white meat separate.
**3** Finely chop the brown crab meat and combine with the lemon juice, mayonnaise and enough of the breadcrumbs to combine. Add the Worcestershire sauce and salt and pepper, to taste.
**4** Press the egg yolks and whites separately through a sieve.
**5** Place the white crab meat inside the dry crab shell, on both the outside edges. Spoon the brown meat mixture into the centre of the shell and arrange the combined parsley and chives, sieved yolks and whites in rows over the brown crab meat. Can be served with bread, lemon wedges and extra mayonnaise.
**NOTE:** When buying fresh crabs, choose ones that seem heavy for their size as they will have the most meat.

## DRESSED CRAB

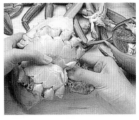

Twist the claws to remove them. Use your thumb as a lever to prise off the hard top shell.

Discard the soft stomach sac from the main body of the crab and remove the grey feathery gills.

Cut the main body of the crab in half lengthways, then remove the white meat from the body using the end of a teaspoon or fork.

*OPPOSITE PAGE: Lobster with parsley mayonnaise (top); Dressed crab*

# SEAFOOD BITES

If you are making a selection of these delicious pieces as part of a buffet, the quantities we have given will be enough to serve about 4 to 6 people.

### SEARED SALMON

Remove the skin and bones from 600 g (1¼ lb) salmon fillet, cut into 3 cm (1¼ inch) cubes and toss the cubes in a mixture of 1 tablespoon cracked black pepper and 1 teaspoon sea salt. Heat 2 tablespoons olive oil in a large frying pan and brown the salmon over high heat. Insert a toothpick in each piece and serve with cocktail sauce (see page 101).

### TEMPURA OCTOPUS

Clean 500 g (1 lb) baby octopus. First, remove the heads from the tentacles with a sharp knife.  Push out the beaks from the centre of the tentacles, then cut the tentacles into sets of two or three. Measure 1 cup (125 g/4 oz) tempura flour into a bowl, make a well in the centre and quickly stir in ¾ cup (185 ml/6 fl oz) iced water,

until just combined—the mixture should still be lumpy. Fill a large saucepan one third full of oil and heat to 180°C (350°F), or until a cube of bread dropped in the oil browns in 15 seconds. Dip the octopus in the batter and deep-fry until lightly golden and crisp. Drain well on crumpled paper towels. Serve immediately. Delicious with ginger and almond sauce (see page 112).

## MUSSELS WITH TOMATO SALSA

Scrub 16–18 mussels with a stiff brush and pull out the hairy beards. Discard any broken mussels, or open ones that don't close when tapped on the bench. Rinse well. Place ¼ cup (60 ml/2 fl oz) each of water and white wine in saucepan and bring to the boil. Add the mussels, cover and cook over high heat for 3–5 minutes, until the mussels are open. Remove from the pan and discard any unopened mussels. Remove and discard one half of each mussel shell and loosen the mussels from the shells with a sharp knife. Combine ¼ small finely diced red onion in a bowl with 1 finely diced small ripe tomato, 1 finely chopped garlic clove, 2 teaspoons balsamic vinegar and 1 tablespoon each of extra virgin olive oil and chopped fresh basil. Season, to taste, and spoon over the mussels.

## WRAPPED PRAWNS WITH JAZZY TARTARE

Peel 500 g (1 lb) cooked medium prawns, leaving the tails intact. Gently pull out the dark vein from each prawn back, starting at the head end. Place 16 long garlic chives in a small pan of boiling water until just wilted. Drain, then refresh in cold water. Wrap one of the chives around each prawn, like a candy cane. Refrigerate while preparing the jazzy tartare sauce. Combine ½ cup (125 g/4 oz) whole-egg mayonnaise in a bowl with 2 small finely chopped pickled gherkins, 1 finely chopped hard-boiled egg, 1 tablespoon chopped fresh parsley, 1 finely chopped spring onion, 1 tablespoon drained bottled capers and 3 teaspoons lemon juice, or to taste. Season with salt and freshly ground black pepper, to taste.

## SEARED SCALLOPS WITH LIME

Remove 16 scallops from their shells and toss in a mixture of 1 tablespoon oil, ¼–½ teaspoon sesame oil, some salt and pepper and 1 tablespoon chopped fresh chives. Rinse and dry the shells. Place the scallops on a hot frying pan for 30 seconds each side, or until just cooked through, being careful not to overcook. Return the scallops to the shells and squeeze lime juice over the top. Sprinkle with chopped fresh chives and some toasted sesame seeds.

*FROM LEFT: Seared salmon; Tempura octopus (top of tray); Mussels with tomato salsa; Wrapped prawns with jazzy tartare; Seared scallops with lime. Sauces in bowls (from left): Jazzy tartare; Cocktail sauce; Ginger and almond sauce*

## FENNEL

Fennel has a light aniseed flavour which goes well with fish. The wild form from Southern Europe, bitter fennel, which was used in ancient times, is now grown mostly for the seeds. The seeds are not only used in cookery but are chewed after a meal in India as a mouth freshener. The sweet fennel, which is now commonly used in cookery, is thought to have been used as far back as the ninth century. It gained popularity and like so many foods, was spread by the Arab traders to the Middle East and India. Gripe water, given to babies to sooth them, contains sweet fennel.

*ABOVE: Seafood pie*

# SEAFOOD PIE

**Preparation time:** 20 minutes
**Total cooking time:** 1 hour 20 minutes
**Serves** 8

★★

2 tablespoons olive oil
3 large salad onions, thinly sliced
1 fennel bulb, thinly sliced
2¹/₂ cups (600 ml/20 fl oz) fish stock
3 cups (750 ml/24 fl oz) cream
1 tablespoon brandy
750 g (1¹/₂ lb) skinless snapper fillets, cut into large pieces
250 g (8 oz) queen scallops
500 g (1 lb) raw medium prawns, peeled and deveined
2 tablespoons chopped fresh flat-leaf parsley
2 sheets ready-rolled puff pastry
1 egg, lightly beaten

**1** Preheat the oven to hot 220°C (425°F/Gas 7). Heat the oil in a deep frying pan, add the onion and fennel and cook over medium heat for 20 minutes or until caramelized.
**2** Add the stock to the pan and bring to the boil. Cook until the liquid is almost evaporated. Stir in the cream and brandy, bring to the boil, then reduce the heat and simmer for 10 minutes, or until reduced by half. Add the seafood and parsley and toss for 3 minutes, or until the seafood just starts to cook.
**3** Lightly grease a 2.5 litre (80 fl oz) pie dish and add the seafood mixture.
**4** Arrange the pastry over the top to cover, trim the excess and press down around the edges. Decorate with any trimmings, making fish or other shapes. Make a steam hole in the top and brush the pastry lightly with beaten egg. Bake for 30 minutes, or until the seafood is cooked through and the pastry is crisp and golden.
**NOTE:** Salad onions are large sweet brown onions particularly suitable for caramelizing because they have a high sugar content.

# SALMON STEAKS WITH HERB SAUCE

**Preparation time:** 25 minutes
**Total cooking time:** 20 minutes
**Serves** 4

 ★ ★

4 salmon steaks (250 g/8 oz each)
2 tablespoons oil

## Herb sauce

1 1/2 cups (375 ml/12 fl oz) fish stock
(see margin note)
1/2 cup (125 ml/4 fl oz) good-quality
white wine
3 tablespoons chopped fresh chives
3 tablespoons chopped fresh parsley
2 tablespoons chopped fresh basil
2 tablespoons chopped fresh tarragon
1 cup (250 ml/8 fl oz) cream
2 egg yolks

**1** Pat the salmon steaks dry with paper towels.
**2** For the herb sauce, combine the stock and wine in a saucepan and bring to the boil. Boil for 5 minutes or until the liquid has reduced by half. Transfer to a blender or food processor, add the chives, parsley, basil and tarragon and blend for 30 seconds. Return to the pan, then stir in the cream and bring to the boil. Reduce the heat to low and simmer for 5 minutes, or until the sauce has reduced by half. Place the egg yolks in a blender or food processor and blend until smooth. With the motor running, gradually drizzle in the hot herb mixture. Process until the sauce is smooth and creamy. Season, to taste.
**3** Heat the oil in a frying pan, add the salmon steaks and cook over medium heat for 3 minutes each side, or until just cooked through (do not overcook). Serve hot with herb sauce.
**NOTE:** You can also serve the salmon cold with a fresh herb mayonnaise. Place 1/2 cup (125 g/ 4 oz) whole-egg mayonnaise, 2 tablespoons sour cream, 1 clove crushed garlic (optional), 3–4 teaspoons lemon juice and 2–3 teaspoons each finely chopped fresh chives, lemon thyme, and parsley in a bowl. Mix until smooth.

## FISH STOCK

Fish stock is used in many seafood recipes, such as the one on this page, and can be bought in some stores. However, it is quick and simple to make. Put 1.5 kg (3 lb) washed bones, heads and tails (from white fish) into a large saucepan with 2 litres (64 fl oz) water, 2 finely chopped onions, 10 peppercorns and a bouquet garni (usually thyme, parsley stalks, celery leaves and a bay leaf wrapped in muslin or tied in a bundle). Bring slowly to the boil, then simmer for 20 minutes, skimming froth from the surface. Strain through muslin.

*ABOVE: Salmon steaks with herb sauce*

## BARBECUED SEAFOOD PLATTER

Thoroughly scrub all the mussels with a stiff brush and pull away the hairy beard from each.

Pull off any vein, membrane or hard white muscle from each scallop, leaving any roe attached.

The Balmain bugs are cooked when the flesh turns white and starts to separate from the shells.

# BARBECUED SEAFOOD PLATTER

**Preparation time:** 40 minutes + 1 hour freezing
**Total cooking time:** 30 minutes
**Serves 6**

⭐ ⭐ ⭐

6 Balmain bugs or slipper lobsters
30 g (1 oz) butter, melted
1 tablespoon oil
12 black mussels
12 scallops on their shells
12 oysters
18 raw large prawns, unpeeled

**Salsa verde, for scallops**

1 tablespoon finely chopped preserved lemon
 (see Note)
1 cup (20 g/$^3$/$_4$ oz) fresh parsley leaves
1 tablespoon drained bottled capers
1 tablespoon lemon juice
3 tablespoons oil, approximately

**Vinegar and shallot dressing, for mussels**

$^1$/$_4$ cup (60 ml/2 fl oz) white wine vinegar
4 French shallots, finely chopped
1 tablespoon chopped fresh chervil

**Pickled ginger and wasabi sauce, for oysters**

1 teaspoon soy sauce
$^1$/$_4$ cup (60 ml/2 fl oz) mirin
2 tablespoons rice wine vinegar
$^1$/$_4$ teaspoon wasabi paste
2 tablespoons finely sliced pickled ginger

**Sweet balsamic dressing, for Balmain bugs or slipper lobsters**

1 tablespoon olive oil
1 tablespoon honey
$^1$/$_2$ cup (125 ml/4 fl oz) balsamic vinegar

**Thai coriander sauce, for prawns**

$^1$/$_2$ cup (125 ml/4 fl oz) sweet chilli sauce
1 tablespoon lime juice
2 tablespoons chopped fresh coriander

**1** Freeze the bugs for 1 hour to immobilize. Cut each bug in half with a sharp knife, then brush the flesh with the combined butter and oil. Set aside while you prepare the rest of the seafood.
**2** Scrub the mussels with a stiff brush and pull out the hairy beards. Discard any broken mussels, or open ones that don't close when tapped on the bench. Rinse well.
**3** Pull off any vein, membrane or hard white muscle from the scallops, leaving any roe attached. Brush the scallops with the combined butter and oil. Cook them shell-side-down on the barbecue.
**4** Remove the oysters from the shells, then rinse the shells under cold water. Pat the shells dry and return the oysters to their shells. Cover and refrigerate all the seafood while you make the dressings.
**5** For the salsa verde, combine all the ingredients in a food processor and process in short bursts until roughly chopped. Transfer to a bowl and add enough oil to moisten the mixture. Season with salt and pepper. Serve a small dollop on each cooked scallop.
**6** For the vinegar and shallot dressing, whisk the vinegar, shallots and chervil in a bowl until combined. Pour over the cooked mussels.
**7** For the pickled ginger and wasabi sauce, whisk all the ingredients in a bowl until combined. Spoon over the cooked oysters.
**8** For the sweet balsamic dressing, heat the oil in a pan, add the honey and vinegar and bring to the boil, then boil until reduced by half. Drizzle over the cooked bugs.
**9** For the Thai coriander sauce, combine all the ingredients in a jug or bowl and drizzle over the cooked prawns.
**10** Cook the seafood on a preheated barbecue grill and flatplate. If necessary, do this in batches, depending on the size of your barbecue. The Balmain bugs will take the longest time to cook, about 5 minutes—they are cooked when the flesh turns white and starts to come away from the shells. The mussels, scallops, oysters and prawns all take about 2–5 minutes to cook.
NOTES: To prepare the preserved lemon, remove the flesh and discard. Wash the skin to remove excess salt and then chop finely.

Mirin, rice wine vinegar and pickled ginger are all available from Asian food speciality stores.

*OPPOSITE PAGE:*
*Barbecued seafood platter*

## PRAWN AND PAPAYA SALAD

Finely slice the red onion and celery.

Thoroughly whisk the dressing ingredients until well combined.

# PRAWN AND PAPAYA SALAD

**Preparation time:** 25 minutes
**Total cooking time:** Nil
**Serves** 4

750 g (1 1/2 lb) large cooked prawns
1 large papaya
1 small red onion, finely sliced
2 celery sticks, finely sliced
2 tablespoons shredded fresh mint leaves

### Dressing

1/2 cup (125 ml/4 fl oz) oil
1/4 cup (60 ml/2 fl oz) lime juice
2 teaspoons finely grated fresh ginger
1 teaspoon caster sugar

1 Peel the prawns, leaving the tails intact. Gently pull out the dark vein from each prawn back, starting at the head end. Place in a large bowl.
2 For the dressing, put all the ingredients in a small bowl and whisk to combine. Season, to taste, with salt and black pepper.
3 Add the dressing to the prawns and toss gently to coat. Peel the papaya and remove the seeds with a spoon. Cut into bite-sized chunks. Add the papaya, onion, celery and mint to the prawns and toss. Serve the salad immediately or cover and refrigerate for up to 3 hours before serving.
**NOTE:** Papayas have bright yellow, smooth skin with a beautiful sweet flesh ranging from deep yellow to pinky-orange, depending on the variety. Papayas contain an enzyme called papain which is used as a tenderizer. Either the fresh fruit is used or, for tenderizing meat, a commercially available powder is used.

## GINGER AND ALMOND SAUCE

Put 1/2 cup (125 ml/4 fl oz) water, 1/2 cup (125 g/4 oz) sugar, 1/4 cup (60 ml/2 fl oz) each of white vinegar and lime juice, 1 chopped clove of garlic and 1 tablespoon grated fresh ginger in a small saucepan. Stir over low heat until the sugar has dissolved, then simmer for 5–8 minutes. Stir in 1 tablespoon each of chopped toasted slivered almonds, chopped fresh coriander and fish sauce. Serve hot or cold with seafood. Makes 3/4 cup (185 ml/6 fl oz).

*ABOVE: Prawn and papaya salad*

# SPICY BAKED FISH WITH VEGETABLES

**Preparation time:** 15 minutes
+ 30 minutes marinating
**Total cooking time:** 45 minutes
Serves 4

★ ★

1 tablespoon cumin seeds

4 cloves garlic

1 small fresh red chilli

90 g (3 oz) fresh coriander (leaves, stems
   and roots), roughly chopped

1 teaspoon salt

1 tablespoon lemon juice

5 tablespoons olive oil

1.5 kg (3 lb), or 2 x 750 g (1½ lb) whole fish,
   (eg. snapper, red emperor, ocean perch,
   monkfish), scaled and cleaned

2–3 ripe tomatoes

450 g (14 oz) new potatoes, sliced

100 g (3½ oz) pitted green olives, cut in halves

**1** Toast the cumin seeds in a dry pan over medium heat for 2–3 minutes, or until fragrant. Grind the seeds to a fine powder in a mortar and pestle, or in a spice grinder.

**2** Mix the ground cumin, garlic, chilli, coriander, salt and lemon juice in a food processor, to form a smooth paste. With the motor running, add 2 tablespoons of the olive oil, in a thin steady stream.

**3** Rinse the fish and pat dry with paper towels. Make 3–4 shallow diagonal slits on both sides of the fish, then rub the spice mixture all over the fish. Put the fish on a dish or plate, then cover with plastic wrap and marinate in the refrigerator for 30 minutes.

**4** Preheat the oven to very hot 240°C (475°F/ Gas 9). Thickly slice the tomatoes and cut the slices in half. Place the fish in the centre of a large baking dish. Scatter the tomato, potato and green olives around the fish. Pour ¼ cup (60 ml/2 fl oz) water and the remaining olive oil over the fish and vegetables. Bake, basting often with the pan juices, for 40 minutes, or until the fish is cooked through. When cooked, the fish will flake apart easily when tested with a fork. Cut in portions for serving.

*BELOW: Spicy baked
fish with vegetables*

# VEGETARIAN

These days, the versatile vegetable can be transformed into an imaginative and richly satisfying meal in its own right. In fact, it seems to be increasingly common for meat-eaters to abandon their meals to sample the tempting array being offered to their vegetarian friends. And with good reason. Vegetarian food has made great strides in the last few years, with cooks all over the world experimenting with new flavour combinations and cooking methods. Spoil your vegetarian guests with the vegetable tart with salsa verde or couscous with pear and vegetable tagine and they're sure to feel as Christmassy as everybody else.

# BAKED RICOTTA

**Preparation time:** 15 minutes
  + overnight draining
**Total cooking time:** 30 minutes
**Serves** 8–10 as an appetizer

★ ★

1 whole fresh ricotta (2 kg/4 lb)
3/4 cup (185 ml/6 fl oz) olive oil
3/4 cup (185 ml/6 fl oz) lemon juice
2 tablespoons thin strips of lemon rind
2 cloves garlic, crushed
6 tablespoons fresh basil leaves, finely shredded
50 g (1 3/4 oz) semi-dried tomatoes, roughly
  chopped

**1** Remove any paper from the base of the ricotta and put the ricotta in a plastic colander. Place over a bowl, ensuring the base of the colander is not touching the base of the bowl. Cover with plastic wrap and leave overnight in the refrigerator, to drain.
**2** Preheat the oven to very hot 250°C (500°F/ Gas 10). Line a baking tray with baking paper. Transfer the ricotta to the tray and brush with a little of the olive oil. Bake for 30 minutes, or until golden brown. Allow to cool slightly.
**3** Mix the remaining olive oil, lemon juice and rind, garlic and basil in a bowl. Season, to taste, with salt and pepper. Place the whole ricotta on a platter, pour on the dressing and scatter with the semi-dried tomatoes. Serve with thin slices of Italian-style bread or bruschetta.

## CHARGRILLED VEGETABLES

Heat a grill and brush with oil. Grill 1 eggplant in 1 cm (1/2 inch) slices, 1 sweet potato in 5 mm (1/4 inch) slices, 1 seeded red and 1 seeded green pepper (capsicum) in large pieces, 1 red onion sliced into wedges, 4 mushrooms and 155 g (5 oz) asparagus for 6–8 minutes (turning halfway), or until tender. The asparagus will only take about 4 minutes. Place the vegetables on a large platter and toss with balsamic vinaigrette. (Whisk together 2 tablespoons balsamic vinegar, 1/3 cup (80 ml/2 3/4 fl oz) extra virgin olive oil, 1 teaspoon crushed garlic, 2 tablespoons shredded fresh basil, salt and freshly ground pepper.) Serves 4.

## RICOTTA

Fresh ricotta is often eaten in Italy as a dessert with sugar or salt as seasoning. However, it is also used in cookery. It is an Italian cheese made from the whey left after the making of other cheeses such as provolone. The word means 'recooked'. The original milk is 'cooked' to separate the curd from the whey. To make ricotta, the whey is then 'cooked' again. A coagulant is then added and the mixture is skimmed and pressed lightly to produce the crumbly, soft-textured moist cheese.

*RIGHT: Baked ricotta*

# RATATOUILLE TARTS

**Preparation time:** 40 minutes + 30 minutes refrigeration + 20 minutes standing
**Total cooking time:** 1 hour 10 minutes
**Makes 12**

3 cups (375 g/12 oz) plain flour

170 g (5½ oz) butter, chilled and chopped

1 eggplant (aubergine), about 500 g (1 lb)

¼ cup (60 ml/2 fl oz) oil

1 onion, chopped

2 cloves garlic, crushed

2 zucchini (courgettes), sliced

1 red pepper (capsicum), chopped

1 green pepper (capsicum), chopped

250 g (8 oz) cherry tomatoes, halved

1 tablespoon balsamic vinegar

1 cup (125 g/4 oz) grated Cheddar

**1** Sift the flour into a bowl and rub in the butter with your fingertips until the mixture resembles fine breadcrumbs. Make a well and add ½ cup (125 ml/4 fl oz) chilled water. Mix with a flat-bladed knife, adding a little more water if necessary, until the dough just comes together. Gather into a ball and divide into 12 portions.
**2** Grease 12 loose-based fluted flan tins measuring 8 cm (3 inches) across the base and 3 cm (1¼ inches) deep. Roll each portion of dough out on a sheet of baking paper to a circle a little larger than the tins. Lift into the tins, press into the sides, then trim away any excess pastry. Refrigerate for 30 minutes. Preheat the oven to moderately hot 200°C (400°F/Gas 6).
**3** Put the tins on baking trays, prick the pastry bases all over with a fork and bake for 20–25 minutes, or until the pastry is fully cooked and lightly golden. Cool completely.
**4** Meanwhile, to make the ratatouille filling, cut the eggplant into 2 cm (¾ inch) cubes, put into a colander and sprinkle with salt. After 20 minutes, rinse, drain and pat dry with paper towels.
**5** Heat 2 tablespoons of the oil in a large frying pan. Cook batches of eggplant for 8–10 minutes, or until browned, adding more oil if necessary. Drain on paper towels. Heat the remaining oil, add the onion and cook over medium heat for 5 minutes, or until very soft. Add the garlic and cook for 1 minute, then add the zucchini and peppers and cook, stirring frequently, for 10 minutes, or until softened. Add the eggplant and tomatoes. Cook, stirring, for 2 minutes. Transfer to a bowl, stir in the vinegar, then cover and cool completely.
**6** Reduce the oven to moderate 180°C (350°F/Gas 4). Divide the mixture among the tart shells with a slotted spoon, draining off any excess liquid. Sprinkle with the Cheddar and cook for 10–15 minutes, or until the cheese has melted and the tarts are warmed through.

**BALSAMIC VINEGAR**
Traditional balsamic vinegar is made in the province of Modena, Italy, by a long, slow process, using a specially cultivated variety of grape. It is aged in wood for at least ten to fifteen years. Although it is quite expensive, only small quantities are used in both sweet and savoury dishes. Balsamic vinegar has a sweet-sour taste and is highly fragrant. Balsam means 'balm', referring to the soothing properties of the vinegar. There are less expensive products that try to imitate the flavour by adding caramel to red wine vinegar.

*LEFT: Ratatouille tarts*

## VEGETABLE TART WITH SALSA VERDE

Preparation time: 30 minutes + 30 minutes
 refrigeration
Total cooking time: 50 minutes
Serves 6

★★★

**Pastry**

1³/4 cups (215 g/7 oz) plain flour
120 g (4 oz) butter, chilled and cubed
1/4 cup (60 ml/2 fl oz) cream

**Salsa verde**

1 clove garlic
2 cups (40 g/1 1/4 oz) fresh flat-leaf parsley leaves
1/3 cup (80 ml/2³/4 fl oz) extra virgin olive oil
3 tablespoons chopped fresh dill
1 1/2 tablespoons Dijon mustard
1 tablespoon red wine vinegar
1 tablespoon drained bottled baby capers

**Filling**

1 large all-purpose potato (eg. desiree, pontiac),
 cubed
1 tablespoon olive oil
2 cloves garlic, crushed

*ABOVE: Vegetable
tart with salsa verde*

1 red pepper (capsicum), chopped
1 red onion, sliced into rings
2 zucchini (courgettes), sliced
2 tablespoons chopped fresh dill
1 tablespoon chopped fresh thyme
1 tablespoon drained bottled baby capers
150 g (5 oz) marinated artichoke hearts, drained
2/3 cup (30 g/1 oz) baby English spinach leaves

**1** Sift the flour and 1/2 teaspoon salt into a large
bowl and rub in the butter with your fingertips
until the mixture resembles fine breadcrumbs.
Add the cream and 1–2 tablespoons iced water
and mix with a flat-bladed knife until the
mixture comes together in small beads. Gather
into a ball and turn out onto a lightly floured
work surface. Flatten into a disc, cover with
plastic wrap, and refrigerate for 30 minutes.
**2** Preheat the oven to moderately hot 200°C
(400°F/Gas 6). Lightly grease a 27 cm (11 inch)
shallow fluted flan tin with a removable base.
**3** Roll the dough out between 2 sheets of
baking paper until large enough to line the flan
tin. Remove the paper and carefully lift the
pastry into the flan tin, pressing it gently into
the fluted sides. Roll the rolling pin over the
tin, cutting off any excess. Line the pastry with
crumpled baking paper large enough to cover
the base and side. Fill with baking beads or
uncooked rice. Place the flan tin on a baking tray

and bake for 15–20 minutes. Remove the beads and paper, reduce the oven to moderate 180°C (350°F/Gas 4) and bake for another 20 minutes, or until the pastry case is dry and golden.

**4** For the salsa verde, blend all the ingredients together in a food processor until almost smooth.

**5** For the filling, boil, steam or microwave the potato until just tender (the point of a sharp knife will come away easily when the potato is ready), but do not overcook. Drain.

**6** Heat the oil in a large frying pan and add the garlic, pepper and onion. Cook over medium-high heat for 3 minutes, stirring frequently. Add the zucchini, dill, thyme and capers and cook for another 3 minutes, stirring often. Add the potato and artichokes, reduce the heat to low and cook for another 3–4 minutes, or until the potato and artichokes are heated through. Season, to taste.

**7** To assemble the tart, spread ¼ cup (60 ml/ 2 fl oz) of the salsa verde over the base of the pastry case. Spoon the vegetable mixture into the case and drizzle with half the remaining salsa verde. Pile the spinach in the centre, drizzle with the remaining salsa verde and serve immediately.

## MUSHROOM NUT ROAST WITH TOMATO SAUCE

**Preparation time:** 30 minutes
**Total cooking time:** 1 hour
**Serves** 6

2 tablespoons olive oil
1 large onion, diced
2 cloves garlic, crushed
300 g (10 oz) cap mushrooms, finely chopped
200 g (6½ oz) raw cashews
200 g (6½ oz) brazil nuts
1 cup (125 g/4 oz) grated Cheddar
¼ cup (25 g/¾ oz) freshly grated Parmesan
1 egg, lightly beaten
2 tablespoons chopped fresh chives
1 cup (80 g/2¾ oz) fresh wholemeal breadcrumbs

### Tomato sauce

1½ tablespoons olive oil
1 onion, finely chopped
1 clove garlic, crushed
400 g (13 oz) can chopped tomatoes
1 tablespoon tomato paste (tomato purée)
1 teaspoon caster sugar

**1** Grease a 14 x 21 cm (5½ x 8½ inch) loaf tin and line the base with baking paper.

**2** Heat the oil in a frying pan and add the onion, garlic and mushrooms. Fry until soft, then cool.

**3** Process the nuts in a food processor until finely chopped, but do not overprocess. Preheat the oven to moderate 180°C (350°F/Gas 4).

**4** Combine the cooled mushrooms, chopped nuts, Cheddar and Parmesan, egg, chives and breadcrumbs in a bowl. Mix well and season, to taste. Press into the loaf tin and bake for 45 minutes, or until firm. Leave for 5 minutes, then turn out and cut into slices.

**5** For the tomato sauce, heat the oil in a saucepan, add the onion and garlic and cook, stirring frequently, for 5 minutes, or until soft but not brown. Stir in the tomato, tomato paste, sugar and ⅓ cup (80 ml/2¾ fl oz) water. Simmer gently for 3–5 minutes, or until slightly thickened. Season with salt and pepper. Serve the tomato sauce with the sliced nut roast.

**NOTE:** For a variation, use a different mixture of nuts and add some seeds. You can use nuts such as pecans, almonds, hazelnuts (without skins) and pine nuts. Suitable seeds to use include sesame, pumpkin or sunflower seeds.

*ABOVE: Mushroom nut roast with tomato sauce*

## MUSHROOMS WITH BEAN PUREE, PUY LENTILS AND RED WINE SAUCE

Pull the stalks from the mushrooms, then very finely chop the stalks.

Simmer the lentil mixture until the lentils are cooked and the liquid is reduced.

Fry both sides of the mushroom caps in the butter and garlic until the mushrooms are tender.

*ABOVE: Mushrooms with bean purée, puy lentils and red wine sauce*

# MUSHROOMS WITH BEAN PUREE, PUY LENTILS AND RED WINE SAUCE

**Preparation time:** 30 minutes
**Total cooking time:** 50 minutes
**Serves** 4

★★

4 large flat field mushrooms
1 tablespoon olive oil
1 red onion, cut into thin wedges
3 cloves garlic, crushed
1 cup (200 g/6 1/2 oz) puy green lentils
3/4 cup (185 ml/6 fl oz) red wine
1 3/4 cups (440 ml/14 fl oz) vegetable stock
1 tablespoon finely chopped fresh flat-leaf parsley
30 g (1 oz) butter

### Bean purée

1 large potato, cut into chunks
2 tablespoons extra virgin olive oil

400 g (13 oz) can cannellini beans, drained and rinsed
2 large cloves garlic, crushed
1 tablespoon vegetable stock

### Red wine sauce

2/3 cup (170 ml/5 1/2 fl oz) red wine
2 tablespoons tomato paste (tomato purée)
1 1/2 cups (375 ml/12 fl oz) vegetable stock
1 tablespoon soft brown sugar

1 Wipe the mushrooms and finely chop the mushroom stalks. Heat the oil in a large saucepan, add the onion and cook over medium heat for 2–3 minutes, or until soft. Add 1 clove of the garlic and the mushroom stalks and cook for 1 minute. Stir in the lentils, red wine and vegetable stock and bring to the boil. Reduce the heat and simmer, covered, for 20–25 minutes, stirring occasionally, or until the liquid is reduced and the lentils are cooked. If the mixture is too wet, uncover and boil until slightly thick. Stir in the parsley. Keep warm.

**2** For the bean purée, bring a small saucepan of water to the boil over high heat and cook the potato for 4–5 minutes, or until tender (pierce with the point of a sharp knife—if the knife comes away easily, the potato is cooked). Drain and mash with a potato masher or fork until smooth. Stir in half the extra virgin olive oil and set aside. Combine the cannellini beans and garlic in a food processor. Add the stock and remaining oil and process until smooth. Transfer to a bowl and fold the mashed potato through. Keep warm.

**3** Melt the butter in a deep frying pan. Add the remaining garlic and the flat mushrooms and cook in batches over medium heat for 3–4 minutes each side, or until the mushrooms are tender. Set aside and keep warm.

**4** For the sauce, add the red wine to the same frying pan, then scrape the bottom to release any sediment. Add the combined tomato paste, stock and sugar and bring to the boil. Cook for about 10 minutes, or until reduced and thick.

**5** Place the mushrooms on individual serving plates and top with warm bean purée. Spoon some lentil mixture over the top and drizzle with the red wine sauce. Season and serve.

**NOTE:** The mushrooms will shrivel if kept warm in the oven.

## PUMPKIN TARTS

**Preparation time:** 20 minutes
+ 30 minutes refrigeration
**Total cooking time:** 35 minutes
**Serves** 6

✷ ✷

2 cups (250 g/8 oz) plain flour
125 g (4 oz) butter, chilled and cubed
1.2 kg (2 lb 6½ oz) pumpkin, cut into
   6 cm (2½ inch) pieces
6 tablespoons sour cream or cream
   cheese
sweet chilli sauce, for serving

**l** Sift the flour and a pinch of salt into a large bowl and rub in the chopped butter with your fingertips until the mixture resembles fine breadcrumbs. Make a well in the centre, add ⅓ cup (80 ml/2¾ fl oz) iced water and mix with a flat-bladed knife, using a cutting action until the mixture comes together in beads. Gently gather the dough together and lift out onto a lightly floured work surface. Press into a ball, then flatten slightly into a disc, wrap in plastic wrap and refrigerate for 30 minutes.

**2** Preheat the oven to moderately hot 200°C (400°F/Gas 6). Divide the pastry into six portions, roll each one out and fit into a 10 cm (4 inch) pie dish. Trim the edges and prick the bases all over. Bake on a baking tray for 15 minutes, or until lightly golden, pressing down any pastry that puffs up. Cool, then remove from the tins.

**3** Meanwhile, steam the pumpkin for about 15 minutes, or until tender.

**4** Place a tablespoon of sour cream in the middle of each pastry case and pile pumpkin pieces on top. Season with salt and cracked black pepper and drizzle with sweet chilli sauce, to taste. Return to the oven for a couple of minutes to heat through. Serve immediately.

*ABOVE: Pumpkin tarts*

3 marinated artichokes, drained and sliced

85 g (3 oz) semi-dried tomatoes, drained
and chopped

100 g (3½ oz) marinated mushrooms, drained
and halved

**1** Line a 23.5 x 13 x 6.5 cm (9 x 5 x 2½ inch) loaf tin with plastic wrap, leaving a generous amount hanging over the sides. Place the ricotta and garlic in a bowl and beat until smooth. Season well and set aside.

**2** Line the base of the tin with half the eggplant, cutting and fitting to cover the base. Top with a layer of half the red pepper, then all the zucchini slices. Spread evenly with the ricotta mixture and press down firmly. Place the rocket leaves on top of the ricotta. Arrange the artichoke, tomato and mushrooms in three rows lengthways on top of the ricotta.

**3** Top with another layer of red pepper and finish with the remaining eggplant. Cover securely with the overlapping plastic wrap. Put a piece of cardboard on top and weigh it down with small food cans. Refrigerate overnight.

**4** To serve, peel back the plastic wrap and turn the terrine out onto a plate. Remove the plastic wrap and cut into thick slices.

NOTE: Chargrilled vegetables and marinated mushrooms and artichokes are available at delicatessens.

## CANDIED PUMPKIN

**Preparation time:** 20 minutes
**Total cooking time:** 35 minutes
Serves 4

500 g (1 lb) pumpkin

30 g (1 oz) butter

2 tablespoons cream

1 tablespoon soft brown sugar

fresh chives, chopped, to garnish

**1** Preheat the oven to moderate 180°C (350°F/ Gas 4). Peel the pumpkin and remove the membrane and seeds. Cut the pumpkin into thin slices and place the slices, overlapping, in a 1 litre (32 fl oz) ovenproof dish. Put the butter, cream and sugar in a small pan over low heat. Stir until smooth, then pour the mixture over the pumpkin. Bake for 35 minutes, or until the pumpkin is tender. Sprinkle with chives.

## CHARGRILLED VEGETABLE TERRINE

**Preparation time:** 30 minutes
+ overnight refrigeration
**Total cooking time:** Nil
Serves 8

★ ★

350 g (11 oz) ricotta

2 cloves garlic, crushed

8 large slices chargrilled eggplant (aubergine),
drained

10 slices chargrilled red pepper (capsicum),
drained

8 slices chargrilled zucchini (courgettes),
drained

*ABOVE: Chargrilled vegetable terrine*

45 g (1½ oz) rocket leaves

Leave the yeast mixture to stand for 10 minutes, or until it is frothy.

Cut the pastry dough into two pieces and roll each into a circle.

Press the edges of the pastry together to seal and pinch to form a pattern.

# FETA AND OLIVE HERB PIE

**Preparation time:** 40 minutes + rising of pastry
**Total cooking time:** 45 minutes
**Serves** 4–6

★★

2 teaspoons sugar

2 teaspoons (7 g/¼ oz) dried yeast

2 tablespoons olive oil

½ cup (60 g/2 oz) plain flour

1 cup (125 g/4 oz) self-raising flour

1 onion, sliced

½ cup (15 g/½ oz) fresh flat-leaf parsley, chopped

1 sprig fresh rosemary, chopped

3 sprigs fresh thyme, chopped

5 fresh basil leaves, torn

¼ cup (40 g/1¼ oz) pine nuts, toasted

1 clove garlic, crushed

175 g (5¾ oz) feta cheese, crumbled

¼ cup (35 g/1¼ oz) pitted olives, chopped

 Dissolve half the sugar in ½ cup (125 ml/ 4 fl oz) warm water and sprinkle the yeast over the top. Leave for 10 minutes, or until frothy (if it doesn't foam, the yeast is dead and you will need to start again), then mix with half the oil. Sift the flours and ½ teaspoon salt into a large bowl. Make a well in the centre and pour in the yeast mixture. Mix well and knead on a floured board until smooth. Cut in half, then roll each half into a 20 cm (8 inch) circle. Place one on a lightly greased baking tray, the other on a baking paper-covered baking tray. Cover the circles with a cloth and put in a warm place for 10–15 minutes, or until doubled in size.

**2** Preheat the oven to moderately hot 200°C (400°F/Gas 6). Heat the remaining oil in a frying pan and cook the onion for 10 minutes, or until golden brown. Sprinkle with the remaining sugar and cook until caramelized. Transfer to a bowl and mix with the herbs, pine nuts, garlic, feta cheese and olives. Spread the mixture over the pastry on the greased tray. Brush the edge with water and put the second pastry circle on top, using the paper to help lift it over. Press the edges together to seal and pinch together to form a pattern. Cut a few slits in the top to allow steam to escape. Bake for 30–35 minutes, or until crisp and golden brown. Serve warm, cut into wedges.

**NOTE:** To toast pine nuts, you can dry-fry them in a frying pan, stirring and watching them constantly so they don't burn.

*ABOVE: Feta and olive herb pie*

123

## EGGPLANT
(AUBERGINE)

The eggplant or aubergine is believed to have originated in India. However, an amazing variety of colours (from purple to white), shapes and sizes are now grown worldwide wherever the climate is suitable. The mild flavour and soft texture make eggplants suitable for all sorts of dishes in combination with other vegetables or meats. The first types to reach Europe from India were the shape of an egg, hence the name. Europeans did not accept it as an edible vegetable at first and grew it simply as a decoration. However, by the sixteenth century, it became popular and spread to America and gradually elsewhere.

*ABOVE: Eggplant, tomato and goats cheese stacks*

# EGGPLANT (AUBERGINE), TOMATO AND GOATS CHEESE STACKS

Preparation time: 15 minutes
Total cooking time: 10 minutes
Serves 4

1/2 cup (125 ml/4 fl oz) olive oil
2 large cloves garlic, crushed
2 small eggplants (aubergines)
2 ripe tomatoes
150 g (5 oz) goats cheese
8 large fresh basil leaves
small rocket leaves, to garnish
extra virgin olive oil, to drizzle

### Dressing

135 g (4 1/2 oz) sun-dried tomatoes in oil
1 clove garlic, crushed
1 tablespoon white wine vinegar
1/4 cup (60 g/2 oz) whole-egg mayonnaise

1 Mix the oil and garlic in a bowl and set aside. Cut each eggplant into six 1 cm (1/2 inch) slices and each tomato into four 1 cm (1/2 inch) slices. Use a sharp knife dipped in hot water to cut the cheese into eight 1 cm (1/2 inch) slices.
2 Brush both sides of the eggplant slices using half the oil. Heat a frying pan and cook the eggplant in batches over high heat for 3–4 minutes each side, or until golden. Remove and keep warm. Brush both sides of the tomatoes using the remaining oil and cook for 1 minute each side, or until sealed and warmed through.
3 For the dressing, drain the sun-dried tomatoes, reserving 1 tablespoon oil. Blend the tomatoes, oil and garlic in a food processor until smooth. Add the vinegar and process until combined. Stir in the mayonnaise and season, to taste.
4 To assemble, place an eggplant slice on each plate. Top each with a slice of tomato, then a basil leaf and a slice of cheese. Repeat with the remaining ingredients to give two layers, finishing with a third piece of eggplant. Add a dollop of dressing and arrange the rocket around each stack. Drizzle a little of the extra virgin olive oil around the stacks. Serve immediately.

# RATATOUILLE TARTE TATIN

Preparation time: 45 minutes
+ 20 minutes refrigeration
Total cooking time: 50 minutes
Serves 6

1½ cups (185 g/6 oz) plain flour

90 g (3 oz) butter, chilled and chopped

1 egg, lightly beaten

1 tablespoon oil

20 g (¾ oz) butter, extra

2 zucchini (courgettes), halved lengthways
and sliced

250 g (8 oz) eggplant (aubergine), cut into
bite-sized cubes

1 large red onion, cut into bite-sized cubes

1 red pepper (capsicum), in bite-sized pieces

1 green pepper (capsicum), in bite-sized
pieces

250 g (8 oz) cherry tomatoes, halved

2 tablespoons balsamic vinegar

½ cup (60 g/2 oz) grated Cheddar

300 g (10 oz) sour cream

¼ cup (60 g/2 oz) good-quality ready-made pesto

**1** Sift the flour into a large bowl and rub in the chopped butter with your fingertips until the mixture resembles fine breadcrumbs. Make a well and add the egg. Mix with a flat-bladed knife, using a cutting action, until the mixture comes together in beads, adding 1 tablespoon water if too dry. Gather together and lift onto a floured work surface. Press into a ball and flatten slightly into a disc. Chill in plastic wrap for 20 minutes.
**2** Preheat the oven to moderately hot 200°C (400°F/Gas 6). Lightly grease a 25 cm (10 inch) springform tin and line the base with baking paper. Heat the oil and extra butter in a large frying pan, add the zucchini, eggplant, onion and peppers and cook over high heat for 8–10 minutes, or until just soft. Add the tomatoes and vinegar and cook for 3–4 minutes.
**3** Place the tin on a baking tray, neatly lay the vegetables in the tin, then sprinkle with cheese. Roll the dough out between two sheets of baking paper to a 28 cm (11 inch) circle. Remove the paper and invert the pastry into the tin over the filling. Use a spoon handle to tuck the edges of the pastry down the side of the tin. Bake for 30–35 minutes (some liquid will leak out), then stand for 1–2 minutes. Remove from the tin and place on a serving plate, pastry-side down. Mix the sour cream and pesto in a small bowl and serve with the tarte tatin.

## RATATOUILLE TARTE TATIN

Mix the combined flour and butter with the egg, using a flat-bladed knife, until it all comes together in beads.

Add the tomato halves and balsamic vinegar to the pan and cook for 3–4 minutes.

Tuck the edges of the pastry down the side of the tin with a spoon handle.

*LEFT: Ratatouille tarte tatin*

ABOVE: Couscous with
pear and vegetable tagine

## TAGINE

Tagine literally means
'stew' and is used in
reference to many
delicious dishes from
Morocco. Common
ingredients of the tagine
are lamb or chicken, often
with preserved lemon
(available at delicatessens
and speciality food stores).
Traditionally, tagine recipes
are cooked slowly over an
open fire or a bed of coals
in a special earthenware
cooking vessel, or *tagine
slaoui*. These vessels often
have elaborate glazing and
bright patterns. However,
the recipes can also be
cooked without using
these special dishes.

# COUSCOUS WITH PEAR
# AND VEGETABLE TAGINE

**Preparation time:** 20 minutes
**Total cooking time:** 1 hour
**Serves** 4–6

1/2 preserved lemon
3 tablespoons oil
2 onions, chopped
1 teaspoon ground ginger
2 teaspoons ground paprika
2 teaspoons ground cumin
1 cinnamon stick
pinch of saffron threads
1.5 kg (3 lb) vegetables (eg. carrot, eggplant,
    orange sweet potato/kumera, parsnip, potato,
    pumpkin), cut into large chunks
400 g (13 oz) can peeled tomatoes
1 cup (250 ml/8 fl oz) vegetable stock
100 g (3 1/2 oz) dried pears, halved
50 g (1 3/4 oz) pitted prunes
2 zucchini (courgettes), cut into large chunks

3 tablespoons chopped fresh flat-leaf parsley
300 g (10 oz) couscous
1/3 cup (30 g/1 oz) flaked or slivered almonds,
    toasted

1 Preheat the oven to moderate 180°C (350°F/
Gas 4). Remove the flesh from the preserved
lemon and thinly slice the lemon rind.
2 Heat 2 tablespoons of the oil in a large saucepan
or ovenproof dish, add the onion and cook over
medium heat for 5 minutes, or until soft. Add
the spices and cook for 3 minutes. Add all the
vegetables, except the zucchini, and stir until
coated with the spices and the outsides begin to
soften. Add the lemon, tomatoes, stock, pears and
prunes. Cover (if using a saucepan transfer to an
ovenproof dish) and bake for 30 minutes. Add
the zucchini and cook, uncovered, for 15 minutes,
or until the vegetables are tender. Remove the
cinnamon stick, then stir in the parsley.
3 Cover the couscous with the remaining oil
and 2 cups (500 ml/16 fl oz) boiling water and
stand until all the water has been absorbed.
Fluff with a fork and serve around the outside
of a platter, with the vegetables in the centre.
Sprinkle with the toasted almonds.

# COUSCOUS VEGETABLE LOAF

**Preparation time:** 20 minutes
  + overnight refrigeration
**Total cooking time:** 15 minutes
**Serves** 6–8

1 litre (32 fl oz) vegetable stock

500 g (1 lb) couscous

30 g (1 oz) butter

3 tablespoons olive oil

2 cloves garlic, crushed

1 onion, finely chopped

1 tablespoon ground coriander

1 teaspoon ground cinnamon

1 teaspoon garam marsala

250 g (8 oz) cherry tomatoes,
  quartered

1 zucchini (courgette), finely chopped

130 g (4¹/₂ oz) can corn kernels,
  drained

8 large fresh basil leaves

150 g (5 oz) sun-dried peppers (capsicums)
  in oil

1 cup (60 g/2 oz) chopped fresh basil, extra

**Dressing**

¹/₃ cup (80 ml/2³/₄ fl oz) orange juice

1 tablespoon lemon juice

3 tablespoons chopped fresh flat-leaf parsley

1 teaspoon honey

1 teaspoon ground cumin

**1** Bring the stock to the boil in a saucepan. Place the couscous and butter in a large bowl, cover with the stock and set aside for 10 minutes.
**2** Meanwhile, heat 1 tablespoon of the oil in a large frying pan and cook the garlic and onion over low heat for 5 minutes, or until the onion is soft. Add the spices and cook for 1 minute, or until fragrant. Remove from the pan.
**3** Add the remaining oil to the pan and fry the tomatoes, zucchini and corn over high heat in batches until soft.
**4** Line a 3 litre (96 fl oz) loaf tin with plastic wrap, allowing it to overhang the side. Arrange basil leaves over the base to form two flowers. Drain the peppers, reserving 2 tablespoons oil, then roughly chop. Add the onion, fried vegetables, sun-dried peppers and extra basil to the couscous and mix. Press into the tin and fold the plastic wrap over to cover. Weigh down with cans of food and refrigerate overnight.
**5** For the dressing, place all the ingredients and the pepper oil in a jar with a lid and shake well.
**6** Turn out the loaf, slice and serve with dressing.

*ABOVE: Couscous vegetable loaf*

127

**VEGETABLE PIE**

Prick the base of the pastry all over with a fork, then bake until dry and golden.

Cook the vegetables until they are soft and almost break up when tested with a knife.

*OPPOSITE PAGE:*
*Vegetable pie (top);*
*Vegetable frittata*

# VEGETABLE PIE

**Preparation time:** 25 minutes
+ 30 minutes refrigeration
**Total cooking time:** 1 hour 10 minutes
Serves 6

## Pastry

1 cup (125 g/4 oz) plain flour
60 g (2 oz) butter, chilled and chopped
1 egg yolk
2 teaspoons poppy seeds

30 g (1 oz) butter
2 tablespoons oil
1 onion, cut into thin wedges
1 leek, sliced
3 potatoes, cut into large chunks
300 g (10 oz) orange sweet potato (kumera),
    cut into large chunks
300 g (10 oz) pumpkin, cut into large chunks
200 g (6½ oz) swede, cut into large chunks
1 cup (250 ml/8 fl oz) vegetable stock
1 red pepper (capsicum), cut into large pieces
200 g (6½ oz) broccoli, cut into large florets
2 zucchini (courgettes), cut into large pieces
1 cup (125 g/4 oz) grated vintage peppercorn
    Cheddar

**1** Preheat the oven to moderately hot 200°C (400°F/Gas 6). For the pastry, sift the flour into a large bowl and rub in the butter with your fingertips until the mixture resembles fine breadcrumbs. Make a well and add the egg yolk, poppy seeds and 1–2 tablespoons iced water and mix with a flat-bladed knife, using a cutting action, until the mixture comes together in beads. Gently gather together and lift out onto a lightly floured work surface. Press into a ball, flatten slightly into a disc, then wrap in plastic wrap and refrigerate for 30 minutes.

**2** Roll the dough between two sheets of baking paper, then remove the top sheet and invert the pastry into a 23 cm (9 inch) pie plate. Use a small ball of pastry to press the pastry in, allowing excess to hang over the sides. Trim any excess pastry. Prick the base with a fork and bake for 15–20 minutes, or until dry and golden.

**3** Meanwhile, for the filling, heat the butter and oil in a large saucepan, add the onion and leek and cook over medium heat for 5 minutes, or until soft and golden. Add the potato, sweet potato, pumpkin and swede and cook, stirring occasionally, until the vegetables start to soften. Add the stock and cook for 30 minutes.

**4** Add the remaining vegetables and cook, partially covered, for 20 minutes, or until the vegetables are soft—some may break up slightly. Season and cool a little. Spoon into the pie shell, sprinkle with cheese and cook under a medium grill for 5 minutes, or until the cheese is golden.

# VEGETABLE FRITTATA

**Preparation time:** 35 minutes + cooling
**Total cooking time:** 35 minutes
Serves 6

1 large red pepper (capsicum)
¼ cup (60 ml/2 fl oz) olive oil
2 leeks, finely sliced
2 cloves garlic, crushed
125 g (4 oz) zucchini (courgettes), thinly sliced
150 g (5 oz) eggplant (aubergine), thinly sliced
150 g (5 oz) orange sweet potato (kumera),
    thinly sliced
7 eggs, lightly beaten
2 tablespoons finely chopped fresh basil
1 cup (100 g/3½ oz) grated Parmesan

**1** Cut the red pepper into large pieces, removing the seeds and membrane. Cook, skin-side-up, under a hot grill until the skin blackens and blisters. Cool in a plastic bag, then peel and cut into thin strips.

**2** Heat 1 tablespoon oil in a deep round 23 cm (9 inch) frying pan, add the leek, garlic and zucchini and stir over medium heat for 5 minutes, or until soft. Remove from the pan and drain on paper towels.

**3** Heat the remaining oil in the same pan and cook the eggplant in batches until golden on both sides. Cook the sweet potato in the pan and drain. Line the base of the pan with half the eggplant and spread with leek mixture. Cover with red pepper, eggplant and sweet potato.

**4** Mix the eggs, basil, Parmesan and some pepper in a jug and pour over the vegetables. Cook over low heat for 15 minutes, or until almost set. Place the pan under a hot grill for 2–3 minutes, or until golden. Cool for about 30 minutes, then turn onto a board. Serve in wedges, cold or at room temperature (it falls apart if eaten hot).

## ROAST VEGETABLE TART

Spread the onion mixture over the pastry, leaving a border all the way around.

Fold the edge of the pastry up and mould into shape to hold in the vegetables.

# ROAST VEGETABLE TART

**Preparation time:** 30 minutes
+ 30 minutes refrigeration
**Total cooking time:** 1 hour 50 minutes
**Serves 4–6**

★ ★

1 eggplant (aubergine), cut into thick slices
350 g (11 oz) pumpkin, cut into large pieces
2 zucchini (courgettes), cut into thick slices
1–2 tablespoons olive oil
1 large red pepper (capsicum), chopped
1 teaspoon olive oil, extra
1 red onion, sliced
1 tablespoon Korma curry paste
natural yoghurt, for serving

### Pastry

1½ cups (185 g/6 oz) plain flour
125 g (4 oz) butter, chilled and chopped
²⁄₃ cup (100 g/3½ oz) roasted cashews,
   finely chopped
1 teaspoon cumin seeds
2–3 tablespoons chilled water

**1** Preheat the oven to moderately hot 200°C (400°F/Gas 6). Put the eggplant, pumpkin and zucchini on a lined baking tray, then brush with oil and bake for 30 minutes. Remove from the oven, turn and add the pepper. Bake for another 30 minutes, then allow to cool.

**2** To make the pastry, sift the flour into a large bowl and rub in the butter with your fingertips until the mixture resembles fine breadcrumbs. Stir in the cashews and cumin seeds. Make a well in the centre and add the water. Mix with a flat-bladed knife, using a cutting action, until the mixture comes together in small beads. Gently gather together and lift out onto a lightly floured work surface. Press together into a ball and flatten slightly into a disc, wrap in plastic wrap and refrigerate for 30 minutes. Roll out between two sheets of baking paper to a circle about 35 cm (14 inch) in diameter.

**3** Heat the extra oil in a frying pan and cook the onion for 2–3 minutes, or until soft. Add the curry paste and cook, stirring, for 1 minute, or until fragrant and well combined. Allow to cool. Reduce the oven temperature to moderate 180°C (350°F/Gas 4).

**4** Lift onto a lightly greased baking tray and spread the onion mixture over the pastry, leaving a 6 cm (2½ inch) border all around. Arrange the

*ABOVE: Roast vegetable tart*

other vegetables over the onion, piling them slightly higher in the centre. Working your way around, fold the edge of the pastry in pleats over the vegetables. Bake for 45 minutes, or until the pastry is lightly golden and cooked. Serve immediately with a dollop of yoghurt.

# BLUE CHEESE AND ONION FLAN

**Preparation time:** 40 minutes
+ 30 minutes refrigeration
**Total cooking time:** 1 hour 40 minutes
**Serves** 8

2 tablespoons olive oil
1 kg (2 lb) red onions, very thinly sliced
1 teaspoon soft brown sugar
1½ cups (185 g/6 oz) plain flour
100 g (3½ oz) cold butter, cubed
¾ cup (185 ml/6 fl oz) cream
3 eggs
100 g (3½ oz) blue cheese, crumbled
1 teaspoon chopped fresh thyme leaves

**1** Heat the oil in a heavy-based frying pan over low heat and cook the onion and sugar, stirring, for 45 minutes, or until the onion is caramelized.
**2** Sift the flour into a large bowl and rub in the butter with your fingertips until the mixture resembles fine breadcrumbs. Make a well in the centre and add 3–4 tablespoons cold water. Mix with a flat-bladed knife, using a cutting action until the mixture comes together in beads. Gently gather together and lift onto a lightly floured work surface. Press into a ball, wrap in plastic wrap and refrigerate for 30 minutes.
**3** Preheat the oven to moderate 180°C (350°F/Gas 4). Roll out the pastry on a lightly floured surface to fit a lightly greased 22 cm (8¾ inch) round loose-based flan tin. Invert the pastry over the tin and press in with a small ball of pastry, allowing excess to hang over the side. Trim any excess pastry, then chill for 10 minutes. Line the pastry shell with baking paper and fill with baking beads or uncooked rice. Bake on a baking tray for 10 minutes. Remove the beads and paper, then bake for 10 minutes, or until lightly golden and dry.
**4** Cool, then gently spread the onion over the base of the pastry. Whisk the cream in a bowl with the eggs, blue cheese, thyme and some pepper. Pour over the onion and bake for 35 minutes, or until firm.

*BELOW: Blue cheese and onion flan*

## MUSHROOM MOUSSAKA

**Preparation time:** 20 minutes
**Total cooking time:** 1 hour
**Serves** 4–6

1 eggplant (aubergine), about 250 g (4 oz),
   cut into 1 cm (½ inch) slices
1 large potato, cut into 1 cm (½ inch) slices
30 g (1 oz) butter
1 onion, finely chopped
2 cloves garlic, finely chopped
500 g (1 lb) flat mushrooms, sliced
400 g (13 oz) can chopped tomatoes
½ teaspoon sugar
40 g (1¼ oz) butter, extra
⅓ cup (40 g/1¼ oz) plain flour
2 cups (500 ml/16 fl oz) milk
1 egg, lightly beaten
40 g (1¼ oz) grated Parmesan

**1** Preheat the oven to hot 220°C (425°F/Gas 7).
Line a baking tray with foil and brush with oil.
Put the eggplant and potato in a single layer on
the tray, sprinkle with salt and pepper and bake

for 20 minutes. Meanwhile, melt the butter in
a large frying pan over medium heat. Add the
onion and cook, stirring, for 3–4 minutes, or
until soft. Add the garlic and cook for 1 minute,
or until fragrant. Increase the heat to high, add
the mushrooms and stir continuously for
2–3 minutes, or until soft. Add the tomato,
reduce the heat and simmer rapidly for
8 minutes, or until reduced. Stir in the sugar.
**2** Melt the extra butter in a large saucepan over
low heat. Add the flour and cook for 1 minute,
or until pale and foaming. Remove from the
heat and gradually stir in the milk. Return to
the heat and stir constantly until the mixture
boils and thickens. Reduce the heat and simmer
for 2 minutes. Remove from the heat and,
when the bubbles subside, stir in the egg
and Parmesan.
**3** Reduce the oven temperature to moderate
180°C (350°F/Gas 4). Grease a shallow
1.5 litre (48 fl oz) ovenproof dish. Spread half
the mushroom mixture over the base of the dish.
Cover with potato and top with half the
remaining mushrooms, then the eggplant. Finish
with the remaining mushrooms, pour on the
sauce and smooth the top with the back of a
spoon. Bake for 30–35 minutes, or until the
edges begin to bubble. Remove from the oven
and leave for 10 minutes before serving.

*ABOVE: Mushroom
moussaka*

# TOFU WITH CARROT AND GINGER SAUCE

**Preparation time:** 25 minutes
+ overnight refrigeration
**Total cooking time:** 30 minutes
Serves 6

★ ★

2 x 300 g (10 oz) packets firm tofu, drained
1/2 cup (125 ml/4 fl oz) orange juice
1 tablespoon soft brown sugar
1 tablespoon soy sauce
2 tablespoons chopped fresh coriander leaves
2 cloves garlic, crushed
1 teaspoon grated fresh ginger
2–3 tablespoons oil
1 kg (2 lb) baby bok choy, quartered lengthways

**Carrot and ginger sauce**

300 g (10 oz) carrots, chopped
2 teaspoons grated fresh ginger
2/3 cup (170 ml/5 1/2 fl oz) orange juice
1/2 cup (125 ml/4 fl oz) vegetable stock

**1** Slice each block of tofu into six lengthways. Place in a single layer in a flat non-metallic dish. Mix the juice, sugar, soy sauce, coriander, garlic and ginger in a jug, then pour over the tofu. Cover and refrigerate overnight, turning once.
**2** Drain the tofu, reserving the marinade. Heat the oil in a large frying pan and cook the tofu in batches over high heat for 2–3 minutes each side, or until golden. Remove and keep warm. Put the marinade in a saucepan and bring to the boil over medium heat. Reduce the heat and gently simmer for 1 minute. Remove from the heat and keep warm.
**3** Heat a wok, add the bok choy and 1 tablespoon water and cook, covered, over medium heat for 2–3 minutes, or until tender. Remove and keep warm.
**4** Put all the sauce ingredients in a saucepan, bring to the boil, then reduce the heat and simmer, covered, for 5–6 minutes, or until the carrot is tender. Transfer to a food processor and blend until smooth.
**5** To serve, divide the bok choy among six plates. Top with some of the carrot and ginger sauce, then the warm tofu and drizzle with a little of the marinade before serving.

**THE ADVENT WREATH**
The custom of having a wreath for Advent, the season including the four Sundays preceding Christmas, is of German origin. These weeks are a time of preparation for the coming of Jesus. The wreaths are used in worship services and family devotions. Four candles, usually lavender in colour, one for each week, are placed around a circle of greenery. Sometimes a pink one is used for the third Sunday. On each of the Sundays prior to Christmas, one of the candles is lit. On Christmas day, a white candle is sometimes added and lit.

*LEFT: Tofu with ginger and carrot sauce*

# VEGETABLES, SOUPS & SALADS

Getting the vegetables exactly right is vital to the success of any self-respecting roast dinner, and never more so than at Christmas time. Crunchy golden hasselback potatoes, roast parsnips drizzled with maple syrup and buttery Brussels sprouts and chestnuts add a delicious jumble of complementary flavours to the main meal. And for a cold meal, such as a seafood platter, caramelized onion and potato salad, tomato and bocconcini salad, or the all-time favourite Caesar salad can join together to create an unbeatable Christmas feast.

## STILTON CHEESE

This cheese is made exclusively in three parts of England: Leicestershire, Nottinghamshire and Derbyshire. The most commonly used is blue-veined Stilton. It has a creamy consistency and distinct tangy flavour and is regarded as the best of all English blue cheeses. It is made in large cylindrical shapes. White Stilton, which does not have the mould, is younger and has a milder flavour. Stilton cheese is traditional fare at Christmas time in England.

*ABOVE: Stilton soup*

# STILTON SOUP

Preparation time: 20 minutes
Total cooking time: 30 minutes
Serves 4–6

### Thyme pitta croutons

2 large Lebanese breads
1 1/2 tablespoons fresh thyme leaves
1/2 cup (50 g/1 1/2 oz) grated Parmesan

30 g (1 oz) butter
2 leeks, white part only, chopped
1 kg (2 lb) potatoes, chopped
   into chunks
1.25 litres (40 fl oz) chicken stock
1/2 cup (125 ml/4 fl oz) cream
100 g (3 1/2 oz) Stilton cheese
fresh thyme sprigs, to garnish

1 Preheat the oven to moderate 180°C (350°F/ Gas 4). Split each Lebanese bread into two, then cut each half into 8 wedges. Put on baking trays, sprinkle with the combined thyme and Parmesan and bake in batches for 5–8 minutes each batch, or until golden and crisp.

2 Melt the butter in a large saucepan, add the leek and cook until softened. Add the potato and chicken stock and bring to the boil. Simmer, covered, for 15 minutes, or until the potato is tender (pierce with the point of a knife—if the potato comes away easily, it is cooked).

3 Transfer the mixture, in batches if necessary, to a blender or food processor and blend until smooth. Return to the saucepan and add the cream and cheese, to taste. Stir over low heat until the cheese has melted, being careful not to let the mixture boil. Ladle into individual dishes and garnish with sprigs of fresh thyme. Serve with the thyme pitta croutons.

NOTE: The croutons can be made up to a week ahead and stored in an airtight container. If they soften, spread on a baking tray and bake in a warm 160°C (315°F/Gas 2–3) oven for 2–3 minutes.

# PIE-CRUST MUSHROOM SOUP

**Preparation time:** 25 minutes
**Total cooking time:** 35 minutes
**Serves** 4

400 g (13 oz) large field mushrooms
60 g (2 oz) butter
I onion, finely chopped
I clove garlic, crushed
¹/₄ cup (30 g/I oz) plain flour
3 cups (750 ml/24 fl oz) chicken stock
2 tablespoons fresh thyme leaves
2 tablespoons sherry
I cup (250 ml/8 fl oz) cream
I sheet frozen puff pastry, thawed
I egg, lightly beaten

**I** Preheat the oven to moderately hot 200°C (400°F/Gas 6). Peel and roughly chop the mushrooms, including the stems. Melt the butter in a large saucepan, add the onion and cook over medium heat for 3 minutes, or until soft. Add the garlic and cook for another minute. Add the mushrooms and cook until soft. Sprinkle with the flour and stir for 1 minute.
**2** Stir in the stock and thyme and bring to the boil. Reduce the heat and simmer, covered, for 10 minutes. Cool before processing in batches. Return the soup to the pan, stir in the sherry and cream, then pour into 4 ovenproof bowls (use small deep bowls rather than wide shallow ones, or the pastry may sag into the soup).
**3** Cut rounds of pastry slightly larger than the bowl tops and cover each bowl with pastry. Seal the pastry edges and brush lightly with the egg. Place the bowls on a baking tray and bake for 15 minutes, or until golden and puffed.

# ROAST PUMPKIN SOUP

**Preparation time:** 20 minutes
**Total cooking time:** 55 minutes
**Serves** 6

1.25 kg (2¹/₂ lb) pumpkin, cut into chunks
2 tablespoons olive oil
I onion, chopped
2 teaspoons ground cumin
I carrot, chopped
I celery stick, chopped
I litre (32 fl oz) chicken or vegetable stock
sour cream, for serving
finely chopped fresh parsley, for serving
ground nutmeg, to garnish

**I** Preheat the oven to moderate 180°C (350°F/ Gas 4). Put the pumpkin on a greased baking tray and lightly brush with half the olive oil. Bake for 25 minutes, or until softened and slightly browned around the edges.
**2** Heat the remaining oil in a large pan. Cook the onion and cumin for 2 minutes over medium heat, then add the carrot and celery and cook for 3 minutes, stirring frequently. Add the pumpkin and stock. Bring to the boil, then reduce the heat and simmer for 20 minutes.
**3** Cool a little then purée in batches in a blender or food processor until smooth. Return the soup to the pan and gently reheat without boiling. Season, to taste, with salt and cracked black pepper. Top with sour cream and sprinkle with parsley and ground nutmeg before serving.
**NOTE:** Butternut and jap pumpkin is often used in soups for a sweeter flavour. If the soup is too thick, thin it down with stock.

*ABOVE: Pie-crust mushroom soup*

## ROAST VEGETABLES

For all these recipes, preheat the oven to moderate 180°C (350°F/Gas 4). Peel all the vegetables. The cooking time will vary, depending on the size and type of vegetable. Vegetables can be placed around the meat roast while it is cooking if oven space is tight. The caramelized meat juices add flavour to the vegetables. While the meat is resting, you can turn the oven up to moderately hot 200°C (400°F/Gas 6) to crisp the vegetables.

## BASIC POTATOES

**Preparation time:** 15 minutes
**Total cooking time:** 55 minutes
**Serves** 4

4 large floury or all-purpose potatoes
  (eg. spunta, sebago, russet, desiree, pontiac)
20 g (³/4 oz) butter, melted
1 tablespoon oil

Cut the potatoes in half and simmer in a pan of water for 5 minutes. Drain, then cool on paper towels. Using a fork, scrape the rounded side of the potatoes to form a rough surface. Place on a greased baking dish and brush with the butter and oil. Roast for 50 minutes, or until golden, brushing halfway through the cooking time with a little more butter and oil.

## ORANGE SWEET POTATO

**Preparation time:** 10 minutes
**Total cooking time:** 25 minutes
**Serves** 4

800 g (1 lb 10 oz) orange sweet potato (kumera)
20 g (³/4 oz) butter, melted
2 teaspoons sesame seeds
¹/2 teaspoon cracked black pepper

Cut the orange sweet potato into 1 cm (¹/2 inch) thick slices. Combine with the butter, sesame seeds and pepper. Toss, then roast in a baking dish for 25 minutes, or until lightly browned and tender, turning once. Sprinkle with salt before serving.

## ROAST ONIONS

**Preparation time:** 20 minutes
**Total cooking time:** 1 hour 10 minutes
**Serves** 6

6 onions
³/4 cup (60 g/2 oz) fresh breadcrumbs
¹/4 cup (25 g/³/4 oz) grated Romano or Parmesan
1 tablespoon chopped fresh basil
20 g (³/4 oz) butter, melted

Peel the onions, leaving the root ends intact. Place in a pan of water, bring to the boil and simmer gently for 20 minutes. Remove and cool. Cut off and discard the top quarter of each onion, and scoop out a third of the inside. Combine the breadcrumbs, cheese, basil and butter in a bowl and season. Spoon into the onions and roast in a lightly greased baking dish for 50 minutes, or until the onions are soft.

## PANCETTA POTATOES

**Preparation time:** 20 minutes
**Total cooking time:** 50 minutes
**Serves** 4

8 medium floury or all-purpose potatoes
  (eg. sebago, spunta, russet, desiree, pontiac)
2 slices pancetta
8 sprigs of fresh rosemary
2 teaspoons butter, softened
oil, for brushing

Cut the potatoes and trim the bases so they sit flat. Cut each pancetta slice lengthways into 4 pieces. Roll a sprig of rosemary in each piece of pancetta. Cut a hole in the centre of the potatoes about halfway through and insert the pancetta. Place on a greased baking dish. Top each potato with ¹/4 teaspoon of the butter. Brush with oil and sprinkle with pepper. Roast for 40–50 minutes, or until golden.
**NOTE:** The texture of potatoes varies from waxy to floury or starchy and it is best to use the type stated in recipes. Sebago and pontiac are good all-rounders and are particularly good for baking. Russet and spunta have a floury texture and are also good baking varieties.

**ROSEMARY**
According to mediaeval legend, fresh rosemary decorating the altar at Christmas time wards off evil spirits and brings special blessings to the people. Sometimes it was strewn on the church floor and it was also burnt instead of expensive incense. Fresh rosemary symbolizes remembrance, friendship and fidelity. It was cultivated in gardens in monasteries for medicine and food. Greek students wore rosemary in their hair at exam time to aid their memories.

*OPPOSITE PAGE, FROM TOP:*
*Basic potatoes; Orange sweet potato; Roast onions; Pancetta potatoes*

## LEEKS

Leeks come from the same family as onions but, because they are milder with a sweeter flavour, they are used when a more delicate taste is desired. They can be cooked as a vegetable in their own right and are especially useful in soups and sauces that don't require a strong flavour. Like onions, they should be cooked slowly so they soften but don't burn. When buying leeks, choose smaller ones as they will be more tender than large leeks. If very young, the whole plant can be used as the green leaves will not be tough.

*ABOVE: Steamed mixed bean bundles*

## STEAMED MIXED BEAN BUNDLES

**Preparation time:** 15 minutes
**Total cooking time:** 8 minutes
**Serves** 4

8 long chives
20 green beans
20 butter beans

**1** Place the chives in a small bowl, cover with boiling water to soften, then drain. Trim the tops and tails from all the beans, divide into 8 bundles and tie them together with a chive. Place the bundles in a steamer over a medium pan half-filled with simmering water, or, alternatively, place them in a medium pan with 3 tablespoons of water.
**2** Cover the steamer and steam the beans over medium heat for 5–8 minutes, or until just tender. Don't allow the water to completely evaporate—add more if necessary. Sprinkle the cooked beans with salt and ground black pepper and serve immediately.

## ROAST LEEK WITH BACON

**Preparation time:** 15 minutes
**Total cooking time:** 25 minutes
**Serves** 6

3 leeks
2 rashers bacon
20 g (³/₄ oz) butter, softened
1 teaspoon chopped fresh thyme

**1** Preheat the oven to moderate 180°C (350°F/ Gas 4). Discard most of the green part from the top section of the leeks, then cut each leek in half lengthways and wash well.
**2** Cut each bacon rasher into 3 long strips and wrap a piece around the middle of each portion of leek.
**3** Place the leeks, rounded-side-up, in a greased shallow baking dish. Combine the butter and thyme and spread over the leeks. Bake for 25 minutes, or until lightly browned and tender.
**NOTE:** Grit tends to stick between the tightly compacted layers of leeks, so rinse carefully.

# BRUSSELS SPROUTS AND CHESTNUTS

**Preparation time:** 30 minutes
**Total cooking time:** 20 minutes
Serves 8

500 g (1 lb) fresh chestnuts or 240 g (7½ oz) can
1 kg (2 lb) Brussels sprouts
30 g (1 oz) butter
grated fresh nutmeg

**1** Make slits in the skins of the chestnuts and put them in a saucepan. Cover with cold water and bring to the boil over high heat. Reduce the heat and simmer for 10 minutes. Drain and leave until cool enough to handle. Peel off the skins.
**2** Trim the sprouts and cut a cross in the base of each. Bring a pan of water to the boil, add the sprouts and simmer for 5–8 minutes, or until just tender. Melt the butter in a large frying pan and add the chestnuts. Cook until they begin to brown, then add the sprouts and toss together until heated through. Season well with salt, pepper and nutmeg.

# HERBED CARROTS

**Preparation time:** 15 minutes
**Total cooking time:** 10 minutes
Serves 6

1 kg (2 lb) carrots
40 g (1¼ oz) butter
2 teaspoons sugar
2 teaspoons lemon juice
2 teaspoons finely chopped fresh
  flat-leaf parsley

**1** Peel the carrots and cut into thick matchsticks. Cook in a saucepan of boiling water for 3–5 minutes, or until tender. Drain well.
**2** Melt the butter in the pan and add the sugar. Return the carrots to the saucepan and toss together until the carrots start to colour a little. Add the lemon juice and parsley and toss together until the carrots are well coated.

## CHESTNUTS

This sweet, edible nut, of which there are many varieties, is popular in Europe, Asia and the United States. In many countries, chestnuts are a traditional cold weather treat and street vendors roast them on small fires to sell to passers-by. The shell has to be pierced before roasting or it will explode. Shelled chestnuts are used in many ways. They are puréed in soups, served as a vegetable, or put in turkey stuffing. Chestnuts are also used in cakes and desserts.

*ABOVE: Brussels sprouts and chestnuts*

141

**2** Combine the apricots, raisins and orange juice in a small pan. Cover and bring to the boil, then remove from the heat and leave for 5 minutes.
**3** Combine the potato, orange sweet potato and undrained fruit in a shallow ovenproof dish. Dot with butter and bake for 45 minutes, or until lightly browned. Stir occasionally. Garnish with chives before serving.
**NOTE:** This dish can be prepared up to baking stage 4 hours ahead.

## SWEET ROAST BEETROOT

**Preparation time:** 15 minutes
**Total cooking time:** 1 hour 30 minutes
**Serves** 6

12 small fresh beetroot
1¹/₂ tablespoons olive oil
20 g (³/₄ oz) butter
1¹/₂ teaspoons ground cumin
1 teaspoon coriander seeds, lightly crushed
¹/₂ teaspoon mixed spice
1 clove garlic, crushed, optional
3–4 teaspoons soft brown sugar
1 tablespoon balsamic vinegar

**1** Preheat the oven to moderate 180°C (350°F/ Gas 4) and brush a baking dish with melted butter or oil. Trim the leafy tops from the beetroot (cut about 3 cm/1¹/₄ inches above the pulp to prevent bleeding), wash the bulbs thoroughly and place on the tray. Bake for 1 hour 15 minutes, or until very tender. Set aside until the bulbs are cool enough to handle.
**2** Peel the beetroot and trim the tops and tails to neaten. Heat the oil and butter in a frying pan, add the cumin, coriander seeds, mixed spice and garlic and cook over medium heat for 1 minute. Add the sugar and vinegar to the pan and stir for 2–3 minutes, or until the sugar dissolves. Add the beetroot, reduce the heat to low and turn the beetroot for 5 minutes, or until glazed all over. Serve warm or at room temperature.
**NOTE:** These are also delicious with some natural yoghurt stirred through and served as a salad. When handling beetroot, take care to prevent them from bleeding. Wash carefully to prevent the skin breaking and don't cut them before cooking.

## FESTIVE FRUITY POTATOES

**Preparation time:** 20 minutes
**Total cooking time:** 50 minutes
**Serves** 8

1 kg (2 lb) new potatoes
1 kg (2 lb) orange sweet potato (kumera)
³/₄ cup (135 g/4¹/₂ oz) dried apricots
³/₄ cup (90 g/3 oz) raisins
²/₃ cup (170 ml/5¹/₂ fl oz) orange juice
60 g (2 oz) butter, cubed
2 tablespoons chopped fresh chives

**1** Preheat the oven to moderate 180°C (350°F/ Gas 4). Peel the potato and orange sweet potato and cut into 3 cm (1¹/₄ inch) pieces. Cook in simmering water for 5 minutes, or until tender, then drain.

*ABOVE: Festive fruity potatoes*

## SANTA CLAUS/ SAINT NICHOLAS

The origin of the story of Saint Nicholas goes back as far as a legend in the fourth century which personifies Santa as a holy man named Nicholas. He entered the priesthood as a teenager and later became a Bishop. It is claimed he performed many miracles. He was made a saint after his death. The anniversary of his death, December 6, became a feast day on the church calendar. He became the patron saint of many people and it was claimed he roamed the earth on his feast day every year leaving sweets and trinkets in children's shoes. Thomas Nast, a cartoonist, depicted the saint in a red suit for *Harper's Weekly* in 1863. This concept of Santa has remained unchanged.

## SPICED RED CABBAGE

**Preparation time:** *20 minutes*
**Total cooking time:** *1 hour 30 minutes*
**Serves 6**

750 g (1 1/2 lb) red cabbage
1 large red onion, chopped
1 green apple, cored and chopped
2 cloves garlic, crushed
1/4 teaspoon ground cloves
1/4 teaspoon ground nutmeg
1 1/2 tablespoons soft brown sugar
2 tablespoons red wine vinegar
20 g (3/4 oz) butter, cubed

**1** Preheat the oven to slow 150°C (300°F/ Gas 2). Quarter the cabbage and remove the core. Finely slice the cabbage and put it in a large ovenproof casserole dish with the onion and apple. Toss well.

**2** Combine the garlic, spices, sugar and vinegar in a small bowl. Pour the mixture over the cabbage, and toss. Dot the top with the butter. Cover and bake for 1 1/2 hours, stirring once or twice. Season, to taste, with salt and freshly ground black pepper, and serve hot.

## CABBAGE WITH PINE NUTS AND PROSCIUTTO

Finely shred half a small green cabbage. Heat 2 teaspoons olive oil and 20 g (3/4 oz) butter in a large pan and fry 1 small finely chopped onion for 5 minutes, or until soft. Add 3 slices chopped prosciutto and fry for another 2 minutes. Add the cabbage and stir for 2–3 minutes, or until just tender. Sprinkle with toasted pine nuts. Serves 4.

*ABOVE: Spiced red cabbage*

## ROAST VEGETABLES

For all these recipes, preheat the oven to moderate 180°C (350°F/Gas 4). Peel all the vegetables except the tomatoes. The cooking time will vary, depending on the size and type of vegetable. Most can be placed around the roast while it is cooking if oven space is tight. The juices add flavour to the vegetables.

## HASSELBACK POTATOES

**Preparation time:** 20 minutes
**Total cooking time:** 50 minutes
**Serves** 4

✶ ✶

8 medium floury or all-purpose potatoes
   (eg. spunta, sebago, russet, desiree, pontiac)
20 g (³/₄ oz) butter, melted
2 teaspoons dry breadcrumbs
2 teaspoons grated Parmesan, optional

Cut a slice off the base of each potato so the potato will sit flat. Place cut-side-down on a board and make thin evenly-spaced cuts about two-thirds of the way through each potato. Place on a lightly greased baking dish. Brush the potatoes with butter, then sprinkle with a mixture of the dry breadcrumbs and Parmesan. Roast for 40–50 minutes, or until golden brown and tender.

## PARSNIPS

**Preparation time:** 10 minutes
**Total cooking time:** 40 minutes
**Serves** 4

✶

4 parsnips, peeled
1 tablespoon oil
20 g (³/₄ oz) butter, melted
1 tablespoon maple syrup

Cut off the thin part of the parsnips, then cut each thick section into quarters lengthways. Toss with the oil and butter in a baking dish and roast for 35 minutes, or until lightly browned, tossing occasionally. Drizzle with maple syrup and roast for 5 minutes.

## PUMPKIN

**Preparation time:** 10 minutes
**Total cooking time:** 40 minutes
**Serves** 4–6

✶

1 kg (2 lb) pumpkin
1 tablespoon oil
20 g (³/₄ oz) butter, melted
¹/₂ teaspoon ground paprika
¹/₂ teaspoon ground cumin

Cut the pumpkin into 8 pieces and toss with the oil, butter, paprika and cumin. Roast in a baking dish for 40 minutes, or until browned and tender, turning once.

## STUFFED TOMATOES

**Preparation time:** 20 minutes
**Total cooking time:** 25 minutes
**Serves** 6

✶

6 ripe tomatoes
20 g (³/₄ oz) butter
2 rashers bacon, finely chopped
75 g (2¹/₂ oz) button mushrooms,
   finely chopped
1 spring onion, finely chopped
1 cup (80 g/2³/₄ oz) fresh breadcrumbs
oil, for drizzling

Cut the tops off the tomatoes, reserving the tops. Scoop out the seeds and soft flesh. Melt the butter over low heat and fry the bacon and button mushrooms for 5 minutes, or until soft. Transfer to a bowl. Stir in the spring onion and breadcrumbs and season with salt and freshly ground black pepper. Fill the tomatoes with the mixture and replace the tops. Place on a baking tray and drizzle with oil. Roast for 20 minutes, or until heated through.

**MISTLETOE**
The delightful tradition of stealing kisses under the mistletoe came from a Scandinavian myth. After each kiss, a berry was to be removed from the mistletoe and given to the kissed lady until no berries remained. Then there was no more power in the spell and no kisses were available. It is thought by some that the tradition began because mistletoe was considered the plant of peace in Scandinavia. If enemies met under the mistletoe, they declared a truce for the day.

*OPPOSITE PAGE, CLOCKWISE, FROM TOP LEFT: Hasselback potatoes; Parsnips; Pumpkin; Stuffed tomatoes*

**2** Mash with a potato masher, adding the butter, milk and cinnamon. Season, to taste, with salt and freshly ground pepper, then spoon into a shallow 1 litre (32 fl oz) capacity casserole dish and smooth the top.

**3** For the crumble topping, remove the crusts from the bread, break the bread into smaller pieces and finely chop in a food processor. Mix in the Parmesan and thyme, then scatter over the mash and bake for 20 minutes, or until the crumble is golden and crispy.

## BRAISED FENNEL

**Preparation time:** 15 minutes
**Total cooking time:** 30 minutes
**Serves** 8

★

4 small fennel bulbs
20 g (³/4 oz) butter
1 tablespoon sugar
¹/3 cup (80 ml/2³/4 fl oz) white wine
²/3 cup (160 ml/5 fl oz) chicken stock
1 tablespoon sour cream

**1** Slice the fennel bulbs into quarters, reserving the fronds. Melt the butter in a frying pan and stir in the sugar. Add the fennel, and cook for 5–10 minutes, until lightly browned all over.

**2** Pour in the wine and stock and bring to the boil, then reduce the heat and simmer, covered, for 10 minutes, or until tender.

**3** Uncover and boil until most of the liquid has evaporated and the sauce has become sticky. Remove from the heat and stir in the sour cream. Garnish with the reserved fennel fronds.

## ORANGE SWEET POTATO CRUMBLE

**Preparation time:** 25 minutes
**Total cooking time:** 40 minutes
**Serves** 6

★

1 kg (2 lb) orange sweet potato (kumera)
50 g (1³/4 oz) butter
¹/3 cup (80 ml/2³/4 fl oz) milk or cream
¹/4 teaspoon ground cinnamon
480 g (15 oz) loaf sourdough bread
¹/2 cup (55 g/2 oz) grated Parmesan
1 teaspoon dried thyme leaves

**1** Preheat the oven to moderate 180°C (350°F/ Gas 4). Cut the orange sweet potato into chunks, put in a saucepan and cook in lightly salted boiling water for 15 minutes, or until tender. Drain and return to the saucepan.

*ABOVE: Orange sweet potato crumble*

## CABBAGE WITH HERBS

Finely shred 850 g (1 lb 12 oz) cabbage (green or red or a combination of both). Melt 60 g (2 oz) butter in a large pan with a lid, add the cabbage and toss to combine with the butter. Put the lid on the pan and 'steam' the cabbage over low heat for 5 minutes. Remove the lid and cook the cabbage over low heat for 3 minutes more, stirring so it cooks evenly. Stir through ²/3 cup (40 g/1¹/4 oz) finely shredded basil. Season with salt and freshly ground black pepper and serve immediately. Serves 4.

# BROCCOLI WITH ALMONDS

**Preparation time:** 10 minutes
**Total cooking time:** 10 minutes
**Serves** 6

500 g (1 lb) broccoli, cut into small florets
2 teaspoons oil
20 g (³/₄ oz) butter
1 clove garlic, crushed
1 tablespoon flaked almonds

**1** Add the broccoli to a saucepan of boiling water and cook for 1–2 minutes, or until just tender. Drain thoroughly. Heat the oil and butter in a large frying pan, add the garlic and almonds and cook for 1–2 minutes, or until the almonds are golden. Remove from the pan and set aside.
**2** Add the broccoli to the frying pan and toss over medium heat for 2–3 minutes, or until the broccoli is heated through. Return the almonds to the pan and stir until well distributed. Serve hot.

# CELERIAC AND TARRAGON PUREE

**Preparation time:** 15 minutes
**Total cooking time:** 15 minutes
**Serves** 6

2 cups (500 ml/16 fl oz) vegetable stock
¼ cup (60 ml/2 fl oz) lemon juice
3 celeriacs, peeled and chopped
40 g (1 ¼ oz) butter
1 tablespoon cream
1 tablespoon finely chopped fresh tarragon

**1** Put the vegetable stock, lemon juice and 2 cups (500 ml/16 fl oz) water in a saucepan and bring to the boil. Add the celeriac and cook for 10–15 minutes, or until tender. You may need to add extra water, depending on the size of the celeriac.
**2** Drain and place in a food processor with the butter and cream. Season with salt and freshly ground pepper and process until smooth. Alternatively, mash until smooth. Stir in the chopped tarragon. If the mixture is too thick, add a little more cream.

# MINTED PEAS

**Preparation time:** 5 minutes
**Total cooking time:** 6 minutes
**Serves** 6

4 cups (620 g/1 ¼ lb) fresh or frozen peas
4 sprigs fresh mint
30 g (1 oz) butter
2 tablespoons shredded fresh mint

**1** Place the peas in a saucepan and pour in water to just cover the peas. Add the mint sprigs.
**2** Bring to the boil and simmer for 5 minutes (only 2 minutes if frozen), or until the peas are just tender. Drain and discard the mint. Return to the saucepan, add the butter and shredded mint and stir over low heat until the butter has melted. Season with salt and cracked pepper.

*ABOVE: Broccoli
with almonds*

# ROAST VEGETABLE MASH

**Preparation time:** 30 minutes
**Total cooking time:** 1 hour 30 minutes
**Serves** 4–6

★

2 large pontiac or sebago potatoes
400 g (13 oz) pumpkin
400 g (13 oz) orange sweet potato (kumera)
2 large parsnips
1 large onion, chopped
2 ripe tomatoes, quartered
6 cloves garlic, unpeeled
2 tablespoons olive oil
30 g (1 oz) butter, chopped

**1** Preheat the oven to moderate 180°C (375°F/ Gas 4). Peel the potatoes, pumpkin, orange sweet potato and parsnip, then cut into large pieces and place in a large baking dish with the onion, tomato and garlic. Drizzle with oil and sprinkle with salt and cracked black pepper.
**2** Bake the vegetables for 1½ hours, or until soft and starting to brown, turning every 30 minutes. Peel the garlic.
**3** Transfer the vegetables to a bowl, add the butter and mash. Season, to taste, with salt and freshly ground pepper.
**NOTE:** You could also substitute swedes, celeriac or Jerusalem artichoke for the parsnips, or carrot for pumpkin or orange sweet potato. Fresh herbs are also a tasty addition—stir through some chopped fresh basil or parsley when mashing the vegetables.

## CHRISTMAS TREE

Of all Christmas traditions, having a tree in the home is probably the most universally accepted. Decorating the tree began in the sixteenth century at the time of Martin Luther. He took a fir tree home and put candles on it to symbolize the starry night in Bethlehem when Christ was born. In 1776, German soldiers taking part in the American War of Independence brought the custom to America. Britain had to wait until 1840 when the German-born Prince Albert, who married Queen Victoria, set up a tree for their children at Windsor Castle and popularized the idea. The custom slowly spread.

*RIGHT: Roast vegetable mash*

## ASPARAGUS WITH BUTTER AND PARMESAN

Preparation time: 15 minutes
Total cooking time: 3 minutes
Serves 4–6

300 g (10 oz) fresh asparagus
40 g (1½ oz) butter, melted
fresh Parmesan shavings
cracked black pepper, for serving

**1** Snap any thick woody ends from the asparagus and discard. Peel the bottom half of each spear with a vegetable peeler if the skin is very thick.
**2** Plunge the asparagus into a pan of boiling water and cook for 2–3 minutes, or until the asparagus is bright-green and just tender. Drain and place on serving plates. Drizzle with a little melted butter. Top with Parmesan shavings and sprinkle with cracked black pepper.
NOTE: You can use green, purple or white asparagus for this recipe, or a combination. Lightly toasted, crushed hazelnuts or pecan nuts can be sprinkled over the top.

## POTATOES WITH ROSEMARY

Preparation time: 10 minutes
Total cooking time: 20 minutes
Serves 6

750 g (1½ lb) baby new potatoes, halved
30 g (1 oz) butter
2 tablespoons olive oil
1 teaspoon cracked black pepper
2 cloves garlic, crushed
1 tablespoon finely chopped fresh rosemary
1 teaspoon sea salt

**1** Lightly boil or steam the potatoes for about 5 minutes, or until just tender (pierce with the point of a small knife—the knife should come away easily). Drain and cool slightly.
**2** Heat the butter and oil in a large heavy-based frying pan. When foaming, add the potatoes and season with half the pepper. Cook over medium heat for 5–10 minutes, or until golden and crisp, tossing to ensure the potatoes are evenly coloured.
**3** Stir in the garlic, rosemary and salt and cook for another minute. Mix in the remaining cracked pepper.

### ASPARAGUS

There are three types of cultivated asparagus, green, purple and white. Green is the one most commonly available in England, Australia and many other countries, while white is more popular in Belgium, Germany and parts of France. Green and white asparagus are the same variety but the white is harvested while the spear is still below the ground. White asparagus spears are usually thick with almost no scales, but only a short part of the length is young enough to be edible. Purple asparagus has a similar flavour to green asparagus but is less commonly available.

*LEFT: Asparagus with butter and Parmesan*

## INDIVIDUAL BAKED ROSTI

**Preparation time:** 20–25 minutes
**Total cooking time:** 55 minutes
**Makes** 12

500 g (1 lb) waxy potatoes, peeled
30 g (1 oz) butter, melted
1 onion

**1** Preheat the oven to hot 220°C (425°F/Gas 7). Cook the potatoes in a pan of boiling salted water for 7 minutes, or until just tender (pierce with the point of a sharp knife—if the knife comes away easily, the potato is ready). Drain and cool.
**2** Brush twelve ½ cup (125 ml/4 fl oz) capacity muffin holes with a little of the butter. Grate the potatoes and onion, mix in a bowl and add the butter. Season with salt and mix well. Divide the mixture among the holes, gently pressing in. Bake for 45 minutes, or until cooked through and golden brown.
**3** With a small palette knife, gently loosen each rosti around the edge and lift out for serving.

*ABOVE: Individual baked rosti*

## LEEKS IN WHITE SAUCE

**Preparation time:** 15 minutes
**Total cooking time:** 15 minutes
**Serves** 6

2 leeks, trimmed
50 g (1¾ oz) butter
1 tablespoon plain flour
1 cup (250 ml/8 fl oz) milk
2 tablespoons grated Cheddar
1 tablespoon dry breadcrumbs

**1** Wash the leeks, cut in half lengthways and then into 5 cm (2 inch) pieces. Heat 30 g (1 oz) of the butter in a heavy-based saucepan, add the leeks and cook for 10 minutes, stirring, until tender. Transfer to an ovenproof serving dish.
**2** Melt the remaining butter in a pan over low heat. Stir in the flour and cook for 1 minute, or until pale and foaming. Remove from the heat and gradually stir in the milk. Return to the heat and stir until the sauce boils and thickens. Pour over the leeks. Sprinkle with cheese and crumbs. Grill for 2–3 minutes, or until golden brown.

## ORANGE POPPY SEED ROASTED VEGETABLES

Preparation time: 20 minutes
Total cooking time: 50 minutes
Serves 8

500 g (1 lb) new potatoes, halved

6 parsnips, peeled and quartered lengthways

500 g (1 lb) orange sweet potato (kumera), cut into large chunks

330 g (11 oz) baby carrots, some with tops on

6 pickling onions, halved

1/3 cup (80 ml/2 3/4 fl oz) oil

2 tablespoons poppy seeds

200 g (6 1/2 oz) triple cream Brie, thinly sliced

### Orange dressing

1/2 cup (125 ml/4 fl oz) orange juice

2 cloves garlic, crushed

1 tablespoon Dijon mustard

1 teaspoon white wine vinegar

1 teaspoon sesame oil

1 Preheat the oven to moderately hot 200°C (400°F/Gas 6). Place all the vegetables and the oil in a large deep baking dish. Toss the vegetables to coat with the oil. Bake for 50 minutes, or until the vegetables are crisp and tender, tossing every 15 minutes. Remove from the oven and sprinkle with the poppy seeds.
2 For the orange dressing, whisk the ingredients together in a small jug.
3 Pour the dressing over the warm vegetables and toss. Transfer to a large bowl, top with the Brie and serve immediately while still warm.

---

## ZUCCHINI (COURGETTES) WITH LEMON AND CAPER BUTTER

Rinse, drain and chop 2 tablespoons bottled capers and put in a small bowl with 100 g (3 1/2 oz) butter, 2 teaspoons grated lemon rind, 1 tablespoon lemon juice and some salt and pepper. Mix until combined. Thinly slice 8 small zucchini (courgettes) lengthways and steam in a saucepan for 3–5 minutes, or until tender. Toss with the caper butter and serve immediately. Serves 4.

---

**REINDEER**
It is thought by some that Scandinavians may have spread the idea of Christmas reindeer to other parts of the world. Reindeers became famous after Dr Clement Moore's poem of 1823, in which Dancer, Prancer, Donder and the other reindeer were introduced as the animals who pulled Santa's sleigh. Goodies such as apples and carrots were left out for the reindeer, continuing the old custom of kindness at this time.

*ABOVE: Orange poppy seed roasted vegetables*

151

**CREAMY POTATO GRATIN**

Sprinkle a little of the grated Cheddar cheese over each layer.

Pour the cream mixture over the top of the potato and onion.

## CREAMY POTATO GRATIN

**Preparation time:** 20 minutes
**Total cooking time:** 40 minutes
**Serves** 6

750 g (1 1/2 lb) waxy or all-purpose potatoes
1 onion
1 cup (125 g/4 oz) grated Cheddar
1 1/2 cups (375 ml/12 fl oz) cream
2 teaspoons chicken stock powder

**1** Preheat the oven to moderate 180°C (350°F/ Gas 4). Thinly slice the potatoes and slice the onion into rings.
**2** Arrange a layer of overlapping potato slices in a baking dish and top with a layer of onion rings. Divide the cheese in half and set aside one half for topping. Sprinkle a little of the remaining cheese over the onion. Continue layering in this order until all the potato and the onion have been used, finishing with a little cheese.

**3** Pour the cream into a small jug, add the chicken stock powder and whisk gently until thoroughly combined. Pour the mixture over the layered potato and onion and sprinkle the top with the reserved cheese. Bake for 40 minutes, or until the potato is tender, the cheese has melted and the top is golden brown.
**NOTES:** A gratin is any dish topped with cheese and/or breadcrumbs and cooked until browned. There are many versions of potato gratin—some are creamy like this one, others less so.

If you prefer, you can use different types of stock, including vegetable, to vary the flavour.

Waxy or all-purpose potatoes are best as they hold their shape better when cooked in this way.

If you have a mandolin, use it to cut the potatoes into thin slices. If not, make sure you use a very sharp knife. Peel the skin very thinly.

*ABOVE: Creamy potato gratin*

# PEAR-SHAPED POTATO CROQUETTES

**Preparation time:** 30 minutes
 + 1 hour 30 minutes refrigeration
**Total cooking time:** 20 minutes
Makes 12

600 g (1 1/4 lb) floury potatoes, peeled
   and chopped

1 egg

1 egg yolk

60 g (2 oz) Parmesan, grated

1/4 cup (40 g/1 1/4 oz) finely chopped ham

3 tablespoons chopped fresh parsley

plain flour, for coating

1 egg, lightly beaten, extra

1 cup (100 g/3 1/2 oz) dry breadcrumbs

2–3 strands raw spaghetti

oil, for deep-frying

**1** Cook the potato for 5–10 minutes, or until tender (pierce with the point of a small knife—if the potato comes away easily, it is ready). Drain and mash thoroughly. While the potato is still hot, gradually stir or fold in the combined beaten egg and egg yolk, Parmesan, ham and parsley. Divide into 12 portions, put on a tray, cover with plastic wrap and refrigerate for at least 1 hour.

**2** Shape the potato portions into small pear shapes and coat each in the flour, egg and then the breadcrumbs. Break the spaghetti into short lengths and insert one piece into the top of each pear shape to represent a stalk. Put on a non-stick tray or a baking tray covered with baking paper. Refrigerate for at least 30 minutes, to firm.

**3** Fill a large heavy-based saucepan one third full of oil and heat to 180°C (350°F), or until a cube of bread browns in 15 seconds. Cook the potato pears, three or four at a time so the pan does not overcrowd, for 2 minutes, or until evenly browned and heated through. Drain on crumpled paper towels. Serve hot or warm.

## PEAR-SHAPED POTATO CROQUETTES

Fold the beaten egg and egg yolk, Parmesan, ham and parsley into the hot mashed potato with a wooden spoon.

Shape each potato portion into a small pear shape and coat each in flour, egg and breadcrumbs.

Break the spaghetti strands into short lengths and insert a piece into the top of each pear shape to represent a stalk.

*LEFT: Pear-shaped potato croquettes*

# HONEY-ROASTED VEGETABLES

**Preparation time:** 20 minutes
**Total cooking time:** 50 minutes
**Serves** 4

4 parsnips

2 carrots

2 small orange sweet potatoes (kumera)

4 beetroot, cut into wedges

8 cloves garlic, unpeeled

1/4 cup (60 ml/2 fl oz) oil

1 tablespoon honey

1 teaspoon cumin seeds

1/2 teaspoon cracked black pepper

1/2 teaspoon rock salt

**1** Preheat the oven to moderately hot 200°C (400°F/Gas 6). Cut the parsnips, carrots and sweet potatoes into 10 cm (4 inch) lengths. Place the vegetables and the unpeeled garlic in a large baking dish, and drizzle with the oil and honey. Sprinkle with the cumin seeds, pepper and salt. Toss to coat.
**2** Bake the vegetables for 40–50 minutes, or until tender inside and golden brown outside.

# DUCHESS POTATOES

**Preparation time:** 20 minutes + refrigeration
**Total cooking time:** 30 minutes
**Serves** 6

860 g (1 lb 12 oz) floury potatoes, quartered

2 eggs

1/4 cup (60 ml/2 fl oz) cream

2 tablespoons freshly grated Parmesan

1/4 teaspoon grated nutmeg

1 egg yolk, for glazing

**1** Boil or steam the potato for 10 minutes, or until just tender (pierce with the point of a small knife—if the potato comes away easily, it is ready). Drain and return to the pan. Turn the heat to very low and shake the pan for 1–2 minutes to dry out the potato. Transfer to a bowl and mash well until smooth.
**2** Beat together the eggs, cream, Parmesan,

nutmeg and some salt and black pepper. Add to the potato and mash to combine. Taste for seasoning and adjust if necessary. Cover and leave for 20 minutes to cool slightly. Preheat the oven to moderate 180°C (350°F/Gas 4).
**3** Put the just warm potato mixture in a piping bag with a 1.5 cm (5/8 inch) star nozzle. Pipe the mixture in swirls, not too close together, onto greased baking trays. Brush lightly all over with the extra egg yolk, to give a golden, crisp finish. Bake for 15–20 minutes, or until golden. Serve hot, sprinkled with a little paprika if desired.
**NOTE:** These can be prepared in advance and refrigerated, covered with plastic. Just before serving, brush with egg yolk and bake.

# RISOTTO-STUFFED ONIONS

**Preparation time:** 15 minutes
**Total cooking time:** 1 hour 40 minutes
**Serves** 8

8 onions (about 200 g/6 1/2 oz each)

1 tablespoon oil

20 g (3/4 oz) butter

70 g (2 1/4 oz) mushrooms, chopped

20 g (3/4 oz) prosciutto, chopped

1/2 cup (110 g/3 1/2 oz) arborio rice

2 1/2 cups (600 ml/20 fl oz) hot chicken stock

2 tablespoons grated Parmesan

2 tablespoons chopped fresh parsley

**1** Preheat the oven to moderately hot 200°C (400°F/Gas 6). Trim the bases of the onions so they sit flat and cut the tops off, leaving a wide opening. Place in a baking dish, drizzle with the oil and bake for 1–1 1/2 hours, or until golden.
**2** Meanwhile, melt the butter in a pan, add the mushrooms and prosciutto and cook for 5 minutes, or until the mushrooms have softened. Add the rice and stir until well coated with the butter. Gradually stir in the hot chicken stock, about 1/2 cup (125 ml/4 fl oz) at a time, making sure the liquid has been absorbed before adding more. When all the stock has been absorbed, stir in the Parmesan and parsley.
**3** Scoop out the flesh from the middle of each onion, leaving at least 3 outside layers on each, to hold the filling. Chop the scooped flesh and stir through the risotto mixture. Spoon the filling into the onion shells, piling a little on top. Bake for 10 minutes to heat through, then serve.

**BOXING DAY**

In many countries, especially Britain and the Commonwealth countries, the day after Christmas Day is known as Boxing Day. Although similar customs can be traced back as far as ancient Rome, its modern origin comes from the tradition of giving apprentices and other tradesmen a gift in a box in appreciation of their service throughout the year. Boxes were also placed in churches as a symbol of charity and their contents distributed to the needy on the day following Christmas which came to be known as Boxing Day.

*OPPOSITE PAGE, CLOCKWISE FROM TOP:*
*Honey-roasted vegetables; Risotto-stuffed onions; Duchess potatoes*

## CAULIFLOWER CHEESE

**Preparation time:** 15 minutes
**Total cooking time:** 20 minutes
**Serves** 4

★

500 g (1 lb) cauliflower, cut into
   small pieces
2 tablespoons fresh breadcrumbs
1/4 cup (30 g/1 oz) grated Cheddar

**Cheese sauce**

30 g (1 oz) butter
30 g (1 oz) plain flour
1 1/4 cups (315 ml/10 fl oz) warm milk
1 teaspoon Dijon mustard
1/2 cup (60 g/2 oz) grated Cheddar
1/2 cup (50 g/1 3/4 oz) grated Parmesan

**1** Lightly grease a 1.5 litre (48 fl oz) heatproof
dish. Cook the cauliflower pieces in a saucepan
of lightly salted boiling water for 10 minutes, or
until just tender. Drain thoroughly, then transfer
to the prepared dish and keep warm.
**2** For the cheese sauce, melt the butter in a pan
over low heat. Stir in the flour and cook for
1 minute, or until pale and foaming. Remove
from the heat and gradually stir in the milk and
mustard. Return to the heat and stir constantly
until the sauce boils and thickens. Reduce the
heat and simmer for 2 minutes, then remove
the pan from the heat. Add the Cheddar and
Parmesan and stir until melted. Do not reheat
or the oil will come out of the cheese. Season
with salt and white pepper, to taste, and pour
over the cauliflower.
**3** Combine the breadcrumbs and Cheddar
and sprinkle over the sauce. Grill under
medium heat until the top is brown and
bubbling. Serve immediately.
**NOTE:** This cheese sauce is also delicious poured
over other vegetables such as broccoli, asparagus,
or a combination of vegetables.

*ABOVE: Cauliflower
cheese*

# TOMATO AND FENNEL IN ROASTED RED PEPPERS
## (CAPSICUMS)

**Preparation time:** 20 minutes
**Total cooking time:** 1 hour
**Serves 6**

2 small fennel bulbs
3 large red peppers (capsicums)
6 ripe Roma (egg) tomatoes
6 cloves garlic, sliced
3 teaspoons fennel seeds
¼ cup (60 ml/2 fl oz) lemon juice
2 tablespoons olive oil

1 Preheat the oven to moderate 180°C (350°F/ Gas 4). Brush a large baking dish with oil.
2 Cut each fennel bulb in half, then cut into thick slices. Place in a pan of boiling salted water, cook for 1 minute, then drain and cool.
3 Cut the red peppers in half lengthways, leaving the stalk attached. Remove the seeds and membrane.

4 Cut the tomatoes in half lengthways and arrange in the pepper halves with the fennel slices. (The amount of fennel used will depend on the size of the peppers and the fennel, but the vegetables should fit firmly inside the peppers.) Add garlic slices to each pepper half and sprinkle with fennel seeds. Season with salt and freshly ground black pepper. Sprinkle the lemon juice and half the oil over the peppers.
5 Bake for 1 hour, or until the peppers are tender, brushing with the remaining oil once or twice during cooking. Serve hot.

## TOMATOES STUFFED WITH FETA

Cut a deep cross in the tops of 6 ripe tomatoes. Combine 150 g (5 oz) crumbled Greek feta in a bowl with 2 teaspoons chopped fresh oregano and 1 tablespoon freshly grated Parmesan. Season with pepper. Stuff each tomato with about 1 tablespoon of the feta mixture. Bake in a moderately hot 200°C (400°F/Gas 6) oven for 20 minutes, or until the skins split and soften. Makes 6.

**FETA**
This famous salty Greek cheese, often found in Greek salads, is now made in other places such as Australia, America and Denmark. Traditionallly made from the milk from sheep or goats, it is now often made using milk from cows. Large blocks are salted, then sliced and salted again. It is packed and left to mature for a month in the salty whey.

*LEFT: Tomato and fennel in roasted red peppers*

## COLESLAW

Preparation time: 20 minutes
Total cooking time: Nil
Serves 10

1/2 green (savoy) cabbage
1/4 red cabbage
3 carrots, coarsely grated
6 radishes, coarsely grated
1 red pepper (capsicum), chopped
4 spring onions, sliced
3 tablespoons chopped fresh flat-leaf parsley
1 cup (250 g/8 oz) good-quality mayonnaise

1 Remove the hard cores from the cabbages and thinly shred the leaves with a sharp knife. Place in a large bowl and add the carrot, radish, red pepper, spring onion and parsley.
2 Add the mayonnaise, season with salt and freshly ground black pepper and toss well.
NOTE: The vegetables can be chopped and refrigerated for up to 3 hours before serving. Add the mayonnaise just before serving.

## COLD POTATO SALAD

Preparation time: 30 minutes
Total cooking time: 10 minutes
Serves 8

1.2 kg (2 lb 6 1/2 oz) waxy white or red potatoes, unpeeled and cut in bite-sized pieces
2 onions, finely chopped
2 green peppers (capsicums), chopped
4–5 celery sticks, chopped
6 tablespoons finely chopped fresh parsley

### Dressing

1 1/2 cups (375 g/12 oz) whole-egg mayonnaise
3–4 tablespoons white wine vinegar or lemon juice
1/3 cup (90 g/3 oz) sour cream

1 Steam or boil the potatoes for 5–10 minutes, or until just tender (pierce with the point of a small sharp knife—if the potato comes away easily it is ready). Don't let the skins break away. Drain and cool completely.

2 Combine the onion, green pepper, celery and parsley with the potato in a large bowl, reserving some parsley for garnish.
3 For the dressing, mix together all the ingredients in a bowl and season with salt and black pepper. Pour over the salad and toss gently. Garnish with the reserved parsley.
NOTE: If you accidentally overcook the potatoes, drain them carefully and spread out on a large flat dish or tray and cool completely. Most of the potatoes will firm up if you do this. In this case, you should also take a little extra care when stirring in the mayonnaise.

## HOT POTATO SALAD

Preparation time: 15 minutes
Total cooking time: 25 minutes
Serves 8

4 rashers bacon
1.5 kg (3 lb) small waxy red potatoes, unpeeled
4 spring onions, sliced
3 tablespoons chopped fresh flat-leaf parsley

### Dressing

2/3 cup (170 ml/5 1/2 fl oz) extra virgin olive oil
1 tablespoon Dijon mustard
1/3 cup (80 ml/2 3/4 fl oz) white wine vinegar

1 Trim the rind and any excess fat from the bacon, then cook under a hot grill until crisp. Chop into small pieces.
2 Steam or boil the potatoes for 10–15 minutes, or until just tender (pierce with the point of a small sharp knife—if the potato comes away easily it is ready). Don't let the skins break away. Drain and cool slightly.
3 For the dressing, whisk all the ingredients together in a jug.
4 Cut the potatoes into quarters and place in a bowl with half the bacon, the spring onion, parsley and some salt and freshly ground black pepper. Pour in half the dressing and toss to coat the potatoes thoroughly. Transfer to a serving bowl, drizzle with the remaining dressing and sprinkle the remaining bacon over the top.
NOTE: The cooking time will depend on the size of the potatoes. The potatoes can be diced instead of quartered if you prefer.

**RADISHES**
Radishes vary considerably in shape, size and even their external colour, which ranges from white to red to black. The white internal flesh is crisp with a slightly peppery taste which can be weak or strong, They are often used raw in salads and in many cuisines they are sculpted into interesting shapes to be used as a decoration on the plate.

*OPPOSITE PAGE,
CLOCKWISE FROM TOP:
Coleslaw; Hot potato
salad; Cold potato salad*

## TOMATO AND BOCCONCINI SALAD

Cut the Roma tomatoes lengthways into three or four thick slices. Discard the outside slices because they won't sit flat.

Use a sharp knife to cut each bocconcini lengthways into three or four thick slices.

Whisk the olive oil and balsamic vinegar together in a small jug.

*ABOVE: Tomato and bocconcini salad*

# TOMATO AND BOCCONCINI SALAD

**Preparation time:** 15 minutes
**Total cooking time:** Nil
**Serves 6–8**

★

12 ripe Roma (egg) tomatoes
10 bocconcini
1 1/3 cups (40 g/1 1/2 oz) fresh basil leaves

**Dressing**

1/2 cup (125 ml/4 fl oz) extra virgin olive oil
1/3 cup (80 ml/2 3/4 fl oz) balsamic vinegar

1 Cut the tomatoes lengthways into 3–4 slices (discard the outside slices, which won't lie flat). Slice each bocconcini lengthways into 3–4 slices.
2 Arrange some tomato slices on a serving plate, place a bocconcini slice on top of each and scatter with some basil leaves. Repeat until all the tomato, bocconcini and basil have been used. Season with salt and pepper.

3 For the dressing, whisk the oil and vinegar together. Drizzle over the salad.
**NOTE:** This salad can also be served with a pesto dressing. Finely chop 1 cup (50 g/1 3/4 oz) fresh basil leaves, 2 tablespoons pine nuts, 1/2 cup (50 g/1 3/4 oz) grated Parmesan and 2 crushed garlic cloves in a food processor. With the motor running, add 1/2 cup (125 ml/4 fl oz) olive oil and 2 tablespoons lemon juice in a steady stream.

## ASPARAGUS AND HAZELNUT SALAD

Toast 2/3 cup (95 g/3 oz) hazelnuts in a frying pan over medium heat for 3 minutes, shaking the pan to prevent the nuts burning. Lightly crush the nuts in a mortar and pestle. Trim the woody ends from 300 g (10 oz) asparagus spears and cook the spears in a large pan of boiling water for 1 minute. Drain and plunge into iced water. Drain. Mix 3 tablespoons olive oil and 3 teaspoons white wine vinegar in a screw top jar. Season and drizzle over the asparagus. Sprinkle with the nuts. Serves 4.

## WALDORF SALAD

**Preparation time:** 20 minutes
**Total cooking time:** Nil
**Serves** 4–6

2 green apples, cut into small pieces
2 red apples, cut into small pieces
2 tablespoons lemon juice
4 celery sticks, sliced
¼ cup (30 g/1 oz) walnut pieces
1 cup (250 g/8 oz) whole-egg mayonnaise
chopped fresh parsley, to garnish, optional

1 Put the apple in a large bowl, drizzle with the lemon juice and toss to coat (this prevents the apples discolouring). Mix in the celery and most of the walnut pieces.
2 Add the mayonnaise to the bowl and toss until well coated. Season, to taste. Spoon the salad into a serving bowl, sprinkle with the remaining walnut pieces and serve. Garnish with parsley.
**NOTE:** This salad is convenient as it can be made up to 2 hours in advance and stored, covered, in the refrigerator.

## QUICK PESTO PASTA SALAD

**Preparation time:** 25 minutes
**Total cooking time:** 15 minutes
**Serves** 6–8

2 cups (100 g/3½ oz) fresh basil leaves
2 cloves garlic, crushed
½ cup (50 g/1¾ oz) grated Parmesan
2 tablespoons pine nuts, toasted
⅓ cup (80 ml/2¾ fl oz) olive oil
500 g (1 lb) penne pasta, cooked
250 g (8 oz) cherry tomatoes, halved
1 small red onion, sliced into thin wedges
150 g (5 oz) black olives
Parmesan shavings, to garnish

1 Process the basil in a food processor with the garlic, Parmesan and pine nuts until roughly chopped. With the motor running, gradually add the olive oil in a thin stream until well combined.
2 Place the pasta in a large bowl, stir in the pesto and mix well. Add the tomatoes, onion and olives and stir gently. Spoon into a serving dish and garnish with Parmesan. Serve while the pasta is still warm or, if you prefer, leave until cold.

### WALNUTS

Walnuts have been eaten since prehistoric times and have been cultivated as long ago as in ancient Greece. There are many species of walnut tree but the most important originated in Persia. The shelled nut is used mostly in cakes, desserts, ice cream, confectionery and, of course, the popular Middle Eastern pastry, baklava. It is also used in savoury dishes such as salads, soups, sauces and dressings for pasta. Oil has been yielded from walnuts since antiquity.

*ABOVE: Waldorf salad*

161

*ABOVE: Bean salad*

## Mustard vinaigrette

1/2 cup (125 ml/4 fl oz) extra virgin olive oil

2 tablespoons white wine vinegar

1 teaspoon sugar

1 tablespoon Dijon mustard

1 clove garlic, crushed

**1** Cut the green beans into short lengths. Bring a small pan of water to the boil and cook the beans for 2 minutes. Drain and rinse, then leave in a bowl of iced water until cold. Drain well.
**2** Drain and rinse the chickpeas, kidney beans, cannellini beans and corn kernels. Mix them in a large bowl with the green beans, spring onion, red pepper, celery, gherkin, mint and parsley. Season with salt and freshly ground black pepper.
**3** For the vinaigrette, whisk together the oil, white wine vinegar and sugar in a small jug. Season with salt and black pepper. Whisk in the mustard and garlic. Drizzle over the salad and toss gently.

## RICE SALAD

**Preparation time:** 30 minutes
  + 1 hour refrigeration
**Total cooking time:** 20 minutes
**Serves 6–8**

1 1/2 cups (300 g/10 oz) long-grain rice

1/2 cup (80 g/2 3/4 oz) fresh or frozen peas

3 spring onions, sliced

1 green pepper (capsicum), finely diced

1 red pepper (capsicum), finely diced

310 g (10 oz) can corn kernels, drained, rinsed

1/4 cup (15 g/1/2 oz) chopped fresh mint

### Dressing

1/2 cup (125 ml/4 fl oz) extra virgin olive oil

2 tablespoons lemon juice

1 clove garlic, crushed

1 teaspoon sugar

**1** Bring a large pan of water to the boil and stir in the rice. Return to the boil and cook for 12–15 minutes, or until tender. Drain and cool.
**2** Cook the peas in a small pan of boiling water for about 2 minutes. Rinse under cold water and drain well.
**3** For the dressing, whisk together the oil, juice, garlic and sugar in a small jug, then season.

## BEAN SALAD

**Preparation time:** 30 minutes
**Total cooking time:** 2 minutes
**Serves 8–10**

250 g (8 oz) green beans, topped and tailed

400 g (12 3/4 oz) can chickpeas

425 g (13 1/2 oz) can red kidney beans

400 g (12 3/4 oz) can cannellini beans

270 g (8 3/4 oz) can corn kernels

3 spring onions, sliced

1 red pepper (capsicum), finely chopped

3 celery sticks, chopped

4–6 bottled gherkins, chopped, optional

3 tablespoons chopped fresh mint

3 tablespoons chopped fresh flat-leaf parsley

**4** Combine the rice, peas, spring onion, peppers, corn and mint in a large bowl. Add the dressing and mix well. Cover and refrigerate for 1 hour. Transfer to a serving dish.

# CARAMELIZED ONION AND POTATO SALAD

**Preparation time:** 20 minutes
**Total cooking time:** 50 minutes
**Serves** 10–12

2 tablespoons oil

6 red onions, thinly sliced

1 kg (2 lb) kipfler, desiree or pontiac potatoes

4 rashers bacon

6 tablespoons chopped fresh chives

**Mayonnaise**

1 cup (250 g/8 oz) whole-egg mayonnaise

1 tablespoon Dijon mustard

2–3 tablespoons lemon juice

2 tablespoons sour cream

**1** Heat the oil in a large heavy-based frying pan, add the onion and cook over low-medium heat for 40 minutes, or until caramelized.
**2** Cut the potatoes into large chunks (if small, leave them whole) and steam or boil for 5–10 minutes until just tender (pierce with the point of a small knife—if the potato comes away easily, it is ready). Drain and cool slightly.
**3** Remove the rind from the bacon and grill until crisp. Drain on crumpled paper towels and cool slightly before roughly chopping.
**4** Put the potato, onion and chives in a large bowl, reserving a few chives for garnish, and toss to combine.
**5** For the mayonnaise, whisk the ingredients together in a bowl. Pour over the salad and toss to coat. Sprinkle with the bacon and garnish with the reserved chives.
**NOTE:** Ideal boiling potatoes are waxy in texture with a high moisture content and low starch content. Examples other than those given in the recipe are sebago, coliban, pink fir apple and jersey royals.

*BELOW: Caramelized onion and potato salad*

163

# MEXICANA SALAD

**Preparation time:** 40 minutes
  + overnight standing
**Total cooking time:** 45 minutes
**Serves** 10–12

 ✵ ✵

250 g (8 oz) dried black-eyed beans
250 g (8 oz) dried red kidney beans
500 g (1 lb) sweet potato
1 large red onion, chopped
1 large green pepper (capsicum), chopped
3 ripe tomatoes, chopped
3 tablespoons chopped fresh basil
3 flour tortillas
1 tablespoon oil
2 tablespoons grated Parmesan
1/4 cup (60 g/2 oz) sour cream

**Dressing**

1 clove garlic, crushed
1 tablespoon lime juice
2 tablespoons olive oil

**Guacamole**

3 ripe avocados
2 tablespoons lemon juice
1 clove garlic, crushed
1 small red onion, finely chopped
1 small red chilli, seeded and chopped
1/4 cup (60 g/2 oz) sour cream
2 tablespoons hot taco sauce

**1** Soak the beans in a large bowl of cold water overnight. Drain and cook in a large pan of rapidly boiling water for 30 minutes, or until just tender. Skim off any scum that appears on the surface during cooking. Do not overcook or the beans will be mushy. Drain and set aside to cool.
**2** Chop the sweet potato into small cubes and cook in boiling water for 5 minutes, or until tender. Drain and allow to cool, then combine with the onion, pepper, tomato and beans. Stir in the basil.
**3** For the dressing, combine all the ingredients in a jar and shake well until combined. Pour over the salad and toss gently to coat.
**4** Preheat the oven to moderate 180°C (350°F/Gas 4). Using a small knife or shaped cutter, cut Christmas tree shapes out of the tortillas, brush lightly with the oil, place on baking trays and and sprinkle with grated Parmesan. Bake for 5–10 minutes, or until crisp and golden.
**5** To make the guacamole, mash the avocados with the lemon juice. Add the garlic, onion, chilli, sour cream and taco sauce and mix well.
**6** Put the salad in a large bowl or on a platter, pile the guacamole in the centre, top with the sour cream and arrange the Christmas tree shapes on top.

# WILD RICE AND WALNUT SALAD

**Preparation time:** 10 minutes
  + 1 hour standing
**Total cooking time:** 5 minutes
**Serves** 6

 ✵

1 1/2 cups (285 g/9 1/2 oz) wild rice
3 oranges
6 spring onions, finely sliced
3/4 cup (90 g/3 oz) walnut pieces, toasted
1 tablespoon chopped fresh flat-leaf parsley

**Dressing**

1/3 cup (80 ml/2 3/4 fl oz) walnut oil
1 tablespoon olive oil
2 tablespoons white wine vinegar
1 tablespoon soy sauce
2 teaspoons honey

**1** Thoroughly rinse the wild rice under cold running water, then put in a saucepan and fill with water to come 2.5 cm (1 inch) above the rice. Bring to the boil and cook for 5 minutes. Remove from the heat, cover and leave for 1 hour. Drain well, transfer to a bowl and leave to cool.
**2** Peel the oranges, reserving the skin from one of them. Separate the flesh into segments and cut into small pieces. Cut the white pith off the reserved skin, cut the rind into julienne strips and reserve for garnish.
**3** Add the orange pieces to the cooled rice with the spring onion, walnut pieces and parsley and lightly toss.
**4** For the dressing, whisk all the ingredients together in a bowl until combined. Pour over the rice mixture and toss gently until well distributed. Garnish with the julienned orange rind.

**POINSETTIAS AND CHRISTMAS**
According to a delightful legend, the red flowering poinsettia first became connected with Christmas during the seventeenth century in Mexico. A boy named Pablo, on his way to church to visit the Nativity scene, had no gift for the Christ child, so he gathered branches from the roadside. The other children laughed at his gift but when he placed it near the manger, brilliant red star-shaped flowers appeared on each branch.

*OPPOSITE PAGE:*
*Mexican salad (top); Wild rice and walnut salad*

# CAESAR SALAD

**Preparation time:** 25 minutes
**Total cooking time:** 20 minutes
**Serves** 6

1 small French bread stick
2 tablespoons olive oil
2 cloves garlic, halved
4 rashers bacon (trimmed of fat)
2 cos lettuces
10 anchovy fillets, halved lengthways
1 cup (100 g/3 1/2 oz) shaved Parmesan
Parmesan shavings, extra, for serving

## Dressing

1 egg yolk
2 cloves garlic, crushed
2 teaspoons Dijon mustard
2 anchovy fillets
2 tablespoons white wine vinegar
1 tablespoon Worcestershire sauce
3/4 cup (185 ml/6 fl oz) olive oil

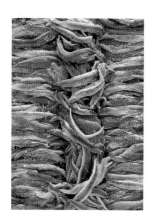

**CAESAR SALAD**
This classic American dish is named after its inventor, Caesar Cardini, who served it in his Tijuana, Mexico, restaurant in the 1920s. It became very popular with people in Hollywood and soon appeared in menus in restaurants in Los Angeles, from where it gradually spread elsewhere.

1 Preheat the oven to moderate 180°C (350°F/Gas 4). To make the croutons, cut the bread stick into 15 thin slices and brush both sides of each slice with oil. Spread them all on a baking tray and bake for 10–15 minutes, or until golden brown. Leave to cool slightly, then rub each side of each slice with the cut edge of a garlic clove. The baked bread can then be broken roughly into pieces or cut into small cubes.

2 Cook the bacon under a hot grill until crisp. Drain on paper towels until cooled, then break into chunky pieces.

3 Tear the lettuce into pieces and put in a large serving bowl with the bacon, anchovies, croutons and Parmesan.

4 For the dressing, place the egg yolks, garlic, mustard, anchovies, vinegar and Worcestershire sauce in a food processor or blender. Season and process for 20 seconds, or until smooth. With the motor running, add enough oil in a thin stream to make the dressing thick and creamy.

5 Drizzle the dressing over the salad and toss very gently until well distributed. Sprinkle the Parmesan shavings over the top and serve immediately.

*RIGHT: Caesar salad*

# CHICKPEA AND ROAST VEGETABLE SALAD

**Preparation time:** 25 minutes
+ 30 minutes standing
**Total cooking time:** 40 minutes
Serves 8

500 g (1 lb) butternut pumpkin, cut
into chunks

2 red peppers (capsicums), halved

4 slender eggplants (aubergines), sliced
in half lengthways

4 zucchini (courgettes), sliced in half
lengthways

4 onions, cut into quarters

olive oil, for brushing

2 x 300 g (10 oz) cans chickpeas, rinsed
and drained

2 tablespoons chopped fresh flat-leaf
parsley

**Dressing**

1/3 cup (80 ml/2 3/4 fl oz) olive oil

2 tablespoons lemon juice

1 clove garlic, crushed

1 tablespoon chopped fresh thyme

**1** Preheat the oven to hot 220°C (425°F/Gas 7). Brush two baking trays with oil and spread the vegetables in a single layer over the trays. Brush the vegetables lightly with the olive oil.

**2** Bake for 40 minutes, or until the vegetables are tender and begin to brown slightly on the edges. Remove and set aside to cool. Remove the skins from the red peppers if you wish. Chop the red peppers, eggplant and zucchini into large pieces, then put all the vegetables in a bowl with the chickpeas and half the parsley.

**3** Whisk together all the dressing ingredients in a bowl. Season, then toss through the vegetables. Set aside for 30 minutes to marinate. Spoon into a serving bowl and sprinkle with the rest of the parsley before serving.

## THE CHIMNEY

As children we are charmed by the idea of a very fat Santa making his way down the chimney without getting stuck, all sooty, or worse still, burnt by the fire. The image was popularized by the American scholar Clement Moore in his famous 1822 poem 'A Visit from St Nicholas'. The idea of entering a home via the chimney dates from prehistoric times, when people lived underground and their smokehole doubled as both the entrance and the exit.

*ABOVE: Chickpea and roast vegetable salad*

167

# SUPPERS & LEFTOVERS

This is always the tricky bit — what to do with the mountain of leftovers, especially when appetites have been completely jaded by the excesses of the last few days and no-one wants to hear the word 'turkey' ever again. Relax. This dilemma can be quickly resolved with the help of the following recipes, where Christmassy ingredients have been cleverly disguised as turkey san choy bau, chicken and asparagus gratin, pea and ham risotto, poached salmon salad with caper dill dressing and many more. You'll be surprised how quickly appreciative appetites can return!

## MUSHROOMS

Fresh button mushrooms are commonly used in cookery, although there are many other types of mushroom available. The flavour of button mushrooms is delicate and they are excellent for use in fillings and sauces or with pasta. You might find it necessary to wipe over fresh mushrooms with a damp cloth to remove any dirt. Don't wash them as this will make them go soggy during cooking. They are best stored in the refrigerator in a paper bag, not in a plastic bag or container, as they will sweat and deteriorate very quickly.

*ABOVE: Turkey filo parcels*

## TURKEY FILO PARCELS

**Preparation time:** 35 minutes
**Total cooking time:** 40 minutes
**Makes** 24

★★

20 g (³/4 oz) butter
200 g (6¹/2 oz) button mushrooms, sliced
4 rashers bacon, diced
350 g (11 oz) cooked turkey, chopped
150 g (5 oz) ricotta
2 spring onions, sliced
3 tablespoons shredded fresh basil
24 sheets filo pastry
butter, melted, extra, for brushing
sesame seeds, for sprinkling

1 Melt the butter in a large saucepan and add the mushrooms and bacon. Cook over high heat for 5 minutes, or until the mushrooms are soft and there is no liquid left. Combine the turkey, ricotta, spring onion and basil in a bowl, add the mushroom mixture, then season, to taste.

2 Preheat the oven to moderate 180°C (350°F/ Gas 4). Cover the pastry with a damp tea towel to prevent drying out. Working with 3 sheets at a time, brush each layer with melted butter. Cut into 3 strips. Place 1 tablespoon of filling at the end of each strip and fold the pastry over to form a triangle. Fold until you reach the end of the pastry. Repeat with the remaining pastry and filling. Place on a greased baking tray, brush with butter and sprinkle with sesame seeds. Bake for 30–35 minutes, or until golden.

## TURKEY AND CORN SOUP

Melt 20 g (³/4 oz) butter in a large saucepan, add 1 thinly sliced leek and stir over medium heat for 5 minutes, or until soft. Mix in 3¹/2 cups (875 ml/28 fl oz) chicken stock and a 420 g (14 oz) can creamed corn. Season. Bring to the boil, then reduce the heat and simmer, covered, for 5 minutes. Add 250 g (8 oz) shredded cooked turkey to the pan and stir until heated through. Serves 4.

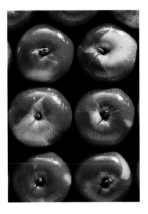

## TURKEY, POTATO AND APPLE SALAD

**Preparation time:** 25 minutes
**Total cooking time:** 15 minutes
**Serves** 6

4 spring onions
2 tablespoons oil
750 g (1 1/2 lb) new baby potatoes
1 red apple
1 tablespoon lemon juice
2 zucchini (courgettes), thickly sliced
400 g (13 oz) cooked turkey meat
2 tablespoons chopped fresh flat-leaf parsley

### Dressing

1/2 cup (125 g/4 oz) whole-egg mayonnaise
3 teaspoons Dijon mustard
1 tablespoon wholegrain mustard
2 tablespoons lemon juice

1 Cut the spring onions into thin strips. Heat the oil in a small frying pan and shallow-fry the spring onion until crisp. Remove and drain on crumpled paper towels.
2 Steam or boil the potatoes for 10 minutes, or until just tender (pierce with the point of a small knife—if the potato comes away easily, it is ready). Drain and allow to cool, then cut in halves.
3 Cut the unpeeled apple into thin wedges and toss with the lemon juice in a bowl (this prevents the apple from discolouring).
4 Boil, steam or microwave the zucchini until tender, then drain and refresh in cold water.
5 For the dressing, stir the ingredients together in a small bowl, then season, to taste.
6 Cut the leftover cooked turkey meat into thin strips and put in a large bowl. Add the potato, apple, zucchini and parsley to the turkey, drizzle the dressing over the top and gently toss until well combined. Serve topped with the crispy spring onion.

### NOISEMAKING

This is one of the earliest Christmas customs and has pagan origins. Long ago, it was believed that creating a dreadful din would scare away evil spirits lurking in the dark and cold of winter. But noisemaking also was held dear by Christians. In colonial times, Christmas Eve revellers roamed the streets blowing horns and whistles, jingling bells, beating drums and shouting. Householders often responded by throwing out coins. Some considered this tradition tiresome and by the late nineteenth century laws were created to keep the noisemakers off the street.

*ABOVE: Turkey, potato and apple salad*

TURKEY EMPANADAS

Brush all around the edges of each pastry circle with water.

Fold the pastry over to enclose the filling, then press the edges together with a fork.

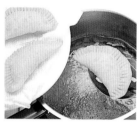

Deep-fry the empanadas until golden brown, then remove them and drain on crumpled paper towels.

# TURKEY EMPANADAS

**Preparation time:** 40 minutes
**Total cooking time:** 25 minutes
**Makes** 18

1 tablespoon oil
1 onion, finely chopped
1 clove garlic, crushed
2 teaspoons paprika
1 teaspoon ground cumin
1/2 teaspoon ground cinnamon
2 tablespoons sherry
400 g (13 oz) can crushed tomatoes
400 g (13 oz) cooked turkey, finely chopped
1/2 cup (110 g/3 1/2 oz) pitted green olives, chopped
3 hard-boiled eggs, chopped
1 tablespoon chopped fresh parsley
4 1/2 sheets ready-rolled shortcrust pastry
oil, for deep-frying

**1** Heat the tablespoon of oil in a frying pan, add the onion and garlic. Cook over medium heat for 2 minutes, then add the paprika, cumin and cinnamon, and stir until fragrant. Add the sherry, tomato and turkey. Boil for about 10 minutes, or until thickened. Remove from the heat and stir in the olives, eggs and parsley. Season, to taste, then transfer to a bowl and allow to cool.
**2** Cut eighteen 12 cm (5 inch) rounds from the pastry. Place 1 1/2 tablespoons of the mixture on one half of each round, brush the edge with water and fold the pastry over to enclose the filling. Press the edges with a fork to seal.
**3** Fill a deep heavy-based saucepan one third full of oil and heat to 180°C (350°F), or until a cube of bread browns in 15 seconds. Deep-fry the empanadas in batches for 2–3 minutes on each side, or until golden brown. Remove from the oil with a slotted spoon, then drain on crumpled paper towels.

# TURKEY SAN CHOY BAU

**Preparation time:** 15 minutes
    + 15 minutes soaking
**Total cooking time:** 5 minutes
**Serves** 4

8 small iceberg lettuce leaves
5 dried Chinese mushrooms
100 g (3 1/2 oz) canned baby corn
1 teaspoon sesame oil
2 teaspoons oil
2 cloves garlic, crushed
1 tablespoon grated fresh ginger
300 g (10 oz) cooked turkey, finely chopped
1/2 cup (90 g/3 oz) water chestnuts, finely chopped
100 g (3 1/2 oz) bean sprouts
2 spring onions, chopped
1 tablespoon chopped fresh coriander
1 teaspoon sugar
1 tablespoon oyster sauce
1 tablespoon soy sauce

**1** Soak the lettuce leaves in cold water while preparing the filling. Soak the Chinese mushrooms in a bowl of boiling water for 15 minutes, or until soft. Drain, discard the stems and finely chop the mushrooms. Thinly slice the baby corn.
**2** Heat the oils in a pan, add the garlic, ginger and corn, and toss over medium heat until fragrant. Add the mushrooms, turkey, water chestnuts, bean sprouts, spring onion, coriander, sugar and oyster and soy sauces. Toss well to heat through.
**3** Drain the lettuce and pat dry with paper towels. Spoon some turkey filling into each lettuce cup and serve.

*OPPOSITE PAGE:*
*Turkey empanadas (top);*
*Turkey san choy bau*

## CHICKEN AND LEEK PIE

Preparation time: 20 minutes
Total cooking time: 40 minutes
Serves 4

★★

50 g (1³/4 oz) butter
2 large leeks, white part only, finely sliced
4 spring onions, sliced
1 clove garlic, crushed
1/4 cup (30 g/1 oz) plain flour
1¹/2 cups (375 ml/12 fl oz) chicken stock
1/2 cup (125 ml/4 fl oz) cream
2 cups (280 g/9 oz) chopped cooked chicken
2 sheets frozen puff pastry, thawed
1/4 cup (60 ml/2 fl oz) milk

1 Melt the butter in a saucepan and add the leek, spring onion and garlic. Cook over low heat for 6 minutes, or until the leek is soft but not browned. Stir in the flour and cook for 1 minute, or until pale and foaming. Remove from the heat and gradually stir in the stock.

Return to the heat and stir constantly until the sauce boils and thickens. Stir in the cream and chicken, then spoon into a shallow 20 cm (8 inch) pie dish and set aside to cool. Preheat the oven to moderately hot 200°C (400°F/Gas 6).
2 Brush around the rim of the pie dish with a little milk. Put 1 sheet of pastry on top and seal around the edge firmly. Trim off any overhanging pastry with a sharp knife and decorate the edge with the back of a fork. Cut the other sheet into 1 cm (1/2 inch) strips and roll each strip up loosely like a snail. Arrange the spirals on top of the pie, starting from the middle and leaving a gap between each one. The spirals may not cover the whole pie. Make a few small holes between the spirals to let out any steam, and brush the top of the pie lightly with milk. Bake for 25–30 minutes, or until the top is crisp and golden. Make sure the spirals look well cooked and are not raw in the middle.
NOTE: Chopped leftover turkey can also be used. You can also make small pies by placing the mixture into 4 greased 1¹/4 cup (315 ml/ 10 fl oz) round ovenproof dishes. Cut the pastry into 4 rounds to fit the tops. Bake for 15 minutes, or until the pastry is crisp.

*ABOVE: Chicken and leek pie*

# CHICKEN AND ASPARAGUS GRATIN

**Preparation time:** 10 minutes
**Total cooking time:** 30 minutes
**Serves** 6

4 cups (540 g/1 lb 2 oz) chopped cooked
   chicken
425 g (14 oz) can asparagus spears, drained
420 g (14 oz) can creamy chicken and corn
   soup, or cream of mushroom soup
1/2 cup (125 g/4 oz) sour cream
2 spring onions, sliced diagonally
1 red pepper (capsicum), thinly sliced
1 cup (125 g/4 oz) grated Cheddar
1/2 cup (50 g/1 3/4 oz) grated Parmesan
1/2 teaspoon sweet paprika

**1** Preheat the oven to moderate 180°C (350°F/ Gas 4). Cover the base of a large, shallow ovenproof dish with the chicken and top with half the asparagus spears.

**2** Combine the soup, sour cream, spring onion and red pepper in a bowl. Season, to taste, and pour over the chicken.

**3** Arrange the remaining asparagus spears on top of the chicken and cover with the combined cheeses. Sprinkle with paprika and bake for 30 minutes, or until golden brown and bubbling. Serve immediately.

---

## TURKEY JAFFLE

Butter a slice of bread and gently press, butter-side-down, onto the base of a lightly-greased, preheated jaffle maker. Spread on some cranberry sauce and top with a couple of slices of turkey, sliced camembert and some lightly mashed left- over baked pumpkin. Top with a second buttered slice of bread, butter-side-up, and cook until golden brown. Makes 1.

---

*BELOW: Chicken and asparagus gratin*

## CORONATION CHICKEN

According to legend, this dish, consisting of cold chicken pieces served with a curried mayonnaise sauce, was devised for the coronation of Queen Elizabeth II in 1953. The unsophisticated dish was meant to appeal to as many tastes as possible. Since then, many chefs have included variations of it on the menu.

# CORONATION CHICKEN

**Preparation time:** 15 minutes
**Total cooking time:** 10 minutes
**Serves** 4–6

500 g (1 lb) cooked chicken
1 tablespoon oil
1 onion, finely chopped
2 teaspoons curry powder
1 tablespoon tomato paste (tomato purée)
2 tablespoons red wine
1 1/2 tablespoons fruit chutney
1/2 cup (125 g/4 oz) whole-egg
    mayonnaise
2 sticks celery, sliced
3 spring onions, finely sliced

*ABOVE: Coronation chicken*

**1** Remove all the skin and any fat from the chicken and cut the flesh into bite-sized pieces. Heat the oil in a saucepan and add the onion. Cover and cook, stirring occasionally, over low heat for 5–10 minutes, or until soft, but not browned. Add the curry powder and stir until fragrant. Add the tomato paste and red wine and stir for 1 minute. Set aside to cool, then mix in a bowl with the chutney and mayonnaise.
**2** Put the chicken, celery and 2 of the spring onions into a large bowl. Add the mayonnaise mixture and toss lightly to coat. Spoon into a serving bowl and sprinkle with finely sliced spring onion.
**NOTE:** Coronation chicken is often accompanied by apricots. The addition of sliced celery is not traditional in this salad but it gives a nice crunchy texture.

# SPLIT PEA AND HAM SOUP

**Preparation time:** 15 minutes
**Total cooking time:** 2 hours 15 minutes
**Serves** 8

500 g (1 lb) yellow split peas
leftover ham bone, about 650 g (1 lb 5 oz)
2 carrots, chopped
2 celery sticks, chopped
1 onion, chopped
2 bay leaves

**1** Rinse the split peas in cold water, then drain. Place the peas, ham bone, carrot, celery, onion, bay leaves and 3 litres (96 fl oz) water in a pan. Cover and bring to the boil. Reduce the heat and simmer, partly covered, for 2 hours, or until the peas are tender. Skim off any scum that rises to the surface.

**2** Remove the ham bone and cut the meat from the bone, discarding any fat or skin. Finely chop the ham and set aside. Remove the bay leaves. Cool the soup slightly, then blend in batches in a blender until smooth, adding a little more water if necessary. Stir in the ham and season with salt and pepper, to taste.

NOTE: This soup thickens on standing. Add vegetable or chicken stock to thin to the desired consistency. The soup can be frozen.

## FRIED HAM AND CHEESE SANDWICH

Butter a slice of bread and on the unbuttered side, spread Dijon mustard, then top with a few slices of ham and Swiss cheese. Place another slice of buttered bread on top, buttered-side-up. Heat a large, heavy-based, non-stick frying pan and add enough vegetable oil to just coat the base. Place the sandwich in the pan and fry over medium heat, turning once, until crisp and brown on both sides. Makes 1.

*ABOVE: Split pea and ham soup*

# HAM AND BEAN SALAD

Preparation time: 30 minutes
Total cooking time: 1 minute
Serves 6

200 g (6¹/₂ oz) green beans

200 g (6¹/₂ oz) sugar snap peas

200 g (6¹/₂ oz) frozen broad beans

200 g (6¹/₂ oz) sliced ham

250 g (8 oz) cherry tomatoes, cut in halves

³/₄ cup (115 g/4 oz) toasted cashews

2 tablespoons chopped fresh parsley

2 tablespoons chopped fresh chives

¹/₄ cup (60 ml/2 fl oz) olive oil

2 tablespoons cider vinegar

¹/₂ teaspoon sugar

2 tablespoons chopped fresh mint

1 Top and tail the green beans and sugar snap peas, then cut the beans diagonally into short lengths. Put the beans, peas and broad beans in a pan of boiling water and cook for 1 minute. Drain and refresh in cold water. Discard the outer skin from the broad beans.
2 Cut the ham into thin strips and combine in a large bowl with the beans and peas, cherry tomatoes, cashews, parsley and chives.
3 For the dressing, combine the oil, vinegar, sugar and mint in a screw top jar, shake, then season, to taste. Pour over the salad and toss well.

# LAYERED COB

Preparation time: 45 minutes
  + overnight refrigeration
Total cooking time: 10 minutes
Serves 6–8

2 red peppers (capsicums)

500 g (1 lb) eggplant (aubergine)

400 g (13 oz) English spinach, trimmed

22 cm (9 inch) cob loaf

2 tablespoons oil

2 cloves garlic, crushed

2 cups (500 g/1 lb) ricotta

2 tablespoons chopped fresh parsley

¹/₄ cup (25 g/³/₄ oz) grated Parmesan

150 g (5 oz) sliced ham

1 Cut the peppers into large flattish pieces. Remove the seeds and membrane. Cook, skin-side-up, under a hot grill until the skins blacken and blister. Cool in a plastic bag, then peel and slice the flesh. Cut the eggplant into 1 cm (¹/₂ inch) slices and grill until golden on both sides. Steam the spinach briefly until wilted, then cool and squeeze out any excess liquid.
2 Cut a large round from the top of the cob loaf and reserve. Scoop out the white bread, leaving a 1 cm (¹/₂ inch) border. Combine the oil and garlic and brush the insides of the loaf and lid.
3 Combine the ricotta, parsley and Parmesan in a bowl. Place half the eggplant slices in the loaf, layer the red pepper on top, then the ham. Top with the ricotta mixture. Season with salt and pepper. Spread the spinach leaves over the top, then add the remaining eggplant. Put the 'lid' on and wrap tightly with plastic wrap. Place a plate on top, weigh down with cans and chill overnight. Serve hot or cold in wedges. To heat, wrap in foil and bake in a moderately hot 200°F (400°C/Gas 6) for 15–20 minutes.

# CHEF'S SALAD

Preparation time: 25 minutes
Total cooking time: Nil
Serves 4

**Dressing**

¹/₂ cup (125 ml/4 fl oz) extra virgin olive oil

2 tablespoons white wine vinegar

1 teaspoon sugar

1 iceberg lettuce

2 tomatoes, cut into wedges

2 celery sticks, cut into julienne strips

1 cooked chicken breast fillet, cut into thin strips

200 g (6¹/₂ oz) ham, cut into thin strips

60 g (2 oz) Swiss cheese, cut into strips

3 hard-boiled eggs, cut into wedges

6 radishes, sliced

1 Whisk the dressing ingredients together in a small jug until well combined. Season, to taste, with salt and freshly ground black pepper.
2 Coarsely shred the lettuce leaves and divide among serving plates. Top with layers of the tomato, celery, chicken, ham, cheese, egg and radish. Drizzle the dressing over the salad and serve immediately.

## LAYERED COB

When the grilled red peppers have cooled, peel the skin away before cutting the flesh into slices.

Scoop out the white bread from the centre of the cob loaf, leaving a border.

Spread the remaining grilled eggplant slices over the top of the spinach leaves.

*OPPOSITE PAGE: Ham and bean salad (top); Layered cob*

179

## HAM, CHEESE AND ONION QUICKBREAD

Use a flat-bladed knife to mix until a soft dough is formed.

After marking into quarters, sprinkle with the remaining onion and Cheddar.

# HAM, CHEESE AND ONION QUICKBREAD

**Preparation time:** 25 minutes
**Total cooking time:** 1 hour 5 minutes
**Serves 6–8**

★ ★

1 tablespoon oil
3 onions, thinly sliced into rings
2 teaspoons soft brown sugar
200 g (6½ oz) sliced ham, finely chopped
3 cups (375 g/12 oz) self-raising flour
100 g (3½ oz) butter, chilled
¾ cup (90 g/3 oz) grated Cheddar
½ cup (125 ml/4 fl oz) milk

**1** Heat half of the oil in a large, heavy-based frying pan. Add the onion and cook over medium heat for 10 minutes, stirring occasionally. Add the sugar and continue to cook for 10–15 minutes, or until the onion is golden brown. Set aside to cool.
**2** Heat the remaining oil in a small frying pan, add the ham and cook over moderately high heat until golden brown. Drain on crumpled paper towels and add to the onion. Allow to cool slightly.
**3** Preheat the oven to hot 210°C (415°F/ Gas 6–7). Lightly grease a baking tray. Sift the flour into a large bowl and rub in the butter with your fingertips until the mixture resembles fine breadcrumbs.
**4** Add three-quarters of the onion mixture and ½ cup (60 g/2 oz) of the Cheddar to the flour and mix well. Make a well in the centre and add the milk and about ½ cup (125 ml/4 fl oz) of water (add enough water to bring the dough together). Using a flat-bladed knife, mix to a soft dough. Gently gather together into a ball.
**5** Lay the dough on the tray and press out to form a 22 cm (8¾ inch) circle. Using a sharp knife, mark the dough into quarters, cutting two-thirds of the way through. Sprinkle with the rest of the onion mixture and the remaining Cheddar. Bake for 15 minutes, then reduce the oven temperature to moderate 180°C (350°F/ Gas 4). Cover the top loosely with foil if it starts getting too brown. Bake for another 20 minutes, or until the base sounds hollow when tapped.

*ABOVE: Ham, cheese and onion quickbread*

## CHRISTMAS HAM AND CIDER CASSEROLE

**Preparation time:** 15 minutes
**Total cooking time:** 25 minutes
**Serves** 4

40 g (1¼ oz) butter

1 onion, chopped

2 leeks, white part only, finely
   sliced

2 cloves garlic, crushed

8 slices ham, chopped

100 ml (3½ fl oz) apple cider

300 g (10 oz) can butter beans,
   rinsed and drained

⅓ cup (25 g/¾ oz) fresh breadcrumbs

1 tablespoon grated Parmesan

**1** Preheat the oven to moderately hot 200°C (400°F/Gas 6). Melt half the butter in a heavy-based frying pan, add the onion and cook over low heat for 2–3 minutes, or until tender. Add the leek and stir until cooked through. Stir in the garlic.

**2** Transfer the onion mixture to an ovenproof dish. Scatter the ham over the top and season with freshly ground black pepper. Pour in the apple cider. Spoon the butter beans over and around the ham and sprinkle with the breadcrumbs and Parmesan. Dot with the remaining butter and bake for 20 minutes, or until lightly golden on top.

**NOTE:** This can also be cooked in individual ramekin dishes—check them after 15 minutes as they may not take as long to cook. Leftover turkey can be chopped and used instead of the ham. For a creamy casserole, stir ½ cup (125 g/4 oz) sour cream into the leek mixture with the garlic.

*ABOVE: Ham and cider casserole*

181

## PEA AND HAM RISOTTO

Add half the wine to the frying pan and simmer, uncovered, until almost all the liquid has evaporated.

Gradually ladle in the hot stock mixture, waiting after each addition until the liquid is absorbed before adding more.

Stir constantly over low heat until all the stock has been absorbed and the rice is creamy and tender.

*ABOVE: Pea and ham risotto*

## PEA AND HAM RISOTTO

**Preparation time:** 25 minutes
**Total cooking time:** 45 minutes
**Serves** 4

 ✷ ✷

1 tablespoon olive oil
1 celery stick, chopped
2 tablespoons chopped fresh flat-leaf parsley
75 g (2¹/2 oz) sliced ham, coarsely chopped
1²/3 cups (250 g/8 oz) frozen green peas
¹/2 cup (125 ml/4 fl oz) dry white wine
3 cups (750 ml/24 fl oz) chicken stock
60 g (2 oz) butter
1 onion, chopped
2 cups (440 g/14 oz) arborio rice
¹/3 cup (35 g/1¹/4 oz) grated Parmesan
shaved Parmesan, for serving

**1** Heat the oil in a frying pan, add the celery, parsley and some freshly ground black pepper and cook, stirring, over medium heat for 2–3 minutes to soften the celery. Add the ham and stir well. Add the peas and half the wine, bring to the boil, then reduce the heat and simmer, uncovered, until almost all the liquid has evaporated. Set aside.
**2** Put the stock, remaining wine and 3 cups (750 ml/24 fl oz) water in a separate pan and keep at simmering point.
**3** Melt the butter in a large heavy-based saucepan. Add the onion and stir until softened. Add the rice and stir well. Gradually stir in the hot stock mixture, ¹/2 cup (125 ml/4 oz) at a time, making sure the liquid has been absorbed before adding more. Stir constantly over low heat with a wooden spoon, until all the stock has been absorbed and the rice is creamy and tender (this will take about 25–30 minutes altogether). Season, to taste.
**4** Add the pea mixture and grated Parmesan to the rice and serve with Parmesan shavings and black pepper.

## HASH HAM CAKE

**Preparation time:** 30 minutes
+ 1 hour refrigeration
**Total cooking time:** 50 minutes
**Serves** 4–6

500 g (1 lb) floury potatoes, such as russet
  or King Edward, peeled and quartered
200 g (6½ oz) ham, finely chopped
4 spring onions, finely chopped
1 small gherkin, finely chopped
2 tablespoons chopped fresh parsley
1 egg, lightly beaten
50 g (1¾ oz) butter

1 Boil or steam the potato for 10–15 minutes, until tender (pierce with the point of a small knife—if the potato comes away easily, it is ready). Drain well, then put the potato in a large bowl and mash.

2 Mix in the ham, spring onion, gherkin, parsley, egg and some freshly ground black pepper. Spread on a plate, cover and refrigerate for at least 1 hour, or overnight, to firm.
3 Heat 30 g (1 oz) of the butter in a 20 cm (8 inch) heavy-based frying pan. Add the potato, spread evenly into the pan and smooth the surface with the back of a spoon. Cook over moderate heat for 15 minutes, then slide out onto a plate. Add the remaining butter to the pan, carefully flip the cake back into the pan and cook for another 15–20 minutes, or until the outside forms a brown crust. Cut into wedges for serving.
NOTE: Floury potatoes have a low moisture and sugar content and lots of starch. This makes them very suitable for mashing as well as baking. If you are not sure, ask your greengrocer which variety is most suitable for your needs. When you buy potatoes, they should be firm, not wrinkled, cracked, sprouting or green. Store away from light in a cool, well-ventilated place. Leave the dirt on unwashed potatoes during storage as it helps to protect them.

*ABOVE: Hash ham cake*

183

## SALMON PIE

**Preparation time:** 25 minutes
+ 30 minutes refrigeration
**Total cooking time:** 1 hour
Serves 4–6

60 g (2 oz) butter

1 onion, finely chopped

200 g (6¹/₂ oz) button mushrooms,
   sliced

2 tablespoons lemon juice

200 g (6¹/₂ oz) cooked poached salmon
   fillet, broken into small pieces, or
   220 g (7 oz) can red salmon

2 hard-boiled eggs, chopped

2 tablespoons chopped fresh dill

3 tablespoons chopped fresh parsley

1 cup (185 g/6 oz) cooked long-grain
   brown rice (see Note)

¹/₄ cup (60 ml/2 fl oz) cream

375 g (12 oz) packet frozen puff pastry

1 egg, lightly beaten

sour cream, optional, for serving

*ABOVE: Salmon pie*

**1** Melt half the butter in a frying pan and cook the onion for 5 minutes until soft but not brown. Add the mushrooms and cook for 5 minutes. Stir in the juice, then remove from the pan.
**2** Melt the remaining butter in the pan, add the salmon and stir for 2 minutes. Remove from the heat, cool slightly and add the egg, dill, parsley, and salt and pepper, to taste. Mix gently and set aside. Mix the rice and cream in a small bowl.
**3** Roll out half the pastry to 15 x 25 cm (6 x 10 inches). Trim the pastry neatly, saving the trimmings, and put on a greased baking tray.
**4** Layer the filling onto the pastry, leaving a 3 cm (1¹/₄ inch) border. Put half the rice into the centre of the pastry, then the salmon and egg mixture, followed by the mushrooms, then the remaining rice. Brush the border with egg.
**5** Roll out the other pastry half to 20 x 30 cm (8 x 12 inches) and place over the filling. Seal the edges. Make two slits in the top. Decorate with the trimmings and chill for 30 minutes.
**6** Preheat the oven to hot 200°C (400°F/Gas 6). Brush the pie with egg and bake for 15 minutes. Reduce the oven to 180°C (350°F/Gas 4) and bake the pie for 25–30 minutes, or until crisp and golden. Serve with sour cream.
**NOTE:** You will need to cook about ¹/₂ cup (100 g/3¹/₂ oz) brown rice for this recipe.

# ROAST VEGETABLE BUBBLE AND SQUEAK

Preparation time: 15 minutes
Total cooking time: 20 minutes
Makes 15

700 g (1 lb 6 oz) leftover mixed roast
    vegetables (eg. potatoes, orange sweet
    potato/kumera, pumpkin)
1¼ cups (185 g/6 oz) chopped cooked
    green vegetables (eg. Brussels sprouts,
    peas, beans)
1 cup (125 g/4 oz) grated Cheddar
1 egg, lightly beaten
40 g (1¼ oz) butter

1 Place the roast vegetables in a large bowl and mash slightly with a fork or potato masher. Add the green vegetables, cheese and egg and stir until well combined. Season, to taste.
2 Melt some of the butter in a large frying pan and place 6 lightly greased egg rings in the pan, spoon some vegetable mixture into each ring and press firmly. Cook over medium heat for 5 minutes on each side, or until golden brown. Wipe the pan clean and repeat with the remaining vegetable mixture and butter.

# VEGETABLE FRITTATA

Preparation time: 25 minutes
Total cooking time: 25 minutes
Serves 4

1 tablespoon olive oil
2 cloves garlic, crushed
1 small red onion, chopped
1 small red pepper (capsicum), chopped
500 g (1 lb) leftover roasted, boiled or
    steamed potatoes, thickly sliced
3 tablespoons chopped fresh parsley
6 eggs
¼ cup (25 g/¾ oz) grated Parmesan

1 Heat the oil in a large heavy-based, non-stick frying pan. Add the garlic, onion and red pepper to the pan and stir over medium heat for 2–3 minutes, or until soft. Add the potato slices to the pan and cook for 2–3 minutes, or until the potato has softened. Stir in the parsley and spread the mixture out evenly over the base of the pan.
2 Beat the eggs in a bowl with 2 tablespoons water and pour into the pan over the vegetables, moving them around slightly so the egg seeps through. Cook over medium heat for 15 minutes, without burning the base.
3 Sprinkle the Parmesan evenly over the frittata and cook under a hot grill for a few minutes to cook the egg and lightly brown the top. Ease a spatula around the edges to loosen and slide onto a plate. Cut into wedges for serving.
NOTE: If you prefer, you can use fewer vegetables and add leftover chopped turkey, chicken, poached salmon or ham. Potatoes are good in frittatas because they help hold the mixture together and make them easy to cut.

*ABOVE: Roast vegetable bubble and squeak*

185

## POACHED SALMON SALAD WITH CAPER DILL DRESSING

Preparation time: 20 minutes
Total cooking time: 10 minutes
Serves 6–8

300 g (10 oz) small new potatoes
200 g (6¹/2 oz) mixed salad leaves, rinsed and dried
100 g (3¹/2 oz) watercress
400 g (13 oz) cooked poached salmon, broken into large flakes
2 Lebanese cucumbers, sliced
¹/2 red onion, thinly sliced
6 gherkins, sliced
6 hard-boiled eggs, quartered
200 g (6¹/2 oz) semi-dried tomatoes, roughly chopped
200 g (6¹/2 oz) feta cheese, crumbled

*ABOVE: Poached salmon salad with caper dill dressing*

### Caper dill dressing

1 tablespoon drained bottled capers, finely chopped
2 tablespoons chopped fresh dill
1 teaspoon finely grated lime rind
2 tablespoons lime juice
1 tablespoon honey mustard
1 tablespoon white wine vinegar
¹/2 cup (60 ml/2 fl oz) olive oil

**1** Steam or boil the new potatoes for 10 minutes, or until just tender (pierce with the point of a small knife—if the potato comes away easily it is ready). Drain well and cut into quarters.
**2** Combine the salad leaves and the watercress and arrange on a large chilled salad plate.
**3** Combine the potato, salmon, cucumber, onion, gherkins, hard-boiled eggs, semi-dried tomatoes and feta in a bowl and toss very gently. Arrange on top of the salad greens.
**4** Place the dressing ingredients in a small bowl and whisk until well combined. Drizzle over the salad and serve immediately.

## SHEPHERD'S PIE

**Preparation time:** 30 minutes
**Total cooking time:** 1 hour 15 minutes
**Serves** 6

750 g (1 1/2 lb) lean cooked roast lamb
25 g (3/4 oz) butter
2 onions, finely chopped
1/4 cup (30 g/1 oz) plain flour
1/2 teaspoon dry mustard
1 1/2 cups (375 ml/12 fl oz) chicken stock
2 tablespoons Worcestershire sauce

### Potato topping

4 large potatoes
1/2 cup (125 ml/4 fl oz) hot milk
30 g (1 oz) butter

1 Brush a 2 litre (64 fl oz) casserole with melted butter or oil. Preheat the oven to hot 210°C (415°F/Gas 6–7). Trim the meat of excess fat, then mince or finely chop. Melt the butter in a large pan, add the onion and stir over medium heat for 5–10 minutes, until golden.

2 Add the flour and mustard to the pan and cook for 1 minute, or until pale and foaming. Remove from the heat and gradually stir in the stock. Return to the heat and stir constantly until the sauce boils and thickens. Reduce the heat and simmer for 2 minutes.

3 Add the meat and Worcestershire sauce to the pan and stir. Season, to taste. Remove from the heat and spoon into the casserole dish.

4 For the potato topping, steam or boil the potatoes for 10–15 minutes, or until just tender (pierce with the point of a small sharp knife—if the potato comes away easily, it's ready). Drain and mash well. Add the milk, butter, and salt and pepper, to taste, to the mashed potato and mix until smooth and creamy. Spread evenly over the meat and rough up the surface with the back of a spoon. Bake for 40–45 minutes, or until the meat is heated through and the topping is golden.

**HOLIDAY FEAST**
For a long time in England, roast boar's head was associated with holiday feasting. Most likely this custom goes back to the Norse practice of sacrificing a boar at Yuletide in honour of the god Freyr. There is a legend that tells of a student at Oxford's Queen College who was attacked on Christmas Day by a wild boar. All he had in his hand to use as a weapon was a copy of Aristotle so he stuck that down the boar's throat. He wanted the book back so he cut off the animal's head and brought it back to the college where it was cooked for dinner.

*ABOVE: Shepherd's pie*

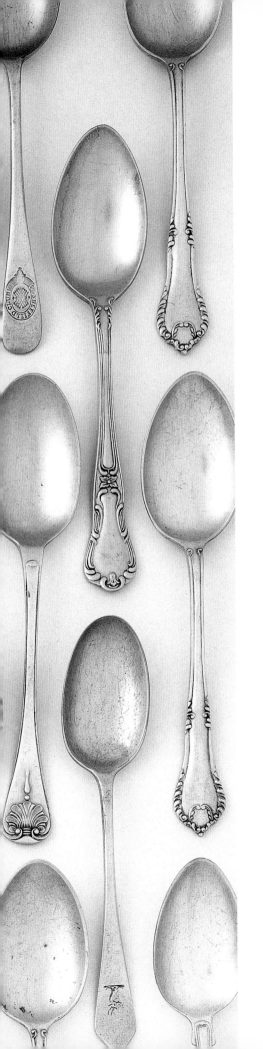

# PUDDINGS & DESSERTS

No matter how enthusiastically you tuck into the savoury part of the meal, room can always be found for dessert. Especially if it's a rich homemade Christmas pudding, full of plump sultanas and raisins, mixed peel and fragrant spices. Add a luscious custard or whisky sauce and it really doesn't get any better than this. That said, why stop at one dessert when you can enjoy a tipsy sherry trifle or a very naughty chocolate hazelnut torte as well? Or, for a lighter but no less decadent option, try the berries in Champagne jelly — the perfect celebration dessert.

# STEAMED PUDDING

These can be made 3 months ahead, wrapped in plastic wrap and foil and kept in a

cool, dark place or the fridge. On the big day, steam in a greased basin for 1 hour.

### PREPARING THE BASIN

It is essential that the capacity of the basin is the correct size for the recipe so the pudding has room to rise and does not expand out of the basin. Check the capacity by filling the basin with water from a measuring jug or cup. Basins are available in many different shapes and sizes and are made of ceramic, glass, steel

or aluminium. Ceramic basins let the pudding cook more slowly, so it cooks through without overcooking the edges. Metal basins cook the pudding more quickly, so it should be checked 30 minutes before the cooking time is up. Most metal basins come with a lid but this is not essential and is often used as well as baking paper and foil.

### STEAMING THE PUDDING

You need a large saucepan which will hold the basin sitting on a trivet and leave space around the basin and enough room to fit the saucepan lid on properly. If you don't have a trivet (a small round or square metal rack, available at speciality stores), you can use a collapsible metal vegetable steamer (unscrew the handle),

or an upturned saucer. Place the empty basin on the trivet in the saucepan and pour water into the saucepan to come halfway up the side of the basin. Remove the basin.

To help prevent the cooked pudding sticking to the basin, brush the basin well with melted butter and line the base with a circle of baking paper (even if your base is very small).

Make the pudding mixture according to the recipe and spoon into the basin, smoothing the top to make it level. Put the saucepan of water on to boil.

To cover the pudding, place a sheet of foil on the bench, top with a piece of baking paper the same size and brush the paper well with melted butter. Fold a pleat across the centre of the foil and paper to allow for expansion. Place the paper and foil, foil-side-up, over the basin (don't press it onto the pudding) and smooth it down the side of the basin. Tie a double length of string firmly around the rim of the basin, then tie a double length of string onto that string to form a handle to lower the pudding into the water. If you have a basin with a lid, clip it on at this stage. The paper/foil lid prevents any moisture getting into the pudding and making it soggy.

Using the handle, carefully lower the pudding into the saucepan and reduce the heat until the water is simmering quickly. Cover the saucepan and cook according to the directions in the recipe. Add more boiling water to the saucepan occasionally to maintain the water level.

## WHEN IS IT COOKED?

When the cooking time is up, carefully remove the pudding from the saucepan using the string handles. Remove the lid and paper/foil and test the pudding— a skewer should come out clean when inserted into the centre (if you hit a piece of fruit, the skewer may come out sticky). You can also check by pressing the top gently—the pudding should be firm in the centre, well risen and moist. If the pudding is not cooked, replace the top and continue cooking until done. When the pudding is cooked, leave it in the basin for 5 minutes before gently turning out onto a large plate. Discard the round of baking paper from the base. If the pudding sticks to the basin, gently loosen around the edges with a palette knife to help release it.

**CHRISTMAS PUDDING**
According to research by Britain's largest producer of Christmas puddings, the Christmas pudding originated as a fourteenth century 'porridge' called frumenty made by boiling beef and mutton with raisins, currants, prunes, wines and spices. It was often more like soup and was eaten as a fasting dish before the festivities. By 1595 the frumenty was evolving into plum pudding, having been thickened with eggs, breadcrumbs and dried fruit and flavoured with ale and spirits. It became the Christmas dessert but the Puritans in 1664 banned it. However, George I tasted and enjoyed it and re-established it as part of Christmas in 1714, despite objections by Quakers. By Victorian times Christmas puddings had evolved into something similar to the ones enjoyed today.

*ABOVE: Steamed pudding*

# STEAMED PUDDING

**Preparation time:** 40 minutes
+ overnight standing
**Total cooking time:** 8 hours
**Serves** 10–12

★ ★

4 cups (640 g/1 1/4 lb) mixed sultanas, currants and raisins
1 2/3 cups (330 g/11 oz) mixed dried fruit, chopped
1/4 cup (45 g/1 1/2 oz) mixed peel
1/2 cup (125 ml/4 fl oz) brown ale
2 tablespoons rum or brandy
1/3 cup (80 ml/2 3/4 fl oz) orange juice
1/3 cup (80 ml/2 3/4 fl oz) lemon juice
1 teaspoon finely grated orange rind
1 teaspoon finely grated lemon rind
225 g (7 oz) suet, grated (see Note)
1 1/3 cups (245 g/8 oz) soft brown sugar
3 eggs, lightly beaten
2 1/2 cups (200 g/6 1/2 oz) fresh white breadcrumbs
3/4 cup (90 g/3 oz) self-raising flour
1 teaspoon mixed spice
1/4 teaspoon grated nutmeg
2/3 cup (100 g/3 1/2 oz) blanched almonds, roughly chopped

**1** Put the sultanas, currants, raisins, mixed dried fruit, mixed peel, brown ale, rum, orange and lemon juices and rinds into a large bowl and stir together. Cover and leave overnight.
**2** Add the suet, brown sugar, eggs, breadcrumbs, flour, spices, almonds and a pinch of salt to the bowl and mix well. The mixture should fall from the spoon—if it is too stiff, add a little more ale.
**3** Place a 2 litre (64 fl oz) pudding basin on a trivet or upturned saucer in a large saucepan with a lid, and pour in enough water to come halfway up the side of the basin. Remove the basin and put the water on to boil.
**4** Prepare the pudding basin as shown on pages 190–1. Fill with the pudding mixture, then cover as shown on the same page. Steam the pudding for 8 hours, replenishing with boiling water when necessary. If you want to keep your pudding and reheat it later, then steam it for 6 hours and steam it for another 2 hours on the day you would like to eat it. Store in a cool, dry place for up to 3 months.
NOTE: Buy suet from your butcher.

# QUICK FRUIT MINCE STEAMED PUDDING

**Preparation time:** 20 minutes
**Total cooking time:** 1 hour 45 minutes
**Serves** 4

1 1/4 cups (155 g/5 oz) self-raising flour
1/4 teaspoon mixed spice
125 g (4 oz) butter, softened
2/3 cup (160 g/5 1/2 oz) caster sugar
3 eggs, lightly beaten
1/3 cup (60 g/2 oz) bottled fruit mince

1 Place a 1 litre (32 fl oz) pudding basin on a trivet or upturned saucer in the base of a large saucepan and pour in enough cold water to come halfway up the side of the basin. Remove the basin and put the water on to boil. Prepare the pudding basin as shown on pages 190–1.

2 Sift the flour and mixed spice into a large bowl. Make a well in the centre, add the butter, sugar, beaten eggs and fruit mince and beat until well combined. Spoon the mixture into the basin and level the top. Cover the basin and make a handle as shown on pages 190–1.

3 Gently lower the basin into the boiling water, cover the saucepan with a tight-fitting lid and cook for 1 hour 45 minutes. Check the water level occasionally and replenish with boiling water when necessary. Leave for 5 minutes before turning onto a serving plate. Serve immediately with custard or flavoured butter.

**NOTE:** The fruit mince used in this pudding is available in most supermarkets. If using home-made fruit mince, the fruit needs to be cut finely and be very moist.

*ABOVE: Quick fruit mince steamed pudding*

## THREE-IN-ONE FRUIT MIX

**Preparation time:** *20 minutes*
**Makes** *enough for 1 cake (use half the mixture),
1 steamed pudding (quarter of the
mixture) and 36 mince tarts (quarter
of the mixture)*

10 cups (1.6 kg/3¼ lb) sultanas

4 cups (640 g/1¼ lb) raisins, chopped

2½ cups (375 g/12 oz) currants

1½ cups (315 g/10 oz) glacé cherries, quartered

2¼ cups (500 g/1 lb) pitted prunes, quartered

1⅓ cups (245 g/7½ oz) mixed peel

2 cups (500 ml/16 fl oz) brandy

½ cup (115 g/4 oz) soft brown sugar

½ cup (160 g/5½ oz) sweet orange marmalade

2 tablespoons cocoa powder

1 tablespoon ground cinnamon

2 teaspoons ground ginger

2 teaspoons mixed spice

Mix the ingredients together in a large bowl,
then store in a sterilized jar or airtight container
in a cool, dark place for up to 1 month before
using. Stir occasionally.

## FRUIT CAKE

Preheat the oven to slow 150°C (300°F/Gas 2).
Grease and line a 23 cm (9 inch) round or square
cake tin as shown on pages 224–5. Beat 250 g
(8 oz) softened unsalted butter, 1 cup (230 g/
7½ oz) soft brown sugar and 2 teaspoons each
of finely grated orange and lemon rind in a small
bowl with electric beaters until just combined.
Add 4 eggs one at a time, beating well after each
addition. Transfer to a large bowl and stir in half
of the soaked fruit mix alternately with 2 cups
(250 g/8 oz) sifted plain flour and ½ cup (60 g/
2 oz) sifted self-raising flour. Mix thoroughly,
then spread evenly into the tin and tap the tin
on the bench to remove any air bubbles. Dip
your fingers in water and level the surface.
Decorate the top of the cake with whole
blanched almonds in a pattern. Sit the cake
on several layers of newspaper on the oven
shelf and bake for 3¼–3½ hours, or until a
skewer comes out clean. Cover the top with
baking paper, seal firmly with foil, then wrap
the cake and tin in a clean tea towel and leave
to cool.

## STEAMED PUDDING

Prepare a 2 litre (64 fl oz) pudding basin as shown
on pages 190–1. Beat 150 g (5 oz) softened
unsalted butter and 1 cup (230 g/7½ oz) soft
brown sugar in a small bowl with electric beaters
until light and fluffy. Add 3 eggs, one at a time,
beating well after each addition. Transfer to a
large bowl and stir in a quarter of the soaked
fruit alternately with 1 cup (125 g/4 oz) each of
sifted plain flour and self-raising flour. Mix well.
Spread into the basin and cover with the lid or as
shown on pages 190–1, then follow the cooking
directions on the same pages (cook for 5 hours).
Replenish the water when necessary with
boiling water. Remove the pudding and test
with a skewer. If it is not cooked, re-cover
and cook until done. Stand the pudding for
5 minutes before turning onto a large plate. If
the pudding sticks, ease down the sides a little
way with a palette knife to help release it. Serve
wedges hot with custard or flavoured butter.

## FRUIT MINCE TARTS

Mix a quarter of the soaked fruit mix with 125 g
(4 oz) grated frozen butter, 1 grated green apple
and ½ cup (115 g/4 oz) soft brown sugar in a
large bowl. For the pastry, sift ½ cup (60 g/2 oz)
custard powder and 4 cups (500 g/1 lb) plain
flour into a large bowl and rub in 360 g (12 oz)
chopped chilled butter with your fingertips until
the mixture resembles fine breadcrumbs. Stir
in ½ cup (60 g/2 oz) icing sugar. Make a well
in the centre and add 1 egg yolk and ¼ cup
(60 ml/2 fl oz) water and mix with a flat-bladed
knife until the mixture comes together in beads.
Gently gather the dough together and lift out
onto a lightly floured work surface. Press into
a ball, flatten slightly into a disc, then wrap in
plastic and refrigerate for 30 minutes. Preheat the
oven to moderate 180°C (350°F/Gas 4). Lightly
grease three 12-hole tartlet tins. Roll two-thirds
of the dough out between 2 sheets of baking
paper to 3 mm (⅛ inch) thick. Cut 36 rounds
from the pastry using a 7 cm (2¾ inch) cutter.
Place in the tins and top with spoonfuls of fruit
mixture. Roll the remaining pastry out between
baking paper and cut 36 rounds with a 6.5 cm
(2½ inch) cutter. Brush the edges with lightly
beaten egg and press the tops on firmly. Crimp
the edges if you wish. Brush with more egg,
then bake for 20–25 minutes, or until well
browned. Leave in the tins for 5 minutes, then
lift onto a wire rack to cool. Dust with icing
sugar before serving.

### FRUIT MINCE

The name mincemeat is
now a misnomer and the
symbolism of these little
pies has been forgotten.
However, they are still a
favourite Christmas treat.
Mincemeat originally
described a mixture of
dried fruit that was added
to leftover meat to make
it go further. The mixture
was used to make oblong
pies, reminiscent of the
crib in the stable in
Bethlehem. A crusty top
with a small pastry doll
representing the Christ-
child was placed in a
hollow in the top. The pie
eventually changed to
round, the meat was
excluded and more fruit
and nuts incorporated.

*OPPOSITE PAGE:*
*Fruit cake*

1/2 cup (80 g/2 3/4 oz) dried dates, chopped

2 eggs, lightly beaten

60 g (2 oz) unsalted butter, melted and cooled

raspberries, for decoration

blueberries, for decoration

icing sugar, for decoration

**Rum butter**

125 g (4 oz) butter, softened

3/4 cup (140 g/4 1/2 oz) dark brown sugar

4 tablespoons rum

**1** Combine the sago and milk in a small bowl, cover and refrigerate overnight.

**2** Prepare a 1.5 litre (48 fl oz) pudding basin as shown on pages 190–1. Place the empty basin in a large saucepan on a trivet or upturned saucer and pour in enough cold water to come halfway up the side of the basin. Remove the basin and put the water on to boil.

**3** Transfer the soaked sago and milk to a large bowl and stir in the bicarbonate of soda until dissolved. Stir in the sugar, breadcrumbs, dried fruit, beaten eggs and melted butter and mix well. Spoon into the basin and smooth the surface with wet hands.

**4** Cover the basin and make a string handle as shown on pages 190–1. Gently lower the basin into the boiling water, reduce to a fast simmer and cover the saucepan with a tight-fitting lid. Cook for 3 1/2–4 hours, or until a skewer inserted into the centre of the pudding comes out clean. Check the water level every hour and top up with boiling water as necessary.

**5** Carefully remove the pudding basin from the saucepan, remove the coverings and leave for 5 minutes before turning the pudding out onto a large serving plate. Loosen the edges with a palette knife if necessary. Serve decorated with raspberries and blueberries and lightly dusted with icing sugar. Serve hot with cold rum butter.

**6** For the rum butter, beat together the butter and sugar with electric beaters for about 3–4 minutes, or until light and creamy. Gradually beat in the rum, 1 tablespoon at a time. You can add more rum, to taste. Transfer to a serving dish, cover and refrigerate until required.

NOTE: Sago is the starch extracted from the sago palm. It is dried and formed into balls by pushing through a sieve. It is often called pearl sago and is available from supermarkets or health food stores. It is white when uncooked but goes transparent when cooked.

## SAGO PLUM PUDDING WITH RUM BUTTER

**Preparation time:** 35 minutes
+ overnight soaking
**Total cooking time:** 4 hours
**Serves** 6–8

★★

1/3 cup (65 g/2 1/4 oz) sago

1 cup (250 ml/8 fl oz) milk

1 teaspoon bicarbonate of soda

3/4 cup (140 g/4 1/2 oz) dark brown sugar

2 cups (160 g/5 1/4 oz) fresh white breadcrumbs

1/2 cup (80 g/2 3/4 oz) sultanas

1/2 cup (75 g/2 1/2 oz) currants

*ABOVE: Sago plum pudding with rum butter*

## FIG PUDDING

**Preparation time:** 40 minutes
**Total cooking time:** 3 hours 40 minutes
**Serves** 8

500 g (1 lb) dried figs, chopped
1³/4 cups (440 ml/14 fl oz) milk
3 cups (240 g/7¹/2 oz) coarse fresh breadcrumbs
³/4 cup (140 g/4¹/2 oz) soft brown sugar
2 cups (250 g/8 oz) self-raising flour, sifted
2 eggs, lightly beaten
150 g (5 oz) unsalted butter, melted and cooled

**1** Prepare a 2 litre (64 fl oz) pudding basin as shown on pages 190–1. Place the empty basin in a large saucepan on a trivet or upturned saucer and pour in enough water to come halfway up the side of the basin. Remove the basin and put the water on to boil.

**2** Put the figs in a small saucepan with the milk. Bring to a simmer, cover and cook over low heat for 10 minutes. The mixture will curdle—stir to combine.

**3** Combine the breadcrumbs, sugar and flour in a large bowl. Stir in the soaked figs and any liquid, the beaten eggs and the melted butter. Spoon into the basin. Cover the basin and make a handle with string as shown on pages 190–1.

**4** Gently lower the basin into the boiling water, reduce to a fast simmer and cover the saucepan with a tight-fitting lid. Cook for 3¹/2 hours, checking the water every hour and topping up with boiling water as necessary. The pudding is cooked when a skewer inserted in the centre comes out clean. Leave for 5 minutes before turning out. Serve with custard or cream.

**CHRISTMAS PUDDING**
Many superstitions have surrounded the Christmas pudding. One states that the puddings should be made by the 25th Sunday after Trinity, prepared with 13 ingredients to represent Christ and His Disciples, and that every member of the family must take a turn at stirring the pudding with a wooden spoon from east to west in honour of the Three Kings.

*ABOVE: Fig pudding*

# PUDDING TOPPINGS

These custards, butters and sauces will complement your rich Christmas pudding,

whether you prefer classic toppings or something different.

### VANILLA CUSTARD

Combine 1 cup (250 ml/8 fl oz) milk and ¼ cup (60 ml/2 fl oz) cream in a saucepan. Bring to the boil, then remove from the heat immediately. In a bowl, whisk 3 egg yolks, ½ cup (125 g/4 oz) caster sugar and 2 teaspoons cornflour. Slowly pour the hot milk and cream into the egg mixture, whisking continuously. Return to the saucepan and stir over low heat for 5 minutes, or until thickened—do not boil. Remove from the heat and stir in ½ teaspoon vanilla essence. Serve. Makes 1½ cups (375 ml/12 fl oz).

### WHISKY SAUCE

Melt 2 tablespoons butter in a saucepan over low heat. Remove from the heat, add ⅓ cup (40 g/1¼ oz) plain flour and stir until combined. Gradually whisk in 2 cups (500 ml/16 fl oz) milk and 2 tablespoons caster sugar. Return to medium heat. Stir until the sauce boils and thickens. Reduce the heat and simmer for 10 minutes, stirring occasionally. Remove from the heat and stir in ⅓ cup (80 ml/2¾ fl oz) whisky, 2 teaspoons butter and 1 tablespoon thick (double) cream. Cover with plastic wrap until ready to serve. Makes 2½ cups (600 ml/20 fl oz).

## CREME A L'ANGLAISE

Whisk 3 egg yolks and 2 tablespoons caster sugar together in a heatproof bowl for 2 minutes, or until light and creamy. Heat 1½ cups (375 ml/12 fl oz) milk until almost boiling, then pour into the bowl, whisking constantly. Return to the clean pan and stir over low heat for 5 minutes, or until thick enough to coat the back of a spoon. Don't let the mixture boil or it will scramble. Remove from the heat. Stir in ½ teaspoon vanilla essence. Transfer to a jug. Makes 2 cups (500 ml/16 fl oz).

## GRAND MARNIER WHIPPED BUTTER

Remove the rind from an orange with a vegetable peeler, avoiding any white pith. Cut the rind into long thin strips, place in a pan of cold water and bring to the boil. Drain and repeat. Return to the pan with ⅓ cup (80 ml/2¾ fl oz) water and 2 tablespoons caster sugar. Stir over low heat until the sugar has dissolved, then boil for 2 minutes until thick and syrupy. Beat 250 g (4 oz) softened unsalted butter in a bowl with electric beaters until light and fluffy. Beat in ⅓ cup (40 g/1¼ oz) icing sugar, ¼ cup (60 ml/2 fl oz) orange juice and 2–3 tablespoons Grand Marnier, to taste, then fold in the orange rind syrup. Don't add the liquid too quickly or the mixture may split. If this happens, beat in enough icing sugar to bring the mixture back together. Dollop on top of hot Christmas pudding. Makes 1 cup (250 g/8 oz).

## BRANDY BUTTER

Beat 250 g (8 oz) softened unsalted butter and 1½ cups (185 g/6 oz) sifted icing sugar with electric beaters until smooth and creamy. Gradually add ¼ cup (60 ml/2 fl oz) brandy, beating thoroughly. Refrigerate until required. Makes 1 cup (250 g/4 oz).

## DARK CHOCOLATE SAUCE

Put 150 g (5 oz) chopped dark chocolate in a bowl. Bring 1¼ cups (315 ml/10 fl oz) cream to the boil in a pan. Stir in 2 tablespoons caster sugar, then pour it over the chocolate. Leave for 2 minutes, then stir until smooth. Add a spoonful of any liqueur. Serve warm. Makes 1½ cups (375 ml/12 fl oz).

*LEFT TO RIGHT: Vanilla custard; Whisky sauce; Crème à l'Anglaise; Grand Marnier whipped butter; Brandy butter; Dark chocolate sauce; Vanilla custard (on pudding)*

## SUGAR-REDUCED PUDDINGS

Stir in the cooled melted butter and the sifted dry ingredients.

Cover each filled mould with a greased circle of foil.

# SUGAR-REDUCED PUDDINGS

**Preparation time:** 30 minutes
  + overnight soaking
**Total cooking time:** 2 hours 30 minutes
**Makes** 10

2²/₃ cups (500 g/1 lb) mixed dried fruit

3 cups (480 g/15 oz) raisins, chopped

1 cup (220 g/7 oz) pitted prunes, quartered

1 cup (200 g/6¹/₂ oz) dried fruit medley

1¹/₃ cups (200 g/6¹/₂ oz) currants

¹/₂ cup (95 g/3 oz) dried figs, chopped

¹/₂ cup (125 ml/4 fl oz) whisky

¹/₂ cup (115 g/4 oz) soft brown sugar

4 eggs, lightly beaten

180 g (6 oz) unsalted butter, melted and cooled

1¹/₂ cups (225 g/7 oz) plain wholemeal flour

¹/₂ cup (60 g/2 oz) self-raising flour

2 teaspoons ground cinnamon

2 teaspoons ground nutmeg

1 teaspoon ground ginger

**1** Mix the fruit and whisky in a large bowl. Cover and leave for several hours or overnight, stirring occasionally, until the whisky is absorbed.

**2** Preheat the oven to moderate 180°C (350°F/ Gas 4). Grease ten ³/₄ cup (185 ml/6 fl oz) moulds with melted butter or oil and line each base with a circle of baking paper.

**3** Add the sugar and eggs to the fruit and mix thoroughly. Stir in the cooled melted butter and the sifted dry ingredients. Mix well until completely combined. Spoon evenly into the moulds. Cover each mould with a greased circle of foil.

**4** Place the puddings in a baking dish, pour in enough boiling water to come halfway up the sides of the moulds. Bake for 2¹/₂ hours, or until cooked when tested.

**5** Stand the puddings in their moulds for 5 minutes before turning out onto serving plates. To reheat, wrap firmly in foil and bake for about 20 minutes, or until warmed through.

**NOTE:** For impressive presentation, these little puddings can be topped with slices of fresh nectarine and some thinly sliced lemon rind.

*ABOVE: Sugar-reduced puddings*

## GLUTEN-FREE PUDDING

**Preparation time:** 30 minutes
  + overnight soaking
**Total cooking time:** 4 hours
**Serves** 8–10

2²/₃ cups (500 g/1 lb) mixed dried fruit

3 cups (480 g/15 oz) raisins, chopped

1 cup (220 g/7 oz) pitted prunes, quartered

1 cup (200 g/6¹/₂ oz) dried fruit medley

1¹/₃ cups (200 g/6¹/₂ oz) currants

¹/₂ cup (95 g/3 oz) dried figs, chopped

¹/₂ cup (125 ml/4 fl oz) sweet sherry

1 tablespoon treacle

1 cup (230 g/7¹/₂ oz) soft brown sugar

4 eggs, lightly beaten

250 g (8 oz) unsalted butter, melted and cooled

1¹/₂ cups (120 g/4 oz) soya flour

³/₄ cup (90 g/3 oz) rice cereal

³/₄ cup (90 g/3 oz) maize cornflour

2 teaspoons ground cinnamon

2 teaspoons ground nutmeg

1 teaspoon ground ginger

**1** Prepare a 2.5 litre (80 fl oz) pudding basin as shown on pages 190–1. Place the empty basin in a large saucepan on a trivet or upturned saucer and pour in enough water to come halfway up the side of the basin. Remove the basin and put the water on to boil.

**2** Mix all the fruit with the sherry in a large bowl. Cover and leave overnight, stirring occasionally, until the sherry is absorbed.

**3** Mix the treacle, sugar and eggs into the fruit. Stir in the cooled butter and sifted dry ingredients until completely combined. Spoon into the pudding basin. Cover with a greased circle of foil. Lower the pudding into the boiling water for 3¹/₂–4 hours, or until cooked when tested. Replenish the water when necessary.

**4** Stand the pudding in the basin for 5 minutes before turning out onto a serving plate. To reheat on the day, steam the pudding for 1 hour, or until heated through.

NOTE: This pudding is suitable for people with coeliac disease. Decorations such as cinnamon sticks or cassia bark and thin slices of lime rind can be added before serving.

*ABOVE: Gluten-free pudding*

¼ cup (60 ml/2 fl oz) orange juice

½ cup (115 g/4 oz) soft brown sugar

3 egg whites, lightly beaten

2 green apples, peeled, cored and grated

1¼ cups (155 g/5 oz) plain flour

½ cup (60 g/2 oz) self-raising flour

2 teaspoons ground cinnamon

2 teaspoons ground nutmeg

1 teaspoon ground ginger

**1** Mix all the fruit with the whisky and juice in a large bowl. Cover and leave for several hours, or overnight, stirring occasionally, until the liquid is absorbed.

**2** Place a circle of baking paper in the base of a 2 litre (64 fl oz) pudding basin. Put the basin on a trivet or upturned saucer in the saucepan and add enough cold water to come halfway up the side of the basin. Remove the basin and put the water on to boil. Bring to the boil, then reduce to a rolling simmer.

**3** Add the brown sugar, egg whites and grated apple to the fruit and mix thoroughly. Mix in the sifted dry ingredients, then spread evenly into the basin and level the surface. Cover the basin (don't grease the paper) and make a string handle as shown on pages 190–1.

**4** Using the handle, lower the pudding into the pan, cover the pan and cook the pudding for 5–5½ hours. Check the water level every hour and top up with boiling water when necessary.

**5** Remove the pudding using the string handle. Remove the lid and paper/foil and test with a skewer (it should come out clean when inserted into the centre). Sometimes it may come out sticky due to the fruit. The pudding should be well risen and moist. If it is not cooked, cover and cook until done. Stand the pudding for 5 minutes before turning onto a large plate. If the pudding sticks, ease down the sides a little way with a palette knife to help release it.

**6** To reheat, return the pudding to a clean basin (with a circle of baking paper in the base), cover as above and steam for about 2 hours, or until heated through. This pudding looks attractive decorated with thinly sliced fruits or candied slices of fruit such as oranges.

## NO-FAT PUDDING

**Preparation time:** 20 minutes
  + overnight soaking
**Total cooking time:** 5 hours 30 minutes
Serves 8–10

★ ★

2⅔ cups (500 g/1 lb) mixed dried fruit

1 cup (200 g/6½ oz) dried fruit medley

1¼ cups (200 g/6½ oz) raisins, chopped

1 cup (150 g/5 oz) currants

½ cup (95 g/3 oz) dried figs, chopped

⅓ cup (75 g/2½ oz) pitted prunes, quartered

¼ cup (60 ml/2 fl oz) whisky

*ABOVE: No-fat pudding*

# LOW-FAT PUDDING

**Preparation time:** 20 minutes
 + overnight soaking
**Total cooking time:** 4 hours 30 minutes
**Serves** 8–10

2²/₃ cups (500 g/1 lb) mixed dried fruit
1 cup (200 g/6¹/₂ oz) dried fruit medley
1¹/₄ cups (185 g/6 oz) currants
1 cup (160 g/5¹/₂ oz) raisins
¹/₂ cup (125 ml/4 fl oz) whisky
¹/₂ cup (115 g/4 oz) soft brown sugar
2 eggs, lightly beaten
1 egg white, lightly beaten
1 green apple, peeled, cored and grated
2 bananas, mashed
1¹/₂ cups (185 g/6 oz) plain flour
¹/₂ cup (60 g/2 oz) self-raising flour
1 teaspoon ground cinnamon
1 teaspoon ground nutmeg
1 teaspoon ground ginger

**1** Mix all the fruit with the whisky in a large bowl. Cover and leave for several hours, or overnight, stirring occasionally until the liquid is absorbed.
**2** Prepare a 2 litre (64 fl oz) pudding basin as shown on pages 190–1.
**3** Place the basin on a trivet or upturned saucer in the saucepan and add enough water to come halfway up the side of the basin. Remove the basin and put the water on to boil while preparing the pudding mixture.
**4** Add the sugar, eggs, egg white, apple and banana to the fruit and mix thoroughly. Stir in the sifted dry ingredients. Mix well, then spread evenly into the basin. Cover the basin and make a string handle as shown on pages 190–1.
**5** Using the handle, lower the pudding into the pan and lower the water to a fast simmer. Cover the saucepan with a lid and cook the pudding for 4–4¹/₂ hours. It may be necessary to replenish the water with more boiling water occasionally, making sure the water is always about halfway up the side of the basin.
**6** Remove the pudding from the saucepan using the string handle. Remove the lid and paper/foil and test the pudding with a skewer (it should come out clean when inserted into the centre). Sometimes it may come out sticky but this could be due to the fruit. It should be well risen and moist. If it is not cooked, cover and cook until done. When cooked, stand the pudding for 5 minutes before inverting onto a large plate. If the pudding sticks, ease down the sides a little way with a palette knife to help release it.
**7** To reheat, return the pudding to a clean buttered basin, cover as above and steam for 2 hours, or until heated through.
**NOTE:** This pudding looks very attractive if presented with decorations on top. Use your favourites, or try a combination of cassia bark or cinnamon sticks and sugar-coated leaves.

*ABOVE: Low-fat pudding*

# BOILED PUDDING

When there is a Christmas pudding hanging in its cloth in the kitchen, everyone

knows that planning has begun and the delicious countdown has started.

Although a little more skill and patience is required to make traditional boiled Christmas puddings than for steamed ones, many people still enjoy making them. A major factor when making a boiled pudding is to ensure the water is on a constant low boil, otherwise you run the risk of having the pudding absorb water and turning into a soggy mass which unfortunately can't be resurrected.

### PREPARING THE CLOTH

You will need a large, deep saucepan with a tight-fitting lid. The pudding must be able to be suspended in the boiling water so it won't touch the base or side of the saucepan during cooking. This helps keep the pudding in shape while it is cooking. Half fill the saucepan with water, cover and bring to the boil. Cut a large square of calico (or follow the

directions in the recipe). You can use a clean old tea towel if it is large enough. Add the calico to the saucepan and simmer for 20 minutes. Wearing rubber gloves and using tongs, remove the calico from the boiling water and wring out well. Cover the pan and keep at a constant simmer. Spread the calico out on a work surface. Cover generously with an even layer of plain flour, using

about ½ cup (60 g/2 oz), leaving a border around the edge. Spread the flour with your hands to get an even covering (this forms a seal between the pudding and the water and prevents the pudding absorbing water). You will need to cover enough calico with flour so that when the cloth is gathered up the pudding mixture is completely enclosed by the floured calico.

## BOILING THE PUDDING

Make the fruit mixture according to the recipe and spoon into the centre of the cloth. Bring the points of the cloth together over the top and gather in all the excess material, easing it in little by little to keep the pleats as small and neat as possible, as these will leave impressions on the pudding when cooked. Pat gently to form a nice round shape. Leaving a small amount of room at the top for

expansion, tie the top tightly with string so there is no gap where water can get into the pudding. Tie another length of string around the top, long enough to tie to the handles on either side of the pan to suspend the pudding (if your saucepan doesn't have suitable handles, suspend a wooden spoon across the saucepan and tie the string to that). Gently lower the pudding into the simmering water. The pudding should float, without touching the bottom. Carefully tie the string tautly across the pan to the opposite handles or the spoon. Cover with a lid and place a couple of large cans of fruit or a brick on the lid if possible. The water needs to be maintained on a low boil constantly for the time stated in the recipe. Replenish the water with boiling water as necessary. When the cooking time is up, remove the pudding from the water and hang it

over a bowl (to catch any drips) in a dry, well-ventilated area (make sure it is not touching anything). Hook up the loose calico ends in the string to help them dry. Leave overnight. The next day, remove the string and if the top is slightly wet, open out and allow to dry. When completely dry, tie with a new piece of string and hang in a cool dark place for up to 4 months. In humid weather, you may need to refrigerate the pudding.

## REHEATING THE PUDDING

To reheat, boil the pudding as above for 2 hours, hang for 15 minutes to dry slightly, then undo the string and carefully peel away some of the calico. Place a plate over the top and invert the plate, pudding and cloth. Ease the calico away from the pudding skin. Serve with your favourite butter or sauce (pages 198–9).

205

## BANANAS

Bananas grow in tropical regions throughout the world. The bunches are known as 'hands', each containing a different number of 'fingers'. They are usually picked while still green and allowed to ripen to yellow before sale. When buying, look for undamaged fruit. Yellow fruit, without green tips, is ripe and black spots on the skin indicate the fruit is very ripe. To store, keep at room temperature until fully ripe, then wrap them in newspaper and refrigerate. They will keep for about 5 days and even though the skins turn black the flesh stays unchanged.

*ABOVE: Sugar-free pudding*

# SUGAR-FREE PUDDING

**Preparation time:** 30 minutes
**Total cooking time:** 1 hour 30 minutes
**Serves** 6–8

6 ripe bananas, mashed
1 egg, lightly beaten
2 cups (370 g/12 oz) mixed dried fruit
1 cup (80 g/3 oz) fresh breadcrumbs

### Orange cream

1¼ cups (315 ml/10 fl oz) cream
2 tablespoons orange juice
1 tablespoon grated orange rind
1 teaspoon vanilla essence

**1** Prepare a 1.25 litre (40 fl oz) pudding basin as shown on pages 190–1.
**2** Place the basin in a large pan, on a trivet or upturned saucer, and pour in enough cold water to come halfway up the side of the basin. Remove the basin and put the water on to boil.
**3** Combine the banana, egg, dried fruit and breadcrumbs in a bowl. Spoon into the prepared pudding basin.
**4** Cover the basin and make a handle as shown on pages 190–1.
**5** Gently lower the basin into the boiling water, reduce the heat to a fast simmer and cover with a tight-fitting lid. Cook for 1½ hours, checking the water after an hour and topping up to the original level with boiling water as needed.
**6** For the orange cream, combine the cream, orange juice, rind and vanilla in a bowl and mix well. Serve over the pudding.

# CHOC-GINGER PUDDINGS

Preparation time: 45 minutes
  + overnight standing
  + overnight hanging
Total cooking time: 1 hour 15 minutes
Makes 10

2 cups (320 g/11 oz) raisins, chopped

1¹/₃ cups (200 g/6¹/₂ oz) currants

²/₃ cup (110 g/3¹/₂ oz) pitted dates, chopped

¹/₃ cup (75 g/2¹/₂ oz) glacé ginger, chopped

1 cup (160 g/5¹/₂ oz) sultanas

100 g (3¹/₂ oz) dried pears, chopped

100 g (3¹/₂ oz) dried apricots, chopped

1 cup (175 g/6 oz) dark chocolate bits

¹/₂ cup (75 g/2¹/₂ oz) pistachios, chopped

¹/₂ cup (125 ml/4 fl oz) brandy

250 g (8 oz) unsalted butter, frozen and grated

1 cup (185 g/6 oz) dark brown sugar

1 tablespoon treacle

¹/₃ cup (80 ml/2³/₄ fl oz) orange juice

1 teaspoon finely grated orange rind

¹/₃ cup (80 ml/2³/₄ fl oz) lemon juice

1 teaspoon finely grated lemon rind

4 eggs, lightly beaten

1 teaspoon bicarbonate of soda

1¹/₂ cups (185 g/6 oz) plain flour

¹/₂ cup (60 g/2 oz) self-raising flour

2 teaspoons mixed spice

2 teaspoons ground cinnamon

1 teaspoon ground nutmeg

1 cup (80 g/2³/₄ oz) fresh breadcrumbs

cream, for serving, optional

**1** Put all the fruit, chocolate and pistachios into a large basin and stir in the brandy. Cover with plastic wrap and leave overnight.

**2** Bring 2 large saucepans of water to the boil. Cut a piece of calico into ten 30 cm (12 inch) squares. Put the calico in one of the saucepans of boiling water for 15 minutes, then remove with tongs and, with gloved hands, wring out the water.

**3** Put the butter in a large bowl and stir in the sugar, treacle, rinds and juices and the eggs. Add the combined sifted bicarbonate of soda, flours and spices in two batches. Stir in the fruit and breadcrumbs.

**4** Place a calico square on a flat surface and rub liberally with plain flour, leaving a border of calico. Place a loosely packed cup of the mixture into the centre of the cloth. Gather and tie the cloth into a neat ball, pleating the calico, as shown on pages 204–5. Tie firmly with string around the top and tie the end of the string to enable you to hang the puddings from a wooden spoon. Repeat with all the mixture and calico. Place half the puddings in each saucepan of boiling water, then sit the lids over the spoons to keep most of the steam in. Simmer for 1 hour. Hang overnight in a cool place to dry, then refrigerate in an airtight container. Keep for up to 1 month.

**5** To reheat, lower the puddings into a pan of boiling water and boil for 30 minutes. Remove the cloths and serve individually, with cream.

*ABOVE: Choc-ginger puddings*

BOILED PUDDING

Dust a calico square with a thick layer of plain flour, spreading it evenly with your hands.

Put the pudding mixture in the centre of the calico square and pull the material up together.

When gathering all the material together, try to keep the folds as neat as possible.

Tie string around the top to seal the pudding, then tie a loop in the string to use as a handle.

*OPPOSITE PAGE:*
*Boiled pudding*

## BOILED PUDDING

Preparation time: 40 minutes
    + overnight soaking + overnight hanging
Total cooking time: 5 hours
Serves 10–12

✫ ✫ ✫

1²/₃ cups (310 g/10 oz) mixed dried fruit

¹/₄ cup (45 g/1¹/₂ oz) mixed peel

4 cups (640 g/1¹/₄ lb) mixed sultanas, currants and raisins

¹/₂ cup (125 ml/4 fl oz) brown ale

2 tablespoons rum or brandy

2 tablespoons orange juice

2 tablespoons lemon juice

1 tablespoon grated orange rind

1 tablespoon grated lemon rind

225 g (7 oz) suet, grated

1¹/₃ cups (245 g/7¹/₂ oz) soft brown sugar

3 eggs, lightly beaten

2¹/₂ cups (200 g/6¹/₂ oz) fresh white breadcrumbs

³/₄ cup (90 g/3 oz) self-raising flour

1 teaspoon mixed spice

¹/₄ teaspoon freshly grated nutmeg

²/₃ cup (100 g/3¹/₂ oz) blanched almonds, chopped

**1** Finely chop the mixed dried fruit and put in a large bowl with the mixed peel, sultanas, currants, raisins, ale, rum, orange and lemon juice and rind. Cover and leave overnight.

**2** Mix the fruit with the remaining ingredients and a pinch of salt. Leave for 10 minutes.

**3** Cut an 80 cm (32 inch) square from a clean piece of calico or an old tea towel and follow the instructions on pages 204–5. Cover, place a couple of large cans of fruit or a brick on the lid if possible, and boil the pudding for 5 hours. Replenish with boiling water when necessary. Remove from the water and hang in a well-ventilated, dry place where it will not touch anything. Hook up the calico ends or open up and loosely place on top of the pudding. Leave the pudding hanging overnight to dry.

**4** Untie the cloth and, if there are damp patches at the top, spread it out to make sure it dries. When it is dry, re-wrap and tie with a new piece of string. The pudding will store hanging in a cool, dry place for up to 4 months. To serve, boil for 2 hours, hang for 15 minutes, then remove from the cloth and cut into wedges.

## CARROT PLUM PUDDING

Preparation time: 25 minutes
    + overnight hanging
Total cooking time: 6 hours
Serves 8

✫ ✫ ✫

1¹/₂ cups (185 g/6 oz) plain flour

1¹/₂ teaspoons bicarbonate of soda

¹/₂ teaspoon ground cloves

1¹/₂ teaspoons ground nutmeg

1¹/₂ teaspoons ground cinnamon

1 teaspoon ground cardamom

1¹/₂ cups (375 g/12 oz) sugar

1¹/₂ cups (240 g/7¹/₂ oz) raisins, chopped

1 cup (125 g/4 oz) chopped walnuts

3 eggs, lightly beaten

60 g (2 oz) unsalted butter, melted and cooled

1 tablespoon finely grated orange rind

1 cup (80 g/2³/₄ oz) fresh breadcrumbs

2¹/₂ cups (390 g/13 oz) coarsely grated carrot

¹/₂ cup (85 g/3 oz) coarsely grated potato

**1** Cut an 80 cm (32 inch) square from a clean piece of calico or an old tea towel and follow the instructions on pages 204–5.

**2** Sift the flour, bicarbonate of soda and spices into a large bowl. Add the sugar and mix well. Mix in the raisins and walnuts.

**3** Make a well in the flour and stir in the eggs and butter. Add the orange rind, breadcrumbs, carrot and potato and stir well. Place the mixture in the centre of the cloth. Fold up, tie and make a string handle following the instructions on pages 204–5. Suspend the pudding in the water and cover the pan. Place a couple of large cans of fruit or a brick on the lid if possible. Simmer for 6 hours or until the pudding feels firm.

**4** Remove the pudding and hang it over a bowl (to catch any drips) in a dry, well-ventilated area not touching anything. Hook up the calico ends or open up and loosely place on top of the pudding. Leave the pudding hanging overnight to dry. The next day, remove the string and if the top is slightly wet, spread out and allow to dry. When completely dry, re-wrap and tie with a new piece of string and hang in a cool dark place for up to 4 months. If the weather is humid you may need to refrigerate the pudding.

**5** When ready to serve, reheat the wrapped pudding in a large saucepan of boiling water for 1¹/₂ hours. Can be served with custard or ice cream.

## ICE CREAM CHRISTMAS PUDDING

Cover the inside and base of the basin with the ice cream and cherry mixture.

Spoon the chocolate ice cream mixture into the bowl, then smooth the top with the back of the spoon.

## ICE CREAM CHRISTMAS PUDDING

**Preparation time:** 1 hour
+ overnight standing + 2 nights freezing
**Total cooking time:** Nil
**Serves** 10

★ ★

1/3 cup (50 g/1 3/4 oz) toasted almonds, chopped
1/4 cup (45 g/1 1/2 oz) mixed peel
1/2 cup (80 g/2 3/4 oz) raisins, chopped
1/2 cup (80 g/2 3/4 oz) sultanas
1/3 cup (50 g/1 3/4 oz) currants
1/3 cup (80 ml/2 3/4 fl oz) rum
1 litre (32 fl oz) good-quality vanilla ice cream
1/2 cup (105 g/3 1/2 oz) red and green glacé
   cherries, quartered
1 teaspoon mixed spice
1 teaspoon ground cinnamon
1/2 teaspoon ground nutmeg
1 litre (32 fl oz) good-quality chocolate
   ice cream

1 Mix the almonds, peel, raisins, sultanas, currants and rum in a bowl, cover with plastic wrap and leave overnight. Chill a 2 litre (64 fl oz) pudding basin in the freezer overnight.
2 Soften the vanilla ice cream slightly and mix in the glacé cherries. Working quickly, press the ice cream around the inside of the chilled basin, spreading it evenly to cover the base and side of the basin. Return the basin to the freezer and leave overnight. Check the ice cream a couple of times and spread it evenly to the top.
3 The next day, mix the spices and chocolate ice cream with the fruit mixture. Spoon it into the centre of the pudding bowl and smooth the top. Freeze overnight, or until very firm. Turn the pudding out onto a chilled plate and decorate. Cut into wedges to serve.
NOTE: If you want to put coins and charms into the pudding, wrap each one in baking paper and poke into the base of the pudding before turning it out. Remember to tell your guests about them before they start eating.

*ABOVE: Ice cream Christmas pudding*

# SUMMER PUDDING

**Preparation time:** 30 minutes
  + overnight refrigeration
**Total cooking time:** 5 minutes
**Serves** 6

150 g (5 oz) blackcurrants
150 g (5 oz) redcurrants
150 g (5 oz) raspberries
150 g (5 oz) blackberries
200 g (6$^1$/$_2$ oz) strawberries, hulled and
  quartered or halved
$^1$/$_2$ cup (125 g/4 oz) caster sugar, or to taste
6–8 slices good-quality sliced white bread,
  crusts removed

**1** Put all the berries, except the strawberries, in a large saucepan with $^1$/$_2$ cup (125 ml/4 fl oz) water and heat gently for 5 minutes, or until the berries begin to collapse. Add the strawberries and remove from the heat. Add the sugar, to taste (this will depend on how sweet the fruit is). Allow to cool.
**2** Line a 1 litre (32 fl oz) pudding basin or six $^2$/$_3$ cup (170 ml/5$^1$/$_2$ oz) moulds with the bread. For the large mould, cut a large circle out of one slice for the base and cut the rest of the bread into wide fingers. For the small moulds, use one slice of bread for each, cutting a small circle to fit the base and strips to fit snugly around the sides. Drain a little of the juice off the fruit mixture. Dip one side of each piece of bread in the juice before fitting it, juice-side-down, into the basin, leaving no gaps. Do not squeeze or flatten the bread or it will not absorb the juices.
**3** Fill the centre of the basin with the fruit and add a little juice. Any fruit that doesn't fit in can be served with the pudding. Cover the top with the remaining dipped bread, juice-side-up, trimmed to fit. Cover with plastic wrap. Place a small plate which fits inside the dish onto the plastic wrap, then weigh it down with heavy cans or a glass bowl. Place on a baking tray to catch any juices. For the small moulds, cover with plastic and sit a small can, or a similar weight, on top of each. Refrigerate overnight. Turn out the pudding/s and serve with any leftover fruit mixture. This is delicious served with dollops of cream.

# MANGO SORBET

**Preparation time:** 20 minutes + freezing
**Total cooking time:** 4 minutes
**Serve** 4–6

1 cup (250 g/8 oz) caster sugar
2 tablespoons lemon juice
2 cups (500 ml/16 fl oz) mango purée,
  or 3 medium mangoes, puréed

**1** Combine the sugar and 1$^1$/$_4$ cups (315 ml/10 fl oz) water in a saucepan and stir over low heat to dissolve the sugar. Bring to the boil and boil for 2 minutes without stirring. Set aside to cool to room temperature.
**2** Add the lemon juice to the mango purée and slowly pour on the sugar syrup. Mix well. Pour into a shallow metal tray, cover with plastic wrap and freeze for 4–6 hours, or until firm.
**3** Break up the mixture with a fork and process in a food processor until soft and smooth (it will be pale). Spoon into an airtight container and freeze for 4–6 hours, or until firm.

*ABOVE: Summer pudding*

ICE CREAM BOMBE

Drape the toffee-coated baking paper over a rolling pin and let it set.

Carefully peel away the toffee bark from the paper in large, irregular shapes.

# ICE CREAM BOMBE

**Preparation time:** 20 minutes + overnight freezing + 25 minutes refrigeration
**Total cooking time:** 3 minutes
**Serves** 8

★ ★ ★

1 large mango, finely chopped
1 cup (160 g/5$^{1}$/2 oz) canned pineapple pieces, drained
1/4 cup (60 ml/2 fl oz) Grand Marnier
250 g (8 oz) fresh strawberries, puréed
400 g (13 oz) can condensed milk
2$^{1}$/2 cups (600 ml/20 fl oz) cream
80 g (2$^{3}$/4 oz) dessert nougat, chopped (see Note)
1/4 cup (35 g/1$^{1}$/4 oz) roughly chopped unsalted pistachios
strawberries, extra, halved, to garnish

**Toffee bark**

1/3 cup (90 g/3 oz) caster sugar

**1** Lightly grease a 2 litre (64 fl oz) pudding basin and line with plastic wrap, allowing it to hang over the side of the basin. Put in the freezer until ready to use. Drain the mango and pineapple in a sieve.
**2** Mix the Grand Marnier, strawberry purée and condensed milk in a large bowl. Whisk the cream to soft peaks, then add to the bowl and continue whisking until thick. Fold in the drained fruits, nougat and pistachios. Pour the mixture into the pudding basin, cover with plastic wrap and freeze overnight, or until firm.
**3** To serve, remove the plastic wrap from the base and invert the pudding onto a chilled serving plate. Remove the bowl, but leave the plastic wrap and refrigerate for 15–25 minutes to soften slightly.
**4** For the toffee bark, line a baking tray with baking paper. Heat the sugar over low heat in a heavy-based saucepan for 2–3 minutes, or until melted and golden. Carefully pour onto the tray. Tilt the tray to get a thin, even layer of toffee over the paper and cool slightly. While still pliable, drape the paper over a rolling pin and allow to cool for 30–60 seconds before peeling away strips of toffee in large irregular shapes. Cool. To serve, remove the plastic and decorate the bombe with toffee bark and strawberries.
**NOTE:** Dessert nougat is a soft nougat available at confectionery shops and some delicatessens.

# SHERRY TRIFLE

**Preparation time:** 30 minutes + refrigeration
**Total cooking time:** 10 minutes
**Serves** 8

★

85 g (3 oz) packet strawberry jelly crystals
300 g (10 oz) jam sponge roll
1/3 cup (80 ml/2$^{3}$/4 fl oz) sherry
825 g (1 lb 11 oz) can sliced peaches, drained
1/4 cup (30 g/1 oz) custard powder
2 cups (250 ml/8 fl oz) milk
1/4 cup (60 g/2 oz) caster sugar
2 teaspoons vanilla essence
1 cup (250 ml/8 fl oz) cream
powdered drinking chocolate, to garnish
strawberries, optional, to garnish

**1** Make the jelly according to the directions on the packet and refrigerate until the mixture reaches the consistency of unbeaten egg white. Meanwhile, cut the sponge roll into 1 cm (1/2 inch) slices and arrange, leaving no gaps, around the side and base of a 2.5 litre (80 fl oz) glass bowl. Drizzle sherry evenly all over the sponge pieces.
**2** Pour the jelly over the cake and refrigerate until set. When set, top with the peach slices and refrigerate.
**3** Blend the custard powder with 1/2 cup (125 ml/4 fl oz) of the milk in a saucepan until smooth. Add the remaining milk, sugar and vanilla to the saucepan. Stir over medium heat for 5 minutes, or until the mixture boils and thickens, then pour into a large bowl and allow to cool, stirring often to prevent a skin forming. When cold but not completely set, pour and spread the custard evenly over the peaches. Refrigerate until cold.
**4** Beat the cream in a large bowl with electric beaters until soft peaks form, spread over the custard, forming peaks, then sprinkle with a little drinking chocolate. Decorate with strawberries if desired.
**NOTE:** You can change the flavour of the jelly and the type of fruit according to your taste.

*OPPOSITE PAGE:*
*Ice cream bombe*

## BERRY TRIFLE

**Preparation time:** 35 minutes
  + overnight refrigeration
**Total cooking time:** 5 minutes
**Serves** 8–10

★ ★

1¹/₂ cups (2 x 225 g/7 oz jars) redcurrant jelly

²/₃ cup (170 ml/5¹/₂ fl oz) fresh orange juice

2¹/₂ cups (600 ml/20 fl oz) cream

250 g (8 oz) mascarpone

¹/₄ cup (30 g/1 oz) icing sugar

1 teaspoon vanilla essence

¹/₄ teaspoon ground cinnamon

250 g (8 oz) thin sponge finger biscuits
   (savoiardi)

1¹/₂ cups (375 ml/12 fl oz) Marsala

400 g (13 oz) fresh raspberries

250 g (8 oz) large fresh strawberries, hulled
   and quartered

400 g (13 oz) fresh blueberries

1 Melt the redcurrant jelly in a small saucepan over medium heat. Remove from the heat, stir in the orange juice and set aside until the mixture reaches room temperature.

2 Put the cream, mascarpone, icing sugar, vanilla essence and cinnamon in a bowl and beat with electric beaters until soft peaks form.

3 Cut each biscuit in half crossways and dip each piece in the Marsala. Arrange half over the base of a 3.25 litre (104 fl oz) serving bowl.

4 Sprinkle a third of the combined berries over the biscuits and drizzle with half the remaining Marsala and a third of the redcurrant sauce. Spoon half the cream mixture over the sauce. Repeat the layering with the remaining half of the dipped biscuits and Marsala, a third of the berries and sauce, and the remaining cream.

5 Arrange the remaining berries over the cream in a mound in the centre of the bowl. Reserve the final third of the redcurrant sauce, cover and refrigerate. Cover the trifle with plastic wrap and refrigerate overnight. Before serving, pour the reserved redcurrant sauce over the berries to glaze. (Gently reheat the sauce if it is too thick.)

*ABOVE: Berry trifle*

# TIRAMISU

**Preparation time:** 30 minutes
+ overnight refrigeration
**Total cooking time:** Nil
**Serves** 6

2 cups (500 ml/16 fl oz) strong black coffee,
  cooled
¼ cup (60 ml/2 fl oz) Marsala or
  coffee-flavoured liqueur
2 eggs, separated
¼ cup (60 g/2 oz) caster sugar
250 g (8 oz) mascarpone
1 cup (250 ml/8 fl oz) cream
16 large sponge finger (savoiardi) biscuits
2 tablespoons dark cocoa powder

**1** Combine the coffee and Marsala in a bowl
and set aside. Beat the egg yolks and sugar in
a bowl with electric beaters for 3 minutes, or
until thick and pale. Add the mascarpone and
mix until just combined. Transfer to a large
bowl. Beat the cream in a separate bowl, with
electric beaters, until soft peaks form, then fold
into the mascarpone mixture.
**2** Place the egg whites in a small, clean, dry
bowl and beat with electric beaters until soft
peaks form. Fold quickly and lightly into the
cream mixture.
**3** Dip half the biscuits into the coffee mixture,
drain off any excess and arrange in the base of
a 2.5 litre (80 fl oz) ceramic or glass serving
dish. Spread half the cream mixture over
the biscuits.
**4** Dip the remaining biscuits into the remaining
coffee mixture and repeat the layers. Smooth
the surface and dust liberally with the cocoa
powder. Refrigerate overnight.
**NOTE:** This delicious rich dessert originated
in Venice. Tiramisu translates as 'pick-me-up'.
It is best made a day in advance to let the
flavours develop but if you don't have time,
refrigerate it for at least 2 hours before serving,
by which time it should be firm.

*ABOVE: Tiramisu*

215

## BERRIES IN
## CHAMPAGNE JELLY

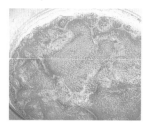

Sprinkle the gelatine over the Champagne in an even layer and leave until spongy.

Slowly pour the jelly into the wine glasses, covering the berries.

*ABOVE: Summer berries in Champagne jelly*

## SUMMER BERRIES IN CHAMPAGNE JELLY

**Preparation time:** 10 minutes + refrigeration
**Total cooking time:** 5 minutes
**Serves** 8

★

1 litre (32 fl oz) Champagne or sparkling
    white wine
1 1/2 tablespoons powdered gelatine
1 cup (250 g/8 oz) sugar
4 strips lemon rind
4 strips orange rind
250 g (8 oz) small strawberries, hulled
250 g (8 oz) blueberries

**1** Pour half the Champagne into a bowl and let the bubbles subside. Sprinkle the gelatine over the top in an even layer. Leave until the gelatine is spongy—do not stir. Pour the remaining Champagne into a large saucepan, add the sugar and rinds and heat gently, stirring constantly, until all the sugar has dissolved.

**2** Remove the saucepan from the heat, add the gelatine mixture and stir until thoroughly dissolved. Leave to cool completely, then remove the rind.

**3** Divide the berries among eight 1/2 cup (125 ml/4 fl oz) stemmed wine glasses and gently pour the jelly over them. Refrigerate until set. Remove from the refrigerator 15 minutes before serving.

# PROFITEROLES WITH DARK CHOCOLATE SAUCE

**Preparation time:** 40 minutes + cooling
**Total cooking time:** 50 minutes
**Serves** 4–6

60 g (2 oz) butter, chopped
¾ cup (90 g/3 oz) plain flour
3 eggs, lightly beaten

### White chocolate filling

¼ cup (30 g/1 oz) custard powder
1 tablespoon caster sugar
1½ cups (375 ml/12 fl oz) milk
150 g (5 oz) white chocolate melts,
   chopped
1 tablespoon Grand Marnier

### Dark chocolate sauce

125 g (4 oz) dark chocolate, chopped
½ cup (125 ml/4 fl oz) cream

1 Preheat the oven to hot 210°C (415°F/ Gas 6–7). Line a baking tray with baking paper. Put the butter and ¾ cup (185 ml/6 fl oz) water in a pan. Bring to the boil, then remove from the heat. Add the flour all at once. Return to the heat and stir until the mixture forms a smooth ball. Set aside to cool slightly. Transfer to a bowl and, while beating with electric beaters, gradually add the eggs a little at a time, beating well after each addition, to form a thick, smooth, glossy paste.

2 Spoon 2 heaped teaspoons of the mixture onto the tray at 5 cm (2 inch) intervals. Sprinkle lightly with water and bake for 12–15 minutes, or until the dough is puffed. Turn off the oven. Pierce a small hole in the base of each profiterole with the point of a knife and return the profiteroles to the oven. Leave them to dry in the oven for 5 minutes.

3 For the filling, combine the custard powder and sugar in a pan. Gradually add the milk, stirring until smooth, then continue to stir over low heat until the mixture boils and thickens. Remove from the heat and add the white chocolate and Grand Marnier. Stir until the chocolate is melted. Cover the surface with plastic wrap and allow to cool. Stir the custard until smooth, then spoon into a piping bag fitted with a 1 cm (½ inch) plain nozzle. Pipe the filling into each profiterole. Serve with the warm chocolate sauce.

4 For the dark chocolate sauce, combine the chocolate and cream in a small saucepan. Stir over low heat until the chocolate is melted and the mixture is smooth. Serve warm.

**NOTE:** The profiteroles can be made a day ahead. Fill just before serving. You can also make miniature profiteroles, using 1 teaspoon of the mixture. Dip the tops of the cooked profiteroles in melted chocolate. When set, fill them with whipped cream.

*ABOVE: Profiteroles with dark chocolate sauce*

**Chocolate topping**
200 g (6¹/₂ oz) dark chocolate, chopped
³/₄ cup (185 ml/6 fl oz) cream
1 tablespoon Frangelico

**1** Preheat the oven to slow 150°C (300°F/
Gas 2). Grease a deep 20 cm (8 inch) round
cake tin and line with baking paper.
**2** Put the chocolate in a heatproof bowl. Half fill
a saucepan with water and bring to the boil.
Remove from the heat and place the bowl over
the pan, making sure it is not touching the
water. Stir occasionally until the chocolate
is melted.
**3** Put the eggs in a large heatproof bowl and
add the Frangelico. Place the bowl over a
saucepan of barely simmering water over low
heat, making sure it does not touch the water.
Beat with an electric mixer on high speed for
7 minutes, or until the mixture is light and
foamy. Remove from the heat.
**4** Using a metal spoon, quickly and lightly fold
the melted chocolate and ground nuts into the
egg mixture until just combined. Fold in the
cream and pour the mixture into the tin. Place
the tin in a shallow baking dish. Pour in enough
hot water to come halfway up the side of the tin.
**5** Bake for 1 hour, or until just set. Remove the
tin from the baking dish. Cool to room
temperature, cover with plastic wrap and
refrigerate overnight.
**6** Cut a 17 cm (7 inch) circle from heavy
cardboard. Invert the chilled cake onto the
disc so that the base of the cake becomes the
top. Place on a wire rack over a baking tray
and remove the baking paper. Allow the cake
to return to room temperature before you start
to decorate.
**7** To make the topping, combine the chopped
chocolate, cream and Frangelico in a small pan.
Heat gently over low heat, stirring, until the
chocolate is melted and the mixture is smooth.
**8** Pour the chocolate mixture over the cake in
the centre, tilting slightly to cover the cake
evenly. Tap the baking tray gently on the bench
so that the top is level and the icing runs
completely down the side of the cake. Place
the hazelnuts around the edge of the cake.
Refrigerate just until the topping has set and
the cake is firm. Carefully transfer the cake
to a serving plate, and cut into thin wedges
to serve.
NOTE: Frangelico is a hazelnut-flavoured
liqueur. Brandy or whisky can also be used, if
preferred. This is a very rich cake so you only
need to serve small portions.

# CHOCOLATE HAZELNUT TORTE

**Preparation time:** 1 hour + overnight
refrigeration
**Total cooking time:** 1 hour 15 minutes
**Serves** 10

★ ★

500 g (1 lb) dark chocolate, chopped
6 eggs
2 tablespoons Frangelico (see Note)
1¹/₂ cups (165 g/5¹/₂ oz) ground hazelnuts
1 cup (250 ml/8 fl oz) cream, whipped
12 whole hazelnuts, lightly roasted

*ABOVE: Chocolate
hazelnut torte*

Line a large baking tray with baking paper and draw a circle on the paper. Turn the paper over.

Beat the egg whites with electric beaters in a dry bowl until soft peaks form.

Spread the stiff mixture onto the paper on the tray inside the drawn circle.

Make furrows all the way round the outside of the meringue mixture by running a palette knife up the edge.

# FRESH FRUIT PAVLOVA

**Preparation time:** 30 minutes
**Total cooking time:** 55 minutes
**Serves** 6–8

 ★ ★

6 egg whites
2 cups (500 g/1 lb) caster sugar
1 1/2 tablespoons cornflour
1 1/2 teaspoons vinegar
2 cups (500 ml/16 fl oz) cream, whipped
2 bananas, sliced
500 g (1 lb) strawberries, sliced
4 kiwi fruit, sliced
4 passionfruit, pulped

**1** Preheat the oven to slow 150°C (300°F/Gas 2). Line a large baking tray with baking paper and draw a 26 cm (10 1/2 inch) circle on the paper. Turn the paper over and place on the tray. Beat the egg whites with electric beaters in a large dry bowl until soft peaks form. Gradually add all but 2 tablespoons of the sugar, beating well after each addition. Combine the cornflour and vinegar with the last of the sugar and beat for 1 minute before adding it to the bowl. Beat for 5–10 minutes, or until all the sugar has completely dissolved and the meringue is stiff and glossy. Spread onto the paper inside the circle.
**2** Shape the meringue evenly, running the flat side of a palette knife along the edge and over the top. Run the palette knife up the edge of the meringue mixture all the way round, making furrows. This strengthens the pavlova and helps prevent the edge from crumbling, as well as being decorative.
**3** Bake for 40 minutes, or until pale and crisp. Reduce the heat to very slow 120°C (250°F/Gas 1/2) and bake for 15 minutes. Turn off the oven and cool the pavlova in the oven, using a wooden spoon to keep the door slightly ajar. When completely cooled, top with cream and fruit. Drizzle with passionfruit pulp and serve.
**NOTE:** This recipe can be made into individual pavlovas. Spoon 6 or 8 rounds of mixture onto 2 baking paper-covered trays. Alternate the trays halfway through cooking time.

*ABOVE: Fresh fruit pavlova*

219

# RASPBERRY MIROIRE

**Preparation time:** 1 hour
+ several hours refrigeration
**Total cooking time:** 30 minutes
**Serves** 8–10

### Sponge base

1 egg

2 tablespoons caster sugar

2 tablespoons self-raising flour

1 tablespoon plain flour

### Raspberry mousse

500 g (1 lb) fresh or frozen raspberries

4 egg yolks

1/2 cup (125 g/4 oz) caster sugar

1 cup (250 ml/8 fl oz) milk

1 1/2 tablespoons gelatine

1/4 cup (60 ml/2 fl oz) crème de cassis liqueur

1 cup (250 ml/8 fl oz) cream

### Raspberry topping

2 teaspoons gelatine

1 tablespoon crème de cassis liqueur

### Chocolate bark

100 g (3 1/2 oz) white chocolate melts, melted

raspberries, to decorate

icing sugar, to dust

cream, for serving, optional

1 Preheat the oven to moderate 180°C (350°F/ Gas 4). Lightly grease a round 22 cm (9 inch) springform tin and line the base with baking paper. Beat the egg and sugar in a small bowl with electric beaters, for 5 minutes, or until thick and fluffy. Sift the flours together three times, then fold into the egg mixture with a metal spoon. Spread evenly into the prepared tin and bake for 10–15 minutes, or until lightly browned and shrunk slightly away from the edge. Remove from the tin and leave to cool on a wire rack. Clean the springform tin, fit the base into the tin upside down and lightly oil the pan and line the base and side with plastic wrap.

2 To make the raspberry mousse, blend or process the raspberries in batches until smooth and press through a plastic strainer (not a metallic one or the raspberries may discolour) to remove the seeds. Reserve 1/2 cup (125 ml/4 fl oz) raspberry purée for the topping. Beat the egg yolks and sugar in a heatproof bowl for 5 minutes, or until thick and pale. Bring the milk to the boil and gradually pour onto the egg mixture, beating continually. Place the bowl over a pan of simmering water and stir for about 10 minutes, or until the mixture thickens slightly and coats the back of a spoon. Allow to cool.

3 Sprinkle the gelatine in an even layer over 1/4 cup (60 ml/2 fl oz) water in a small heatproof bowl and leave to go spongy. Do not stir. Put a small saucepan of water on to boil. When it boils, remove from the heat and place the bowl in the water (it should come halfway up the side of the bowl), then stir until clear and completely dissolved. Cool slightly. Stir the gelatine mixture, raspberry purée and liqueur into the custard mixture, then refrigerate until thick but not set. Beat the cream until soft peaks form and fold into the raspberry mixture with a metal spoon. Place the sponge into the base of the prepared tin and pour the raspberry mixture evenly over the top. Refrigerate for several hours, or until firm.

4 For the topping, sprinkle the gelatine in an even layer over 1/3 cup (80 ml/2 3/4 fl oz) water in a heatproof bowl and leave to go spongy. Do not stir. Put a small saucepan of water on to boil. When it boils, remove from the heat and place the bowl in the water (it should come halfway up the side of the bowl), then stir until clear and completely dissolved. Cool slightly. Stir in the reserved raspberry purée and the liqueur, pour evenly over the set mousse, then refrigerate until set.

5 To make the chocolate bark, cover a baking tray firmly with plastic wrap, spread the chocolate thinly over the plastic and allow to set. When set, break into large angular pieces.

6 To serve, cut the Raspberry miroire into wedges, place pieces of chocolate on the back of each slice and keep in place with a dob of cream. Decorate with extra raspberries, dust lightly with icing sugar and serve with cream if desired.

**NOTE:** Miroire denotes the shiny jelly topping, meaning 'mirror' in French.

**RASPBERRIES**
The raspberry is a relatively soft berry usually seen in the red variety but occasionally in black or white. The fruit has a fine down covering and tastes sweet, although it has a slightly acid effect on the palate. It is a rambling plant that prefers to grow in a cool climate. As the fruit has a tendency to go mouldy and soften, it is best used as soon as possible after purchase. Raspberries are also available frozen.

*OPPOSITE PAGE:*
*Raspberry miroire*

# CAKES & BAKING

Baking is the area where Christmas tradition has its strongest influence. Many people can happily waltz through the entire festive season without so much as a turkey sandwich but would absolutely draw the line at missing out on the Christmassy flavour of fresh fruit mince. It simply wouldn't be right to go through December without the beloved and familiar mince pie or the traditional fruit cake, rich with glacé fruit, mixed peel and nuts. Generously covered with marzipan icing and beautifully decorated, the Christmas cake deserves pride of place in every festive table setting.

# LINING CAKE TINS

If you put a little extra time and effort into the preparation of the tins, you shouldn't end up with misshapen cakes or round edges on square cakes.

### CHOOSING THE CAKE TIN

Choose and prepare the cake tin well before you make the mixture. Cake tins not only come in the round and square type traditionally used at Christmas time but also in the shape of bells, flowers, hearts and diamonds. Most tins are aluminium, but some are made of tin, specially treated to make them food safe. The size of tins given in recipes is for the measurement across the base. If you want to use a different tin from the one stated you will need to use a tin with the same capacity. So if the recipe asks for a 20 cm (8 inch) round cake tin, fill a tin this size with water, gradually transfer the water into the chosen tin, and keep doing so until the chosen tin is full. In this way, you can work out how many quantities of mixture are required to fill the tin.

### HOW MUCH LINING?

Average-sized cakes or fruit cakes that are not in the oven for extended cooking times only require a single layer of baking paper to line the base and side. However, cakes that are much larger or those that require long cooking times (most fruit cakes) need extra protection from burning, both around the side and under the base of the tin. Extra layers of baking

paper are used inside the tin and newspaper is wrapped around the outside. Several layers of newspaper are also put under the tin, on the oven shelf.

## SUCCESSFUL LINING

Lightly grease the cake tin with melted butter or a mild-flavoured vegetable oil. This helps keep the paper in place. Cut a double layer of paper into a strip long enough to fit around the outside of the tin and tall enough to come 5 cm (2 inches) above the edge of the tin. Fold down a cuff about 2 cm (³/4 inch) deep along the length of the strip, along the folded edges. Make diagonal cuts up to the fold line on each strip about 1 cm (¹/2 inch) apart. Fit the strip around the inside of the tin, with the cuts on the base, pressing the cuts out at right angles so they sit flat around the base. Place the

cake tin on a doubled piece of baking paper and draw around the edge. Cut it out and sit it on the base of the tin, over the cuts. Most cake tins can be lined successfully this way. Before you turn on the oven, prepare your cake tin following these instructions and have the oven shelves in the correct position to accommodate the lined tin. Cakes are normally cooked on the third shelf. Spoon the prepared cake mixture into the tin, ensuring it is pushed well into corners and edges. Tap the tin on the bench to remove any air bubbles. Smooth the top with fingers dipped in water and decorate the top with fruit or nuts if desired. To prevent the cake burning on the outside, fold over several sheets of newspaper long enough to wrap around the side of the cake tin and to come a little higher than the baking

paper. Tie around the tin securely with string and sit the tin on several layers of folded newspaper on the oven shelf. Because the oven temperature is low, it is quite safe to have the paper in the oven. Some people also like to use a layer of brown paper and a layer of baking paper.

When the cake is completely cold, remove it from the tin, then remove the paper. If there is a wet spot on the base of the cake, return the cake to the tin and cook for another hour, or until dried out. If the edges and side of the cake feel a little dry, brush well all over with extra brandy or rum and wrap in plastic wrap. When you are happy with the cake and it is cold, wrap firmly in plastic wrap and store in an airtight container. Most fruit cakes will keep for 8–12 months. Cakes containing nuts only keep for up to 3 months. Fruit cakes can be frozen.

225

**CHRISTMAS CAKE**

Make decorations in the shape of Christmas trees using green icing.

Paint small pieces of icing different colours to put on the cake to represent wrapped presents.

Write your greeting on baking paper and leave until dry. Carefully remove and attach to the cake.

*OPPOSITE PAGE:*
*Christmas cake*

# CHRISTMAS CAKE

**Preparation time:** 40 minutes + overnight soaking
**Total cooking time:** 3 hours 40 minutes
**Makes** 1

★★★

2 cups (320 g/11 oz) sultanas
2 cups (320 g/11 oz) raisins, chopped
2 cups (300 g/10 oz) currants
1 cup (185 g/6¹/2 oz) mixed peel
¹/2 cup (100 g/3¹/2 oz) red glacé cherries, quartered
¹/2 cup (110 g/3¹/2 oz) chopped glacé ginger
²/3 cup (160 g/5¹/2 oz) chopped glacé apricots
¹/2 cup (125 ml/4 fl oz) brandy
¹/2 cup (125 ml/4 fl oz) orange juice
1¹/2 cups (150 g/5 oz) walnuts
250 g (8 oz) unsalted butter, softened
1 cup (230 g/7¹/2 oz) soft brown sugar
¹/2 cup (160 g/5¹/2 oz) orange marmalade
5 eggs
2 cups (250 g/8 oz) plain flour
1 teaspoon bicarbonate of soda
1 teaspoon ground cinnamon
1 teaspoon ground nutmeg

**Icing and decorations**

2 tablespoons apricot jam
800 g (1 lb 10 oz) marzipan icing
1 egg white
1 kg (2 lb) ready-made soft icing
icing sugar
assorted food colourings

1 Put all the fruit in a large bowl, separating any clumps with your fingers. Stir in the brandy and orange juice. Cover with plastic wrap and leave overnight (or for at least 4 hours) so the fruit can absorb most of the liquid. Stir occasionally.
2 Preheat the oven to warm 160°C (315°F/ Gas 2–3). Grease and line a 23 cm (9 inch) round or 20 cm (8 inch) square cake tin as shown on pages 224–5.
3 Bake the walnuts on a baking tray for 8–10 minutes (don't let them burn), or until lightly toasted. Cool, then roughly chop.
4 Beat the butter, sugar and marmalade in a large bowl with electric beaters until the mixture is light and creamy. Scrape down the sides of the bowl with a rubber spatula. Add the eggs one at a time, beating well after each addition.

The mixture will appear curdled but don't worry. Add the butter mixture and walnuts to the soaked fruit. Sift the flour, bicarbonate of soda and spices over the top, then mix gently but thoroughly. Make sure there are no pockets of flour in the mixture, but don't beat too vigorously.
5 Spoon into the tin, tap the tin on the bench to remove any air bubbles and smooth the surface with wet fingers. Wrap the outside of the tin as shown on pages 224–5. Sit the tin on several layers of newspaper in the oven and bake for 3–3¹/2 hours, or until a skewer inserted into the centre of the cake comes out clean and the cake has shrunk slightly from the edge of the tin. Cool in the tin before turning the cake out.
6 Ice the cake by following the instructions on pages 234–5.
7 To decorate:
**Christmas trees:** Colour various sized pieces of icing green and roll into cone shapes. Use scissors to make snips into the side of the cone all over. Leave to dry. Cut small stars out of yellow tinted icing and leave to dry. Stick the stars to the top of the tree with a little egg white mixed to a paste with sifted pure icing sugar. Dust with sifted icing sugar.
**Presents:** Make shapes of icing in various sizes and leave to dry. Paint in different colours and leave to dry. Paint on bows and ribbons, stripes and spots. Arrange on the cake, attaching with royal icing. You can also tie a ribbon or frill around the cake and write a Christmas greeting.
**Runout letters:** Trace a Christmas greeting from a lettering book or Christmas card onto a piece of paper in simple, easy-to-read letters. Place the paper on a board and cover with baking paper. Make up some icing using an egg white and enough pure icing sugar to make a smooth icing which will hold its shape. Tint with colour and spoon into a paper piping bag. Pipe around the outline of the letters, then fill in the centre. If the icing is too stiff and doesn't sit flat, brush it with a paintbrush dipped in egg white. Dry overnight, then peel the letters off and stick them to the cake with a little egg white mixed to a paste with sifted pure icing sugar.
**Leaves:** Use a holly-shaped cutter to cut leaves out of the icing. Shape the leaves and leave to dry. When dry, paint green. Roll small amounts of icing into balls to represent holly berries. Paint red and leave to dry. Holly leaves can be used alone as a wreath around the edge of the cake.
**NOTE:** Never use real holly berries to decorate your cake—they are toxic!

Keep your decorated cake in an airtight container in a cool, dry place for 4–5 months. Do not refrigerate or the icing will go sticky.

## BOILED FRUIT CAKE

Stir thoroughly to ensure the sugar dissolves and the butter melts evenly through the mixture.

Add the eggs, flour and mixed spice and mix through thoroughly.

Smooth over the top of the cake with wetted hands before baking.

*ABOVE: Boiled fruit cake*

## BOILED FRUIT CAKE

**Preparation time:** 20 minutes
**Total cooking time:** 2 hours 10 minutes
**Makes** 1

✫ ✫

2 cups (320 g/11 oz) raisins, chopped

2 cups (320 g/11 oz) sultanas

1 cup (150 g/5 oz) currants

2/3 cup (100 g/3 1/2 oz) blanched almonds, chopped

1/2 cup (100 g/3 1/2 oz) red glacé cherries

1 cup (230 g/7 1/2 oz) soft brown sugar

125 g (4 oz) unsalted butter, chopped

1/4 cup (60 ml/2 fl oz) brandy

2 eggs, lightly beaten

3/4 cup (90 g/3 oz) plain flour

3/4 cup (90 g/3 oz) self-raising flour

2 teaspoons mixed spice

**1** Put the dried fruits, almonds, glacé cherries, sugar, butter, brandy and 1 cup (250 ml/8 fl oz) water in a large saucepan. Bring to the boil, stirring occasionally until the sugar has dissolved and the butter has melted. Remove from the heat and set aside to cool to room temperature.
**2** Preheat the oven to warm 160°C (315°F/Gas 2–3). Grease and line a 20 cm (8 inch) round or 18 cm (7 inch) square cake tin as shown on pages 224–5.
**3** Add the eggs to the fruit, then sift in the flours and spice. Mix together, working quickly and lightly, but don't overmix. Spoon into the tin, tap the tin on the bench to remove any air bubbles, then smooth the surface with wet fingers. Wrap newspaper around the outside of the tin as shown on pages 224–5. Sit the tin on several more layers of newspaper in the oven and bake for 1 1/2–2 hours, until a skewer inserted into the centre of the cake comes out clean. Cool completely in the tin, covered with a clean tea towel, then turn out. Store in an airtight container or wrapped in plastic for 2–3 months.

# BOILED GINGER FRUIT CAKE

**Preparation time:** 20 minutes
**Total cooking time:** 2 hours
**Makes** 1

1¼ cups (155 g/5 oz) self-raising flour

1¼ cups (155 g/5 oz) plain flour

250 g (8 oz) unsalted butter

1 cup (230 g/7½ oz) dark brown sugar

1 cup (160 g/5½ oz) pitted dried dates, chopped

1²/₃ cups (270 g/9 oz) raisins, chopped

1²/₃ cups (270 g/9 oz) sultanas

½ cup (110 g/3½ oz) chopped glacé ginger

²/₃ cup (170 ml/5½ fl oz) green ginger wine

⅓ cup (80 ml/2¾ fl oz) apple juice

2 teaspoons ground ginger

½ teaspoon bicarbonate of soda

2 eggs, lightly beaten

2–3 tablespoons green ginger wine, extra

1 Sift the flours into a large bowl and make a well in the centre. Combine the butter in a large saucepan with the sugar, fruit, green ginger wine, apple juice and ground ginger. Stir over low heat until the butter has melted and the sugar has dissolved. Bring to the boil, then reduce the heat and simmer for 5 minutes. Remove from the heat, stir in the bicarbonate of soda and set aside to cool.

2 Preheat the oven to moderate 180°C (350°F/ Gas 4). Grease and line a deep 20 cm (8 inch) square or 23 cm (9 inch) round cake tin as shown on pages 224–5.

3 Mix one egg at a time into the fruit, then add the mixture to the well in the flour and stir until just combined—don't overmix. Spoon into the tin, tap the tin on the bench to remove any air bubbles and smooth the surface with wet fingers. Wrap newspaper around the outside of the tin as shown on pages 224–5. Sit the tin on several layers of newspaper in the oven and bake for 1½–1¾ hours, or until a skewer inserted into the centre of the cake comes out clean.

4 Drizzle the hot cake with green ginger wine. Cool in the tin, covered with a clean tea towel, then store in an airtight container or plastic wrap for up to 2 months.

## DATES

Dates are a popular snack at Christmas time in Europe and are also used to flavour and sweeten cakes. They have been an important part of the diet in North African, Middle Eastern and Arabian countries for thousands of years. Dates are usually sold in the dried form although fresh dates are also becoming more readily available. Dried dates have a darker skin than fresh ones and are sweeter. When buying dates, look for soft, plump ones. They are best eaten at room temperature and do not usually need to be refrigerated.

*LEFT: Boiled ginger fruit cake*

FROSTED FRUIT CAKE

Paint the fruit with a little egg white, then sprinkle with the caster sugar.

For the icing, whisk the egg white until just foamy, then beat in the lemon juice and, gradually, the icing sugar.

Use a palette knife to smooth the icing over the cake, allowing it to run slowly down the side.

*OPPOSITE PAGE:*
*Frosted fruit cake*

# FROSTED FRUIT CAKE

**Preparation time:** 30 minutes + overnight soaking + 1–2 hours decorating
**Total cooking time:** 3 hours 30 minutes
**Makes** 1

★ ★ ★

4 cups (640 g /1 1/4 lb) sultanas

3 cups (480 g/15 oz) raisins, chopped

2 cups (300 g/10 oz) currants

1 1/4 cups (265 g/8 oz) glacé cherries, quartered

1 cup (250 ml/8 fl oz) brandy or rum

250 g (8 oz) unsalted butter, chopped, softened

1 cup (230 g/7 1/2 oz) dark brown sugar

2 tablespoons apricot jam

2 tablespoons treacle or golden syrup

1 tablespoon grated lemon or orange rind

4 eggs

2 3/4 cups (340 g/11 oz) plain flour

1 teaspoon mixed spice

1 teaspoon ground cinnamon

1 teaspoon ground ginger

1 tablespoon brandy or rum, extra

## Decorations

selection of seasonal fruits such as white and dark cherries, small bunches of red, white and black currants, apricots, tiny plums or pears

1 egg white

caster sugar

## Icing

1 egg white

1–3 teaspoons lemon juice

1 cup (125 g/4 oz) pure icing sugar, sifted

**1** Put the fruit in a large bowl with the brandy and leave to soak overnight. Preheat the oven to slow 150°C (300°F/Gas 2). Grease and line an oval cake tin 18 x 25 cm (7 x 10 inch), or a 23 cm (9 inch) round cake tin, as shown on pages 224–5.

**2** Beat the butter and sugar in a small bowl with electric beaters until just combined. Beat in the jam, treacle and rind. Add the eggs one at a time, beating well after each addition. Transfer to a large bowl.

**3** Stir the fruit and the combined sifted flour and spices alternately into the mixture. Spoon into the tin, tap the tin on the bench to remove any air bubbles and smooth the surface with wet fingers. Wrap newspaper around the outside of the tin as shown on pages 224–5. Sit the tin on several layers of newspaper in the oven and bake for 3 1/4–3 1/2 hours, or until a skewer inserted into the centre comes out clean. Drizzle with the extra brandy while hot. Cover the top with baking paper, cover tightly with foil and wrap the tin in a clean dry tea towel until the cake is completely cold.

**4** Remove from the tin and store in an airtight container or wrapped in plastic wrap for up to 8 months.

**5** Wash the fruit to be used for decorating several hours in advance so it is completely dry. Line a tray with paper towels. Place the egg white in a shallow bowl and whisk until just foamy. Put some caster sugar on a large plate and working with one portion of fruit at a time, brush the egg white lightly all over the fruit. Sprinkle the sugar over the fruit, shaking off any excess and leave to dry on the paper-covered tray for about 1–2 hours, depending on the humidity. Frost more fruit than you think you will need so you have a good selection.

**6** For the icing, whisk the egg white until just foamy, beat in 1 teaspoon of lemon juice and then gradually beat in the icing sugar, beating well after each addition. The icing should be thick and white—add a little more lemon juice if necessary, but don't make it too runny. Place the fruit cake on a serving plate and working quickly pour the icing over the top. Using a palette knife smooth the icing to the edge of the cake, allowing it to run slowly down the side of the cake. Leave for at least 10 minutes to let the icing set a little before arranging the frosted fruits on the top. The iced cake will keep for up to a month.

**NOTE:** The cake can be iced several days ahead and the frosted fruit prepared when you are ready to use it. Mix up a little extra icing and use to secure the fruit to the dried icing. Don't have the icing too thin when you pour it over the cake, otherwise it may discolour from the cake underneath. If you don't want to frost fruit, top the cake with fresh fruit and dust all over with icing sugar. Alternatively, decorate with bought Christmas decorations.

INDIVIDUAL BOURBON
CHRISTMAS CAKES

For the holly leaves, knead the almond icing until soft, then cut out holly leaves with a cutter or template.

Paint the edges of the tiny leaves with colouring. Don't use too much or it will bleed further into the icing.

Roll out the soft icing for each cake individually, until it is large enough to cover one of the cakes.

For the cakes with the royal icing, spread a tablespoon of icing over each with a palette knife, letting some drizzle down the side.

*OPPOSITE PAGE:*
*Individual bourbon*
*Christmas cakes*

# INDIVIDUAL BOURBON CHRISTMAS CAKES

**Preparation time:** 40 minutes + overnight
soaking + decorating
**Total cooking time:** 1 hour 15 minutes
**Makes** 12

★ ★ ★

1/4 cup (60 g/2 oz) chopped glacé apricots

1/2 cup (110 g/3 1/2 oz) chopped glacé pineapple

1/2 cup (100 g/3 1/2 oz) chopped glacé figs

2 cups (320 g/11 oz) raisins, chopped

1 2/3 cups (250 g/8 oz) currants

3/4 cup (180 ml/6 fl oz) bourbon

250 g (8 oz) unsalted butter, chopped

1 cup (230 g/7 1/2 oz) dark brown sugar

1/2 cup (180 g/6 oz) treacle

4 eggs

2 1/2 cups (310 g/10 oz) pecans, chopped

1 1/2 cups (185 g/6 oz) plain flour

1/2 cup (60 g/2 oz) self-raising flour

2 teaspoons ground nutmeg

2 teaspoons ground ginger

2 teaspoons ground cinnamon

6 tablespoons bourbon, extra

**Holly leaves and berries**

60 g (2 oz) ready-made almond icing

pure icing sugar

green and red food colouring

**Soft icing-covered cakes**

1/3 cup (105 g/3 1/2 oz) apricot jam, warmed,
sieved

1.2 kg (2 lb 6 1/2 oz) ready-made soft icing

pure icing sugar

thin ribbon

**Royal icing-covered cakes**

1 egg white

2 cups (250 g/8 oz) pure icing sugar, sifted

2–3 teaspoons lemon juice

**1** Cut the glacé fruits and raisins into small pieces. Place in a large bowl with the currants and bourbon and mix well. Cover and leave to soak overnight, stirring occasionally.

**2** Preheat the oven to slow 150°C (300°F/Gas 2). Lightly grease twelve 1 cup (250 ml/8 fl oz)

muffin holes and line the bases with a circle of baking paper. Beat the butter, sugar and treacle in a small bowl until just combined. Add the eggs one at a time, beating well after each addition. Transfer to a large bowl, stir in the soaked fruit mixture, pecans and then the sifted dry ingredients and mix well.

**3** Spoon the mixture evenly into the tins, and smooth the surface with fingers dipped in cold water. Bake for 1–1 1/4 hours, or until a skewer inserted into the centre comes out clean. Cover the top of the cakes lightly with foil if over-browning. Brush the tops of the cakes with half the extra bourbon while hot, cover with baking paper, then seal firmly with foil and cool in the tins before turning out. Brush with the remaining bourbon, wrap firmly in plastic and leave for two weeks before decorating. When decorating, the base will become the top.

**4** To make the holly leaves, knead 50 g (1 3/4 oz) of the almond icing until it is soft. Roll out on a surface lightly dusted with icing sugar until very thin. Cut out the leaves using a cutter or template. Pinch the leaves in half, open out and press the edges gently to curl in different directions. Dry on baking paper. Brush the edges with green food colouring. Knead a little red colouring into the remaining almond icing and roll into small balls to make berries. Paint or roll the berries in colouring to coat thoroughly. Allow to dry.

**5** For the soft icing-covered cakes, melt the jam until runny, strain and brush some all over each cake. Roll out 100 g (3 1/2 oz) of the soft icing on a surface lightly dusted with icing sugar until large enough to cover one cake. If there are any holes in the cake, use a little extra icing to fill the holes and make a smooth surface. Place the icing over the cake and ease over the side, pressing lightly, then trim from around the base. Mix together a little icing sugar and water into a smooth paste. Wrap a ribbon around the base of the cake and seal with a little paste. Use the paste to secure 2 holly leaves and berries to the top. Repeat with remaining cakes and icing.

**6** For the royal icing-covered cakes, lightly beat the egg white with a wooden spoon just to break down a little. Gradually add the icing sugar, beating to a smooth paste. Slowly add the lemon juice until slightly runny. Spread a tablespoon of icing over each cake, using a palette knife to smooth and letting some drizzle down the sides. Secure holly leaves and berries on the top just before the icing sets.

**NOTE:** Iced cakes can be kept for up to a month in an airtight container, or un-iced for up to 8 months.

# ICING YOUR CAKE

Careful preparation when icing your cake will make decorating easy. Organize

yourself well, have patience and a beautiful cake will be your reward.

### BEFORE YOU START
A truly beautiful iced cake starts with careful preparation when making the cake. The more perfectly shaped the cake, the better the result. Use the correct tin size as stated in the recipe and line the tin properly before filling with the mixture (see pages 224–5). Spread the mixture evenly into corners, tap the tin on the bench to remove air bubbles and smooth the surface with wet fingertips.

Bake as instructed in the recipe and ice when completely cold. Trim the dome from the top of the cake evenly with a large sharp knife to make a flat surface. Don't use a serrated knife as the fruit may drag and tear the cake. Turn the cake over so you can use the smooth base as the top of the cake. You will need about 1 kg (2 lb) ready-made almond icing and 1 kg (2 lb) ready-made soft icing for a 22 cm (9 inch) cake. Both almond icing

and soft icing (known as ready-roll fondant in the UK) are available in packets at supermarkets or specialty cake-decorating shops. Keep icings covered with plastic wrap until you are ready to use to prevent them drying out.

### ALMOND ICING OR MARZIPAN
Almond icing and marzipan are interchangeable. Briefly knead the almond icing until smooth and pliable on

a clean work surface lightly dusted with icing sugar. Fill any holes that have formed on the surface of the cake (the result of an air bubble, the tin lining not being smooth, or the fruit drying out) with small pieces of almond paste. Warm about 2 tablespoons apricot jam with 1 teaspoon water in a small pan over low heat, then push it through a fine sieve and brush it all over the cake with a pastry brush. This acts as a 'glue' to hold the icing in place. Roll out the almond icing into a circle large enough to just cover the base and side of the cake—don't roll it out too big or you may end up with unwanted folds.

To prevent tearing the icing as you lift it and so you have more control, roll it over a rolling pin, then carefully move it across onto the cake, unrolling and smoothing it over the base and side and pressing out any folds and wrinkles with

icing sugar-dusted hands. Carefully pierce any air bubbles with a large pin. Keep your hands and rolling pin lightly dusted with icing sugar to prevent sticking. Trim the almond icing around the base of the cake with a sharp knife and leave the cake overnight in a cool, dry place to dry a little. This layer makes a firm base for the soft icing.

Lightly beat an egg white, to break it up slightly, and brush a thin layer all over the surface of the almond icing with a pastry brush. This will 'glue' the soft icing to the almond layer.

## SOFT ICING

Briefly knead the soft icing on a work surface dusted lightly with icing sugar until the icing is smooth and pliable. If you would like to colour the icing, now is the time—add the liquid colour one drop at a time using a toothpick. Roll

out the icing and cover the cake using the same method as the almond icing, gently pressing the icing over the cake. Dust your hands with icing sugar and smooth out any wrinkles and folds. You can also use a 'smoother', available from cake-decorating shops or you can make your own with a smooth-edged piece of laminex and a wooden block glued to the back as a handle. Trim the icing around the base of the cake with a sharp knife and leave the cake in a cool, dry place overnight.

Leftover icing can be wrapped in plastic and stored in an airtight container for 1–2 months. To finish the cake, shape decorations out of leftover icing, let them dry, then paint with food colouring and allow to dry. Secure to the cake with a little egg white mixed to a paste with sifted pure icing sugar. See the next page for some simple decorating ideas.

# EASY DECORATING

Don't be thrown into a spin by the thought of decorating cakes such as these. They are made beautiful using simple ideas and ribbon and a little imagination.

### A MINIMUM OF FUSS

Once you have made your favourite fruit cake, you can transform it into something special by following our instructions or using them as a guide to create your own extravaganza with inspiration from things such as books, tree decorations, greeting cards and photos in magazines. Use covered cake boards to make the cake look professional, though a large glass or white platter is also suitable as a base. Place the iced cake on the base before decorating, securing it with a little paste made with egg white and sifted pure icing sugar (this is called royal icing). Pure icing sugar is best as it sets hard— icing sugar mixture has cornflour mixed with it to prevent it setting hard.

### SILVER CAKE

Follow the directions on pages 234–5 to cover the cake with almond icing and soft icing, reserving a little soft icing for decoration. On a surface lightly dusted with pure icing sugar, roll the reserved icing into several long thin sausages. Twist two of the sausages together to form a rope. Brush a little egg white

around the bottom edge of the cake and wrap the 'rope' around the cake, hiding any joins you may need to make (try and make these at the back of the cake). Set aside for a few hours, or overnight, to dry. Cut a length of ribbon long enough to go from the base on one side of the cake to the other and gently tuck under the 'rope'. Cut 2 more lengths of ribbon long enough to tuck under the 'rope' edge and be tied together into a big bow. In a small bowl, mix a little egg white with sifted pure icing sugar to make a paste (royal icing). Place into the corner of a small plastic bag and pipe dots randomly all over the cake. Secure assorted sized silver dragees or cachous (available at gourmet food or cake specialty stores and some supermarkets) onto the icing and leave to set.

## GOLD TREE CAKE

Cover the cake with almond icing as shown on pages 234–5. Beat some egg white in a small bowl with enough sifted pure icing sugar to make a sticky paste. Spread over the top of the almond icing and form peaks using a spatula. Place a bought tree or similar suitable decoration in one corner with some artificial holly and berries. Dust with sifted icing sugar. Tie a large thick decorative ribbon, or two overlapping thinner ones, around the side of the cake, securing the ribbon at the back with a little of the royal icing (the egg white and pure icing sugar paste) and some pins. Once set, remember to carefully remove the pins. Add a coloured bow, made from organza or similar material, to the front corner.

## PARCEL CAKE

Cover a round cake in almond icing as on pages 234–5. Lightly tint ready-made icing with egg-yellow food colouring and roll into a round (large enough to cover the side of the cake and form the folds of the sack when brought together) on a surface dusted with icing sugar. Brush the almond icing all over with egg white and place the cake in the centre of the rolled icing. Gather the icing up the side of the cake and pleat to form the neck (leave an opening). You may need to press the icing onto the egg white. Tie a cord or ribbon around the neck. Dust with sifted icing sugar and fill with decorations, wrapped lollies and chocolates.

*FROM LEFT: Silver cake;*
*Gold tree cake; Parcel cake*

237

# GLUTEN-FREE CAKE

**Preparation time:** 30 minutes + overnight soaking
**Total cooking time:** 3 hours 30 minutes
**Makes** 1

1 kg (2 lb) mixed dried fruit

2/3 cup (160 g/5 1/2 oz) chopped glacé apricots

2/3 cup (140 g/5 1/2 oz) chopped glacé pineapple

1/4 cup (60 ml/2 fl oz) orange juice

1/2 cup (125 ml/4 fl oz) sweet sherry

250 g (8 oz) unsalted butter, softened

1 cup (230 g/7 1/2 oz) soft brown sugar

5 eggs, lightly beaten

1 tablespoon coffee and chicory essence

1 tablespoon molasses

1 tablespoon orange marmalade

1 tablespoon grated orange rind

3/4 cup (90 g/3 oz) slivered almonds

2 cups (180 g/6 oz) soya flour

2 cups (90 g/3 oz) baby rice cereal

2/3 cup (90 g/3 oz) maize flour

1 teaspoon bicarbonate of soda

1 teaspoon ground cloves

1 teaspoon ground nutmeg

1 teaspoon ground cinnamon

1 teaspoon mixed spice

2/3 cup (100 g/3 1/2 oz) blanched whole almonds,
  for decoration

2 tablespoons sweet sherry, extra

1 Mix the fruit in a large bowl with the orange juice and sherry. Cover and leave overnight, stirring occasionally. Grease and line a deep 23 cm (9 inch) square or 24 cm (9 1/2 inch) round cake tin as on pages 224–5. Preheat the oven to slow 150°C (300°F/Gas 2).
2 Beat the butter and sugar to just combine. Add the eggs one at a time, beating well after each addition. Add the essence, molasses, marmalade and rind and beat until well combined.
3 Transfer the mixture to a large bowl and stir in the fruit, almonds and sifted dry ingredients. Spoon into the tin and tap the tin on the bench to remove air bubbles. Smooth the surface with wet fingertips. Decorate with the almonds (in circles), pressing in slightly. Wrap the cake tin as shown on pages 224–5 and bake for 3–3 1/2 hours, or until a skewer inserted into the centre of the cake comes out clean—sometimes the fruit may stick to the skewer. Remove from the oven and sprinkle with the extra sherry.

Cover the top with baking paper, then cover tightly with foil and wrap in a thick tea towel. Cool completely in the tin. Store in an airtight container or in plastic wrap for up to 6 months.

# SUGAR-REDUCED CAKE

**Preparation time:** 30 minutes + overnight soaking
**Total cooking time:** 3 hours
**Makes** 1

1.25 kg (2 1/2 lb) mixed dried fruit

1 cup (250 ml/8 fl oz) brandy

180 g (6 oz) unsalted butter, softened

1/2 cup (115 g/4 oz) soft brown sugar

4 eggs, lightly beaten

2 tablespoons coffee and chicory essence

1 tablespoon finely grated orange rind

2 cups (250 g/8 oz) plain flour

1/2 cup (60 g/2 oz) self-raising flour

1 teaspoon ground nutmeg

1 teaspoon ground cinnamon

1 teaspoon mixed spice

1/4 teaspoon ground cloves

1 1/4 cups (125 g/4 oz) whole pecans,
  for decoration

1 Mix the fruit in a large bowl with the brandy. Cover and leave overnight, stirring occasionally. Grease and line a deep 23 cm (9 inch) round or 20 cm (8 inch) square tin as on pages 224–5. Preheat the oven to slow 150°C (300°F/Gas 2).
2 Beat the butter and sugar to just combine. Add the eggs one at a time, beating well after each addition. Add the essence and rind and beat until combined. Transfer to a large bowl and stir in the fruit and sifted dry ingredients. Spoon into the cake tin, tap the tin on the bench to remove any air bubbles, and smooth the surface with wet fingertips. Decorate with the pecans, pressing into the mixture slightly. Wrap the outside of the tin as shown on pages 224–5.
3 Sit the cake on several layers of newspaper in the oven and bake for 2 3/4–3 hours, or until a skewer inserted into the centre of the cake comes out clean—sometimes the fruit may stick to the skewer. Remove from the oven and cover the top with baking paper, then cover tightly with foil and wrap in a thick tea towel. Cool completely in the tin. Store in an airtight container or in plastic wrap for up to 6 months.

**PECANS**
Pecans are a nut native to North America. Most are now cultivated but there are still many old wild trees producing nuts which are marketed. Pecan nuts are also now being grown in Australia, Israel and South Africa. The trees sometimes grow to 50 metres and the nuts have to be harvested by shaking the trees. The nut shell has a smooth surface. Pecan nuts are used mostly in sweet dishes, especially the famous American dessert, pecan pie, and confectionery.

*OPPOSITE PAGE:*
*Sugar-reduced cake*

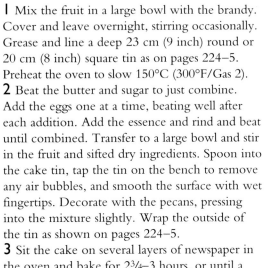

# LIGHT FRUIT CAKE

**Preparation time:** 30 minutes
**Total cooking time:** 2 hours
**Makes** 1

185 g (6 oz) unsalted butter, softened
1/2 cup (125 g/4 oz) caster sugar
3 eggs
1 cup (160 g/5 1/2 oz) sultanas
2/3 cup (100 g/3 1/2 oz) currants
1/4 cup (60 g/2 oz) chopped glacé apricots
1/4 cup (45 g/1 1/2 oz) chopped glacé figs
1 cup (240 g/7 1/2 oz) coarsely chopped
　glacé cherries
1/2 cup (80 g/2 3/4 oz) macadamia nuts,
　coarsely chopped
1 1/2 cups (185 g/6 oz) plain flour
1/2 cup (60 g/2 oz) self-raising flour
1/2 cup (125 ml/4 fl oz) milk
1 tablespoon sweet sherry
nuts or glacé cherries, for decoration

1 Preheat the oven to warm 160°C (315°F/ Gas 2–3). Grease and line a deep 20 cm (8 inch) round or 18 cm (7 inch) square cake tin as shown on pages 224–5.
2 Cream the butter and sugar in a small bowl until just combined. Add the eggs, one at a time, beating well after each addition.
3 Transfer the mixture to a large bowl and stir in the fruit and nuts. Sift in half the flours and half the milk, stir to combine, then stir in the remaining flours and milk, and the sherry. Spoon into the prepared tin and tap the tin on the bench to remove any air bubbles. Smooth the surface with wet fingers and decorate the top with nuts or cherries, or both. Wrap the outside of the tin as shown on pages 224–5. Sit the tin on several layers of newspaper in the oven and bake for 1 3/4–2 hours, or until a skewer inserted into the centre of the cake comes out clean. The top may need to be covered with a sheet of baking paper if it colours too much.
4 Remove from the oven, remove the top baking paper and wrap the tin in a thick tea towel until cool. Remove the paper tin lining and wrap the cake well in aluminium foil, or store in an airtight container. Keeps for up to 2 weeks.

# LOW-CHOLESTEROL CAKE

**Preparation time:** 30 minutes + overnight
　soaking
**Total cooking time:** 3 hours 30 minutes
**Makes** 1

1 kg (2 lb) mixed dried fruit
2/3 cup (160 g/5 1/2 oz) chopped glacé apricots
2/3 cup (140 g/4 1/2 oz) chopped glacé pineapple
1 cup (250 ml/8 fl oz) brandy
1 cup (230 g/7 1/2 oz) soft brown sugar
1/3 cup (80 ml/2 3/4 fl oz) vegetable oil
3 egg whites, lightly beaten
1 teaspoon vanilla essence
1 tablespoon molasses
1 tablespoon orange marmalade
1/4 cup (60 ml/2 fl oz) orange juice
1 tablespoon finely grated orange rind
2 cups (250 g/8 oz) plain flour
1/2 cup (60 g/2 oz) self-raising flour
1 teaspoon ground nutmeg
1 teaspoon ground cinnamon
1 teaspoon ground cloves
1 teaspoon mixed spice

1 Mix the fruit in a large bowl with the brandy. Cover and leave overnight, stirring occasionally.
2 Preheat the oven to slow 150°C (300°F/ Gas 2). Grease and line a deep 20 cm (8 inch) square or 23 cm (9 inch) round cake tin as shown on pages 224–5.
3 Beat the sugar, oil and egg whites until combined. Add the essence, molasses, marmalade, juice and rind and beat until combined. Transfer to a large bowl and stir in the fruit and sifted dry ingredients. Spoon into the tin, tap the tin on the bench to remove any air bubbles and smooth the surface with wet fingers. Wrap the outside of the tin as shown on pages 224–5. Sit the tin on several layers of newspaper in the oven and bake for 3–3 1/2 hours, or until a skewer inserted into the cake comes out clean—sometimes the fruit may stick to the skewer.
4 Remove from the oven and cover the top with baking paper. Cover tightly with foil and wrap in a thick tea towel. Cool in the tin. Store in an airtight container or in plastic wrap for up to 6 months.

**RAISINS**
Raisins, sultanas and currants are all dried grapes. Although 'raisin' is sometimes used as the generic term for all three, it usually refers to certain types of dried grape. Raisins come in many different shapes and sizes, depending on the grape. Originally, most raisins came from Turkey, the Mediterranean region and Afghanistan. They are still grown in these places but most come from California.

*OPPOSITE PAGE:*
*Light fruit cake (top);*
*Low-cholesterol cake*

## YULETIDE

Yuletide is another name for the Christmas season. In Scandinavia in pre-Christian days, people celebrated Juul at the same time of the year as people now celebrate Christmas. Juul, or wheel, represented a revolution of the sun and at Yuletide the sun was at its lowest. The yule log was a magical source of fuel for the sun. Christianity adopted the yule log and it later became a custom to put one on the hearth on Christmas Eve and burn it for the next twelve hours, adding warmth to the home. The log that was used had to be taken from a tree on the property, or be a gift, or just picked up, but not bought. A part of it was kept and used as kindling for the following year's yule log. A popular cake (see page 246) is made to represent the log.

*ABOVE: Golden glacé cake*

# GOLDEN GLACE CAKE

**Preparation time:** 15 minutes
**Total cooking time:** 1 hour 45 minutes
**Makes** 1

★★★

1/2 cup (120 g/4 oz) chopped glacé orange slices
1/2 cup (120 g/4 oz) chopped glacé pears
1 cup (240 g/8 oz) chopped glacé apricots
1 cup (240 g/8 oz) chopped glacé pineapple
1/3 cup (60 g/2 oz) chopped mixed peel
1/2 cup (80 g/2 3/4 oz) blanched almonds, coarsely chopped
1 1/2 cups (185 g/6 oz) plain flour
1/2 cup (60 g/2 oz) self-raising flour
250 g (8 oz) unsalted butter, softened
1 tablespoon finely grated orange rind
1 tablespoon finely grated lemon rind
1 cup (250 g/8 oz) caster sugar
5 eggs
1/4 cup (60 ml/2 fl oz) sweet sherry

**1** Preheat the oven to moderate 180°C (350°F/ Gas 4). Grease and line a deep 20 cm (8 inch) square or 23 cm (9 inch) round cake tin as shown on pages 224–5.

**2** Combine the fruits, peel and almonds, then toss with 1/4 cup (30 g/1 oz) of the plain flour to keep the fruits separate. Sift together the remaining flours.

**3** Beat the butter and rind in a small bowl with electric beaters, gradually adding the sugar, until light and fluffy. Beat in the eggs, one at a time, beating well after each addition. Transfer to a large bowl, stir in the flour alternately with sherry, then fold in the fruit, nut and flour mixture.

**4** Spoon into the tin, tap the tin on the bench to remove any air bubbles and smooth the surface with wet fingers. Sit the tin on several layers of newspaper and bake for 30 minutes. Reduce the heat to warm 160°C (315°F/ Gas 2–3) and bake for 1–1 1/4 hours, or until cooked when a skewer inserted in the centre comes out clean. Cool completely in the tin, covered with a clean tea towel, before turning onto a wire rack to cool. Store in an airtight container or in plastic wrap for up to 4 weeks.

# GLACE FRUIT AND NUT LOAF

**Preparation time:** 30 minutes
**Total cooking time:** 1 hour 45 minutes
**Serves** 12

50 g (1³/₄ oz) unsalted butter, softened

¹/₄ cup (55 g/2 oz) soft brown sugar

2 tablespoons breakfast marmalade

2 eggs

1 cup (125 g/4 oz) plain flour

1 teaspoon baking powder

1 teaspoon ground nutmeg

1¹/₄ cups (200 g/6¹/₂ oz) pitted dried dates

1¹/₂ cups (240 g/7¹/₂ oz) raisins, chopped

1 cup (155 g/5 oz) brazil nuts

²/₃ cup (140 g/4¹/₂ oz) red, yellow and green
    glacé cherries, quartered

¹/₂ cup (120 g/4 oz) chopped glacé pears
    or pineapple

¹/₂ cup (120 g/4 oz) chopped glacé apricots

¹/₂ cup (120 g/4 oz) chopped glacé peaches

¹/₃ cup (120 g/4 oz) chopped glacé figs

1 cup (100 g/3¹/₂ oz) walnut halves

²/₃ cup (100 g/3¹/₂ oz) blanched almonds

## Topping

2 teaspoons gelatine

2 tablespoons breakfast marmalade

150 g (5 oz) glacé pineapple or pear rings

100 g (3¹/₂ oz) red, yellow and green
    glacé cherries

¹/₄ cup (40 g/1¹/₄ oz) blanched almonds, toasted

**1** Grease a deep 20 x 8 cm (8 x 3 inch) bar tin and line the base and sides with baking paper. Preheat the oven to slow 150°C (300°F/Gas 2).
**2** Beat the butter, sugar and marmalade together until pale and creamy. Add the eggs and beat until combined.
**3** Sift the flour, baking powder and nutmeg into a large bowl. Add the fruit and nuts and mix until each piece is coated in the flour. Stir into the egg mixture.
**4** Put the mixture in the tin, pushing well into each corner. Bake for 1¹/₂–1³/₄ hours, or until a skewer inserted into the centre comes out clean. Cool in the tin for 10 minutes before turning out. Remove the baking paper and transfer to a wire rack to cool.

**5** For the topping, sprinkle the gelatine over 2 tablespoons water and the marmalade in a small bowl. Bring a pan of water to the boil, then remove from the heat. Stand the bowl in the pan and stir until the gelatine has dissolved. Brush the top of the cake with some of the gelatine mixture, top with arranged pineapple, cherries and almonds. Brush or drizzle with more gelatine mixture and allow to set.
**NOTE:** This type of cake is known in some places as an American-style fruit cake, or a stained glass fruit cake.

*ABOVE: Glacé fruit and nut loaf*

FRESH FRUIT
MINCE TARTS

Mix the pastry with a knife
until the mixture comes
together in beads.

Cut 24 pastry rounds and
fit them into the holes in
the tartlet pans.

Place a pastry shape on top
of each tart before baking.

## FRESH FRUIT MINCE TARTS

**Preparation time:** 1 hour + 30 minutes
refrigeration
**Total cooking time:** 50 minutes
**Makes** 24

★ ★ ★

1¾ cups (215 g/7 oz) plain flour
150 g (5 oz) butter, chilled and chopped
¾ cup (80 g/2¾ oz) ground hazelnuts
2 tablespoons caster sugar
1–2 tablespoons iced water
icing sugar, for dusting

### Filling

¾ cup (115 g/4 oz) blueberries
1 cup (200 g/6½ oz) peeled, finely chopped apple
½ cup (80 g/2¾ oz) raisins, chopped
½ cup (75 g/2½ oz) currants
½ cup (80 g/2¾ oz) sultanas
¼ cup (30 g/1 oz) slivered almonds, toasted
¼ cup (60 g/2 oz) caster sugar
2 tablespoons mixed peel
½ cup (125 ml/4 fl oz) brandy
1 teaspoon grated lemon rind
½ teaspoon mixed spice
½ teaspoon ground ginger

**1** For the pastry, sift the flour into a large bowl and rub in the butter with your fingertips until the mixture resembles fine breadcrumbs. Stir in the nuts and sugar. Make a well and mix in the water with a flat-bladed knife until the mixture comes together in beads. Gather into a ball and turn out onto a lightly floured surface. Press into a ball and flatten slightly into a disc. Cover with plastic wrap and chill for 30 minutes.

**2** Preheat the oven to moderate 180°C (350°F/ Gas 4). Roll out the dough between sheets of baking paper to 3 mm (⅛ inch) thick. Using a 7 cm (2¾ inch) round pastry cutter, cut 24 pastry rounds and line two deep 12-hole tartlet pans with the rounds. Line each pastry case with baking paper and fill with baking beads. Bake for 10 minutes, remove the paper and beads and bake for another 10 minutes.

**3** Meanwhile, press together the pastry scraps and roll to 3 mm (⅛ inch) thick. Using 4.5 cm (1¾ inch) star, bell or holly-shaped cutters, cut 24 shapes from the pastry for the tart lids.

**4** For the filling, put all the ingredients in a saucepan and simmer, stirring, for 5–10 minutes, or until thick and pulpy. Cool slightly. Divide among the pastry cases, then top each with a pastry lid. Bake for 20 minutes, or until the lids are golden. Leave in the pans for 5 minutes before transferring to a wire rack to cool. Dust with sifted icing sugar before serving. Store in an airtight container for up to a week.

*ABOVE: Fresh fruit
mince tarts*

# TRADITIONAL MINCE TARTS

**Preparation time:** 40 minutes + 35 minutes
refrigeration + 3 weeks bottling
**Total cooking time:** 15 minutes
**Makes** 48

★★★

### Fruit mince

2 large green apples (about 440 g/14 oz),
    peeled, cored and finely chopped
250 g (8 oz) packet suet mix
1 1/2 cups (345 g/11 oz) soft brown sugar
2 1/3 cups (375 g/12 oz) raisins, chopped
1 1/2 cups (240 g/8 oz) sultanas
1 1/2 cups (225 g/7 oz) currants
3/4 cup (140 g/5 oz) mixed peel
100 g (3 1/2 oz) slivered almonds, chopped
1 tablespoon mixed spice
1/2 teaspoon ground nutmeg
1/2 teaspoon ground cinnamon
2 teaspoons grated orange rind
1 teaspoon grated lemon rind
1 cup (250 ml/8 fl oz) orange juice
1/2 cup (125 ml/4 fl oz) lemon juice
150 ml (5 fl oz) brandy

### Pastry

800 g (1 lb 10 oz) plain flour
1 teaspoon caster sugar
400 g (13 oz) unsalted butter, chilled, chopped
4 eggs, lightly beaten
4 drops vanilla essence
1 egg white, lightly beaten, to glaze

1 Combine all the fruit mince ingredients with
1/2 cup (125 ml/4 fl oz) of the brandy in a large
bowl. Mix thoroughly. Spoon into sterilized,
warm jars. Use a skewer to remove air bubbles
and to pack the mixture in firmly. Leave a
1.5 cm (5/8 inch) space at the top of the jar and
wipe the jar clean with a cloth. Spoon a little
brandy over the surface of the mince and seal.
Label and date. Set aside for at least 3 weeks,
or up to 6 months, before using in pies and
tarts. Refrigerate the mince in hot weather.
2 For the pastry, in a large bowl, sift together
the flour, sugar and a large pinch of salt. Rub
the butter into the flour with your fingertips
until the mixture resembles fine breadcrumbs.
3 Make a well in the centre and pour in the
combined egg, vanilla and 2–3 teaspoons water.

4 Bring the mixture together with a flat-bladed
knife or pastry scraper to form a rough ball. If it
is slightly sticky, add a little more flour. Turn
out onto a lightly floured cool surface, gather
into a ball and flatten slightly. Wrap in plastic
wrap and chill for 20 minutes.
5 Separate one third of the pastry, re-wrap in
plastic and return to the fridge. Roll the remaining
pastry to 3 mm (1/8 inch) and cut out 48 rounds
using a 7 cm (2 3/4 inch) plain or fluted cutter.
6 Line four 12-hole, 7 cm (2 3/4 inch) diameter,
shallow tart tins. Fill each with 1 level tablespoon
fruit mince. Return to the fridge.
7 Preheat the oven to moderately hot 200°C
(400°F/Gas 6). Roll out the remaining pastry
and cut 48 round shapes for pastry lids using a
6 cm (2 1/2 inch) round cutter. Cut shapes out of
the centre of some of the tops if you wish.
Gather the scraps and re-roll. Place one on top
of each pie and refrigerate for 15 minutes.
8 Brush with egg white, dust with sugar if you
wish, and bake for 12–15 minutes.

*ABOVE: Traditional
mince tarts*

## YULE LOG

Beat the eggs and sugar until light and fluffy, using electric beaters.

Pour the sponge mixture into the prepared tin and spread evenly.

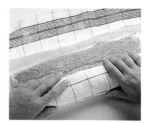

Roll the sponge up lengthways in a tea towel and leave until cool.

*ABOVE: Yule log*

# YULE LOG

**Preparation time:** 40 minutes
**Total cooking time:** 15 minutes
**Serves** 8

★ ★ ☆

1/2 cup (60 g/2 oz) plain flour
2 tablespoons cocoa powder
3 eggs
1/3 cup (90 g/3 oz) caster sugar
50 g (1 3/4 oz) unsalted butter, melted and cooled
1 tablespoon caster sugar, extra

**Filling**
125 g white chocolate, chopped
1/2 cup (125 ml/4 fl oz) cream
50 g (1 3/4 oz) hazelnuts, toasted and finely chopped

**Topping**
125 g (4 oz) dark chocolate, chopped
1/2 cup (125 ml/4 fl oz) cream, extra
icing sugar, to dust

**1** Preheat the oven to moderate 180°C (350°F/Gas 4). Brush a 30 x 35 cm (12 x 14 inch) swiss roll tin with oil or melted butter and line the base and sides with baking paper. Sift the flour and cocoa powder together twice. Using electric beaters, beat the eggs and sugar for 5 minutes, or until light and fluffy and increased in volume.
**2** Sift the flour over the eggs and pour the butter around the edge of the bowl. Using a large metal spoon, gently fold the mixture together to incorporate the flour and butter. Take care not to overmix and lose too much volume.
**3** Spread the mixture into the tin and bake for 12 minutes, or until the sponge springs back when lightly touched with your fingertips. Sprinkle the extra caster sugar over a clean tea towel. Turn the sponge out onto the tea towel

246

close to one end. Roll the sponge and tea towel together lengthways and leave to cool.

**4** For the filling, put the white chocolate in a small heatproof bowl. Bring a small pan of water to the boil, then remove from the heat. Add the cream to the chocolate and stand the bowl over the pan of water, making sure the base of the bowl does not touch the water, until the chocolate is soft. Stir until smooth. Repeat with the dark chocolate and cream for the topping. Leave the white chocolate mixture until it has cooled to room temperature and is the consistency of cream. Leave the dark chocolate mixture until it cools to a spreadable consistency.

**5** Beat the white chocolate mixture with electric beaters until soft peaks form—do not overbeat or the mixture will curdle. Unroll the sponge, remove the tea towel and spread with the filling, finishing 2 cm (³/₄ inch) from the end. Sprinkle with the hazelnuts. Re-roll the sponge and trim the ends. Cut off one end on the diagonal and place it alongside the log to create a branch.

**6** Place the yule log on a serving plate and spread the dark chocolate topping all over it. Run the tines of a fork along the length of the roll to give a 'bark' effect. Just before serving, dust with icing sugar. Decorate with some fresh green leaves.

## STAINED-GLASS WINDOW BISCUITS

**Preparation time:** 1 hour + 15 minutes refrigeration
**Total cooking time:** 10 minutes
**Makes** about 20

★ ★

150 g (5 oz) unsalted butter, cubed, softened
¹/₂ cup (60 g/3 oz) icing sugar
1 egg
1 teaspoon vanilla essence
¹/₃ cup (40 g/1 ¹/₄ oz) custard powder
2 cups (250 g/8 oz) plain flour
¹/₄ cup (30 g/1 oz) self-raising flour
200 g (6¹/₂ oz) assorted boiled lollies
beaten egg, to glaze

**1** Line two baking trays with baking paper. Beat the butter and icing sugar until light and creamy. Add the egg and vanilla and beat until fluffy, then beat in the custard powder. Fold in the combined sifted flours.

**2** Turn onto a lightly floured surface and knead until smooth. Roll between 2 sheets of baking paper to 3 mm (¹/₈ inch) thick. Refrigerate for 15 minutes, or until firm.

**3** Preheat the oven to moderately hot 200°C (400°F/Gas 6). Separate the lollies into their different colours and crush using a rolling pin. Cut out the dough with a 9.5 cm (3¹/₂ inch) fluted round cutter. Lay on the trays. Use small cutters to cut shapes from inside the circles.

**4** Glaze the biscuits with the beaten egg and bake for 5 minutes. Don't let the glaze drip into the cutout sections of the biscuits or the stained glass will be cloudy. Fill each cut-out section with a different-coloured lolly. Bake for 5–6 minutes, or until the lollies melt. Leave for 10 minutes, then cool on a wire rack.

*ABOVE: Stained-glass window biscuits*

# GINGERBREAD HOUSE

If you are feeling creative and like a challenge, delight your family with an attractive

gingerbread house that can be decorated as simply or intricately as you wish.

### MAKING THE MIXTURE

The first thing to do is to make the mixture. Place 250 g (8 oz) softened unsalted butter, 2/3 cup (155 g/5 oz) soft brown sugar and 1/2 cup (175 ml/6 fl oz) golden syrup in a bowl and beat until light and creamy. Gradually add 2 lightly beaten eggs, beating thoroughly after

each addition. Sift 5 cups (625 g/1 1/4 lb) plain flour, 2 tablespoons ground ginger and 2 teaspoons bicarbonate of soda into the bowl and stir until combined. Bring the dough together with your hands, turn it out onto a well-floured work surface, then knead until smooth. Cover with plastic wrap and refrigerate for 30 minutes.

### CUTTING THE SHAPES

Meanwhile, cut a paper pattern for each part of the house (when cutting the gingerbread you will need to cut two pieces of each paper pattern). The pattern for the sides should measure 10 x 20 cm (4 x 8 inches), the roof 15 x 20 cm (6 x 8 inches) and the front/back

16 x 20 cm (6½ x 8 inches). Measure 10 cm (4 inches) down from the centre of the front/back piece and draw a line across the rectangle. Turn the paper so the smaller rectangle is at the top, then draw a diagonal line from the centre of the top of the rectangle to each side, joining with the line already drawn across (this will give you a triangular end to the rectangle), then cut off the corners. Preheat the oven to moderate 180°C (350°F/Gas 4). Roll out the dough between two sheets of baking paper, in two batches if necessary, to 5 mm (¼ inch) thick. Using the paper templates as a guide, cut out two roof pieces, a front and back piece and two sides of the house. Cut 4 rectangular pieces for the chimney 5 x 4 cm (2 x 1½ inches), then

cut a wedge out of 2 of them so they will sit on the roof when joined together. If you would like windows or a door, cut these from the gingerbread. Line four baking trays with baking paper. Lift the pieces onto the trays, refrigerate for 20 minutes, then bake each tray for 12 minutes. Set aside to cool. For stained glass windows, crush assorted coloured boiled lollies and fill the cut-out windows about 5 minutes before the gingerbread is cooked. They will melt together.

## ICING AND ASSEMBLY

To make the icing, place 1 egg white in a bowl and gradually add about 2¼ cups (280 g/9 oz) sifted pure icing sugar until you have a smooth mixture which will stay in place when piped—if it is too

runny, add more icing sugar. To assemble the house, join the front and sides of the house together with a piped line of icing and leave to dry. Add the back to the house in the same way, hold for a few minutes, then stand up to dry. Decorate the outside seam with more piped icing to strengthen it. Join the chimney pieces together with a little icing. Attach the roof pieces and chimney using more piped icing. Leave everything to dry before decorating. Decorate the roof by attaching sweets with icing or piping decorations such as roof tiles or ivy onto the house.

**NOTE:** This quantity of mixture is also enough to make about 30 gingerbread people. Extra mixture can be made and cut into tree shapes to decorate the scene.

*ABOVE: Individual panettone*

## INDIVIDUAL PANETTONE

**Preparation time:** 30 minutes + 1 hour soaking
and 1 hour 40 minutes rising
**Total cooking time:** 35 minutes
**Makes 8**

★ ★

¹/₂ cup (95 g/3 oz) chopped dried apricots

¹/₂ cup (75 g/2¹/₂ oz) currants

¹/₂ cup (80 g/2³/₄ oz) sultanas

¹/₂ cup (125 ml/4 fl oz) Marsala

2 x 7 g (¹/₄ oz) sachets dried yeast
(see Note)

³/₄ cup (185 ml/6 fl oz) milk, warmed

¹/₂ cup (125 g/4 oz) caster sugar

180 g (6 oz) butter, softened

2 teaspoons vanilla essence

3 eggs

2 egg yolks

4 cups (500 g/1 lb) plain flour

1 teaspoon ground aniseed

**1** Combine the fruit and Marsala in a bowl, cover with plastic wrap and stand for 1 hour, or until most of the liquid is absorbed. Put the yeast, milk and 1 teaspoon of the sugar in a bowl and leave in a warm place for about 10 minutes, until foamy.

**2** Place the butter, vanilla and the remaining sugar in a bowl and beat with electric beaters until light and fluffy. Add the eggs and yolks one at a time, beating well after each addition.

**3** Sift the flour and aniseed into a bowl, make a well in the centre and add the yeast mixture, butter mixture and fruit mixture. Mix with a flat-bladed knife, until the mixture forms a soft, sticky dough. Cover and leave in a warm place for 40 minutes, or until the dough has doubled in size.

**4** Lightly oil the base and sides of eight ¹/₂ cup (125 ml/4 fl oz) soufflé dishes. Cut a strip of brown paper long enough to fit around the inside of each dish and tall enough to come 10 cm (4 inches) above the edge. Fold down a cuff about 2 cm (³/₄ inch) deep along the length of each strip. Make diagonal cuts up to the fold line on each strip, about 1 cm (¹/₂ inch) apart. Fit the strips around the inside of the dishes, pressing the cuts so they sit flat around the bottom edge of the dish. Cut circles of brown paper using the dish as a guide, place in the base of each dish, and grease the paper.

**5** Turn the dough out onto a floured surface and knead for 3 minutes, or until smooth. You will need more flour, up to ¹/₂ cup (60 g/2 oz), and the dough should be soft but not sticky. Divide into eight equal portions and press into the dishes. Cover with a tea towel and place in a warm place for an hour, or until doubled in size.

**6** Preheat the oven to moderately hot 200°C (400°F/Gas 6). Bake for 30–35 minutes, or until golden brown and cooked through when tested with a skewer. Remove from the soufflé dishes, leaving the paper attached. Dust with icing sugar, if desired. Serve warm or cold.

**NOTE:** If you are using fresh yeast, you will need double the amount of the dry yeast stated in the recipe.

This special cake from Milan can be made in various sizes. These individual ones are delightful to serve but if you prefer to make a large one and serve it in portions, you will find a recipe on page 272.

## SHORTBREAD BELLS

**Preparation time:** 30 minutes
+ 15 minutes refrigeration
**Total cooking time:** 25 minutes
**Makes** about 40

250 g (8 oz) butter, softened
1/2 cup (125 g/4 oz) caster sugar
2 cups (250 g/8 oz) plain flour
1/2 cup (90 g/3 oz) rice flour
1 egg white, lightly beaten
edible gold leaf (see Note)

**1** Line two baking trays with baking paper. Place the butter and sugar in a bowl and beat with electric beaters until light and creamy.
**2** Sift the flours into the butter mixture, and mix together with a flat-bladed knife to make a crumbly dough. Gather together and turn out onto a sheet of baking paper. Press together gently. Cover with another sheet of baking paper and roll out to 7 mm (1/4 inch) thick.
**3** Peel off the top sheet of baking paper and cut shapes from the dough using bell-shaped cutters of varying sizes. Cut as many as possible, then gently press the leftovers together, re-roll and cut out more. Lift onto the trays and refrigerate for 15 minutes. Preheat the oven to warm 160°C (315°F/Gas 2–3), then bake for 20–25 minutes, or until golden underneath. Cool on a wire rack.
**4** Lightly brush the top of some of the biscuits with egg white and lay a piece of gold leaf on top. Rub gently with your finger to transfer the gold leaf from the tissue paper to the biscuit. The gold leaf will give a decorative effect.
**NOTE:** Edible gold leaf is available from art supply shops and some cake-decorating shops.

## SCOTTISH SHORTBREAD

**Preparation time:** 15 minutes
**Total cooking time:** 35 minutes
**Makes** one 28 cm (11 inch) round

250 g (8 oz) butter, softened
2/3 cup (160 g/5 1/2 oz) caster sugar
1 2/3 cups (210 g/7 oz) plain flour
1/2 cup (90 g/3 oz) rice flour
1 teaspoon sugar, for sprinkling

**1** Preheat the oven to warm 160°C (315°F/Gas 2–3). Brush a 28 cm (11 inch) round pizza tray with melted butter or oil. Line with baking paper. Beat the butter and sugar with electric beaters in a small bowl until light and creamy. Transfer to a large bowl and add the sifted flours. Mix to a soft dough with a flat-bladed knife. Lift onto a lightly floured surface and knead for 30 seconds, or until smooth.
**2** Transfer to the pizza tray and press into a 25 cm (10 inch) round (the tray must be larger than the uncooked shortbread as the mixture will spread during cooking). Pinch and flute the edge decoratively with your fingers. Prick the surface lightly with a fork and mark into 16 segments with a sharp knife. Sprinkle with sugar and bake on the middle shelf for 35 minutes, or until firm and lightly golden. Cool on the tray.

*ABOVE: Shortbread bells*

# SWEETS, CHOCOLATES & GIFTS

For many reasons, it's such a good idea to make up a couple of batches of home-made goodies to give away as presents. It shows that you care enough about your family and friends to make something with your own hands, and it also gives you a reprieve when people unexpectedly turn up bearing gifts (as they inevitably do!). Best of all, you get to keep any leftovers if you find you 'accidentally' overcatered — something that can happen remarkably easily when temptations such as buttered brazil nuts and chocolate mallow fudge are on the 'to do' list!

## CHRISTMAS PRESENTS

It is believed the tradition of exchanging gifts at Christmas time began with the story of the Three Magi who offered the Christ child frankincense, gold and myrrh. Since then, giving has worked its way into many stories. St Nicholas and his friends were known for their charity. Gift-giving in their honour started in the thirteenth century when provincial French nuns gave presents to poor children on December 6, St Nicholas's feast day. In some places in Europe, presents are still given at this time. However, in most places, gifts are exchanged on either December 24 or 25.

*ABOVE: White Christmas*

## WHITE CHRISTMAS

**Preparation time:** 15 minutes
+ 30 minutes refrigeration
**Total cooking time:** 5 minutes
**Makes** 24

1½ cups (45 g/1½ oz) puffed rice cereal
1 cup (100 g/3½ oz) milk powder
1 cup (125 g/4 oz) icing sugar
1 cup (90 g/3 oz) desiccated coconut
⅓ cup (80 g/2¾ oz) chopped red glacé cherries
⅓ cup (80 g/2¾ oz) chopped green glacé cherries
⅓ cup (55 g/2 oz) sultanas
250 g (8 oz) white vegetable shortening (Copha)

**1** Line a shallow 28 x 18 cm (11 x 7 inch) tin with foil. Put the puffed rice, milk powder, icing sugar, coconut, glacé cherries and sultanas in a large bowl and stir. Make a well in the centre.
**2** Melt the shortening over low heat, cool slightly, then add to the well in the puffed rice mixture. Stir with a wooden spoon until all the ingredients are moistened.
**3** Spoon into the tin and smooth down the surface. Refrigerate for 30 minutes, or until completely set. Remove from the tin and discard the foil. Cut into small triangles to serve.

## BUTTERED BRAZIL NUTS

**Preparation time:** 20 minutes
**Total cooking time:** 30 minutes
**Makes** about 24

2 cups (500 ml/16 fl oz) sugar
2 tablespoons liquid glucose
125 g (4 oz) butter, chopped
1 tablespoon white vinegar
2 cups (310 g/11 oz) whole Brazil nuts

**1** Line two 32 x 28 cm (13 x 11 inch) baking trays with foil and brush the foil with melted butter or oil.

**2** Combine the sugar, liquid glucose, butter, vinegar and ½ cup (125 ml/4 fl oz) water in a medium, heavy-based saucepan. Stir over medium heat without boiling, until the butter has melted and the sugar has completely dissolved. Brush the sugar crystals from the sides of the pan with a wet pastry brush. Bring to the boil, then reduce the heat slightly and boil without stirring for 25 minutes, or until a teaspoon of the mixture dropped into cold water reaches small-crack stage (forming little sticky threads) or, if using a sugar thermometer, it must reach 138°C (275°F). Remove from the heat immediately.

**3** Put one nut at a time onto a wooden spoon and dip into the caramel mixture. Place on the tray to set. Put sheets of waxed paper between layers of the nuts and store in an airtight container at room temperature for up to 7 days.

NOTE: While Brazil nuts are traditionally used in this recipe, different types of nuts or a combination can be used. Use the quantity given (by weight). If using smaller nuts, dip a few at a time to form clusters.

## FLORENTINES

Preparation time: 25 minutes
Total cooking time: 7 minutes each batch
Makes 24

¼ cup (30 g/1 oz) plain flour
2 tablespoons chopped walnuts
2 tablespoons chopped flaked almonds
2 tablespoons finely chopped glacé cherries
2 tablespoons finely chopped mixed peel
75 g (2½ oz) unsalted butter, chopped
¼ cup (45 g/1½ oz) soft brown sugar
180 g (6 oz) dark chocolate, chopped

**1** Preheat the oven to moderate 180°C (350°F/Gas 4). Line a baking tray with baking paper.

**2** Sift the flour into a bowl. Add the walnuts, almonds, cherries and mixed peel. Stir, then make a well in the centre.

**3** Combine the butter and sugar in a small pan and stir over low heat until the butter has melted and the sugar has dissolved. Remove from the heat and add to the dry ingredients. Stir with a wooden spoon until just combined, being careful not to overbeat. Measure teaspoons of mixture at a time onto the tray, pushing off the spoon with a palette knife, and spreading with the palette knife. Leave about 7 cm (2¾ inches) between each one as they will spread. Press into neat 5 cm (2 inch) rounds. Bake for 5–7 minutes. Remove from the oven and while still soft, use a flat-bladed knife to push the biscuits into neat rounds. Cool on the tray for 5 minutes before transferring to a wire rack to cool thoroughly.

**4** Put the chocolate in a heatproof bowl. Bring a saucepan of water to the boil, then remove from the heat. Sit the bowl over the saucepan, making sure the bowl does not touch the water. Stir until the chocolate has melted. Carefully spread with a flat-bladed knife on the underside of the Florentines. Make a swirl pattern on the tops with a fork if you wish. Place the biscuits chocolate-side up on a wire rack, to set.

NOTE: Florentines can be made several days before required and stored in an airtight container. You can use white chocolate melts instead of dark chocolate.

*ABOVE: Florentines*

## SPICED TREACLE GINGERBREADS

Knead the dough on a lightly floured surface until smooth.

Cut out a hole from the top of each shape so a ribbon can be threaded through to use for hanging.

*ABOVE: Spiced treacle gingerbreads*

# SPICED TREACLE GINGERBREADS

**Preparation time:** 45 minutes + 25 minutes refrigeration
**Total cooking time:** 10 minutes per batch
**Makes** about 36

★ ★

140 g (4¹/₂ oz) unsalted butter, softened
¹/₂ cup (115 g/4 oz) dark brown sugar
¹/₄ cup (90 g/3 oz) treacle, preferably black
1 egg
2 cups (250 g/8 oz) plain flour
¹/₄ cup (30 g/1 oz) self-raising flour
3 teaspoons ground ginger
2 teaspoons ground cinnamon
³/₄ teaspoon ground cloves
³/₄ teaspoon ground nutmeg
1 teaspoon bicarbonate of soda

### Icing

1 egg white
¹/₂ teaspoon lemon juice
1 cup (125 g/4 oz) icing sugar, sifted
assorted food colourings

**1** Lightly grease two baking trays. Beat the butter and sugar in a bowl with electric beaters until light and creamy, then beat in the treacle and egg. Fold in the combined sifted flours, spices and bicarbonate of soda. Turn out onto a lightly floured surface and knead for 2–3 minutes, or until smooth. Cover with plastic wrap and chill for 10 minutes.
**2** Divide the dough in half and roll out between two sheets of baking paper to 4 mm (¹/₄ inch) thick. Lay on the trays and chill for 15 minutes until just firm. Preheat the oven to moderate 180°C (350°F/Gas 4).
**3** Cut out the dough using a 7 cm (2³/₄ inch) heart-shaped cutter (or whatever shapes you prefer). Using a sharp knife, cut out a 1 cm (¹/₂ inch) hole at the top of each shape (you can thread ribbon through these holes to hang up the biscuits). Place on the trays and bake for 10 minutes. Remove from the oven and leave on the trays for 5 minutes before transferring to a wire cake rack to cool. When the biscuits are cold, decorate with the icing.
**4** For the icing, whisk the egg white until foamy. Add the lemon juice and sugar and stir until glossy. Tint the icing any colour you want, then spoon into paper piping bags or a small plastic bag, seal the end and snip off the tip. When decorated, leave the icing to set.

# ROCKY ROAD

**Preparation time:** 20 minutes + several
hours refrigeration
**Total cooking time:** 5 minutes
**Makes** about 30 pieces

250 g (8 oz) pink and white marshmallows,
halved
1 cup (160 g/5½ oz) unsalted peanuts,
roughly chopped
½ cup (105 g/3½ oz) glacé cherries,
halved
1 cup (60 g/2 oz) shredded coconut
350 g (11 oz) dark chocolate, chopped

**1** Line the base and two opposite sides of a
shallow 20 cm (8 inch) square cake tin with foil.
**2** Put all the marshmallows, peanuts, cherries
and coconut into a large bowl and mix until
well combined.
**3** Put the chocolate in a heatproof bowl. Half
fill a saucepan with water and bring to the boil.
Remove from the heat and place the bowl over
the pan, making sure it is not touching the
water. Stir occasionally until the chocolate
is melted.
**4** Add the chocolate to the marshmallow
mixture and toss until well combined. Spoon
into the cake tin and press evenly over the base.
Refrigerate for several hours, or until set.
Carefully lift out of the tin, then peel away
the foil and cut the rocky road into small
pieces. Store in an airtight container in
the refrigerator.

# CHOCOLATE MALLOW FUDGE

**Preparation time:** 20 minutes
+ overnight refrigeration
**Total cooking time:** 10 minutes
**Makes** about 40 pieces

70 g (2¼ oz) butter, chopped
150 g (5 oz) dark chocolate,
chopped
250 g (8 oz) white marshmallows
1 teaspoon vanilla essence
50 g (1¾ oz) milk chocolate, melted

**1** Line the base and two long sides of an
8 x 26 cm (3 x 10½ inch) bar tin with foil.
**2** Put the chopped butter, dark chocolate
and white marshmallows in a saucepan.
Stir constantly over low heat until the
chocolate and marshmallows are melted.
Remove the saucepan from the heat and
stir in the vanilla essence.
**3** Pour the mixture into the tin and refrigerate
for several hours, or overnight, until firm.
Remove the fudge from the tin and remove
the foil. Cut into 2 cm (¾ inch) slices, then
cut each slice into 3 pieces. Drizzle the fudge
with the melted milk chocolate, then set aside
until set.

*ABOVE: Rocky road (top);
Chocolate mallow fudge*

## WHITE CHOCOLATE LEMON TRUFFLES

**Preparation time:** 25 minutes
  + 4 hours refrigeration
**Total cooking time:** 2 minutes
**Makes** about 40

1/4 cup (60 ml/2 fl oz) cream
250 g (8 oz) white chocolate melts, chopped
1 tablespoon finely grated lemon rind
2 teaspoons lemon juice
1/2 cup (45 g/1 1/2 oz) desiccated coconut
3/4 cup (45 g/1 1/2 oz) toasted shredded
  coconut

**1** Heat the cream and white chocolate melts in a saucepan over low heat until the chocolate has just melted. Remove the pan from the heat and stir in the lemon rind, lemon juice and desiccated coconut. Leave to cool, then refrigerate for 1 1/2–2 hours, until firm.
**2** Place teaspoons of the mixture on a foil-lined tray and refrigerate for 2 hours, or until very firm. Roll into balls, then coat with toasted shredded coconut. Keep refrigerated until ready to serve.

## RUM TRUFFLES

**Preparation time:** 20 minutes
  + 50 minutes refrigeration
**Total cooking time:** 1 minute
**Makes** about 25

200 g (6 1/2 oz) dark cooking chocolate,
  finely chopped
1/4 cup (60 ml/2 fl oz) cream
30 g (1 oz) butter
1/2 cup (50 g/1 3/4 oz) chocolate cake crumbs
2 teaspoons dark rum, brandy or whisky
1/2 cup (95 g/3 oz) chocolate sprinkles

**1** Line a baking tray with foil. Put the chocolate in a heatproof bowl. Combine the cream and butter in a small pan and stir over low heat until the butter melts and the mixture is just boiling. Pour the hot cream mixture over the chocolate and stir until the chocolate melts and the mixture is smooth.

**2** Stir in the cake crumbs and rum. Refrigerate for 20 minutes, stirring occasionally, or until firm enough to handle. Roll heaped teaspoons of the mixture into balls.
**3** Spread the chocolate sprinkles on a sheet of greaseproof paper. Roll each truffle in sprinkles, then place on the baking tray. Refrigerate for 30 minutes, or until firm. Serve in small paper patty cups, if desired.
**NOTE:** Truffles can also be rolled in dark cocoa powder. They can be made up to a week in advance and refrigerated in an airtight container.

## MINI FRUIT TRUFFLE PUDDINGS

**Preparation time:** 40 minutes
**Total cooking time:** Nil
**Makes** about 44

500 g (1 lb) fruit cake
2 tablespoons desiccated coconut
1/3 cup (80 ml/2 3/4 fl oz) dark rum
1/3 cup (30 g/1 oz) flaked almonds, toasted
  and crushed
400 g (13 oz) dark chocolate buttons, melted
2 teaspoons oil
150 g (5 oz) white chocolate, melted
1 stick of angelica (see Note), chopped
8 red glacé cherries, chopped

**1** Finely chop the fruit cake in a food processor. Combine in a bowl with the coconut, rum, almonds and 150 g (5 oz) of the melted dark chocolate buttons and mix thoroughly. Roll two teaspoons of the mixture at a time into balls and place on a baking tray covered with baking paper.
**2** Place the remaining melted dark chocolate buttons and oil in a small bowl and stir well. Sit each truffle on a fork and dip in the chocolate to coat. Carefully remove, allowing any excess to drain away. Place back on the paper and leave to set. Do not refrigerate.
**3** When the chocolate is set, spoon the white chocolate into a small piping bag or a small plastic bag, snip off the end of the bag and drizzle chocolate on top of each pudding and down the sides (to look like custard). Before the chocolate sets, decorate with small pieces of angelica and cherry.
**NOTE:** Angelica, sold in health-food stores, is candied stems or leaf ribs of a parsley-like plant.

**CHRISTMAS STOCKINGS**
In 300 AD a young bishop in Asia Minor became famous for his kindness. Later known as Saint Nicholas, the kind bishop often distributed gifts but didn't wait for thanks. According to one of many legends, one night he climbed onto a rooftop and dropped a gift down the chimney. The gift fell into a stocking that had been hung to dry. After this, children began leaving things such as shoes or stockings to be filled with goodies on Christmas Eve.

*OPPOSITE PAGE, CLOCKWISE FROM LEFT: White chocolate lemon truffles; Rum truffles; Mini fruit truffle puddings*

## CHRISTMAS TREE

Having a real Christmas tree in the house engages not only our senses of sight, touch and smell but also our sense of hope, goodwill and tradition. Like so many Christmas traditions, there are conflicting theories about the origins. One legend states that in the eighth century an English missionary was travelling in Germany when he came upon an oak tree where a human sacrifice was to take place. He stopped the sacrifice and chopped down the oak. In its place a fir tree grew and the missionary took this as a sign that Christianity would replace paganism and dedicated the tree to the Holy Infant.

*ABOVE: Creamy coconut ice*

## CREAMY COCONUT ICE

**Preparation time:** 20 minutes
 + 2 hours refrigeration
**Total cooking time:** Nil
**Makes** 30 pieces

★★

2 cups (250 g (8 oz) icing sugar
¼ teaspoon cream of tartar
400 g (13 oz) can condensed milk
3½ cups (315 g/10 oz) desiccated coconut
2–3 drops pink food colouring

1 Grease a 20 cm (8 inch) square cake tin and line the base with baking paper.
2 Sift the icing sugar and cream of tartar into a bowl. Make a well and add the condensed milk. Using a wooden spoon, stir in half the coconut, then the remaining coconut. Mix well with your hands. Divide in half and tint one half pink. Using your hand, knead the colour through evenly.
3 Press the pink mixture over the base of the tin, cover with the white mixture and press down firmly. Refrigerate for 1–2 hours, or until firm. Remove from the tin, remove the paper and cut into pieces. Store in an airtight container in a cool place for up to 3 weeks.

## CHOCOLATE CLUSTERS

**Preparation time:** 25 minutes + setting
**Total cooking time:** 10 minutes
**Makes** about 40

★

155 g (5 oz) dark chocolate melts
155 g (5 oz) white chocolate melts
⅔ cup (125 g/4 oz) dried mixed fruit
125 g (4 oz) glacé ginger, chopped

1 Put 125 g (4 oz) of the dark chocolate melts in a heatproof bowl. Half fill a pan with water and bring it to the boil. Remove from the heat and place the bowl over the pan, making sure it is not touching the water. Stir until melted. Allow to cool slightly. Repeat with 125 g (4 oz) of the white chocolate melts.
2 Stir the mixed fruit into the cooled dark chocolate. Combine the ginger with the cooled white chocolate.
3 Drop spoonfuls of the mixtures separately onto foil-lined trays, and leave to set at room temperature. Melt the remaining chocolate separately and drizzle over the tops.

# HARD CARAMELS

**Preparation time:** 25 minutes + setting
**Total cooking time:** 15 minutes
**Makes** 49

1 cup (250 g/8 oz) sugar
90 g (3 oz) butter
2 tablespoons golden syrup
1/3 cup (80 ml/2³/4 fl oz) liquid glucose
1/2 cup (90 ml/3 fl oz) canned condensed milk
250 g (8 oz) dark chocolate, chopped

**1** Grease the base and sides of a 20 cm (8 inch) square cake tin, then line with baking paper and grease the paper. Combine the sugar, butter, golden syrup, liquid glucose and condensed milk in a heavy-based saucepan. Stir over medium heat without boiling until the butter has melted and the sugar has dissolved completely. Brush the sugar crystals from the sides of the saucepan with a wet pastry brush.

**2** Bring to the boil, reduce the heat slightly and boil, stirring, for about 10–15 minutes, or until a teaspoon of mixture dropped into cold water reaches hard ball stage (forming a firm ball that holds its shape). If using a sugar thermometer, the mixture must reach 122°C (250°F). Remove from the heat immediately. Pour into the tin and leave to cool. While the caramel is still warm, mark into 49 squares with an oiled knife. When cold, cut through completely into squares.

**3** Line two baking trays with foil. Place the chocolate in a small heatproof bowl. Bring a saucepan of water to the boil, then remove the saucepan from the heat. Sit the bowl over the saucepan, making sure the bowl doesn't touch the water. Stir until the chocolate has melted. Remove from the heat and cool slightly. Using two forks, dip the caramels one at a time into the chocolate to coat. Lift out, drain the excess chocolate, then place on the trays and leave to set.

**NOTE:** Store hard caramels in an airtight container in a cool, dark place for up to 4 weeks.

## COMPOUND CHOCOLATE

Compound chocolate melts, buttons and drops contain vegetable fat instead of cocoa butter. They are ideal for cooking and decorations because they have a lovely shiny surface when moulded and dipped and they set well.

*LEFT: Hard caramels*

*ABOVE: Crackle cookies*

# CRACKLE COOKIES

**Preparation time:** 20 minutes + 3 hours refrigeration
**Total cooking time:** 25 minutes per batch
**Makes** about 60

125 g (4 oz) unsalted butter, softened

2 cups (370 g/12 oz) soft brown sugar

1 teaspoon vanilla essence

2 eggs

60 g (2 oz) dark chocolate, melted

1/3 cup (80 ml/2¾ fl oz) milk

2¾ cups (340 g/11 oz) plain flour

2 tablespoons cocoa powder

2 teaspoons baking powder

1/4 teaspoon ground allspice

2/3 cup (85 g/3 oz) chopped pecans

icing sugar, to coat

**1** Lightly grease two baking trays. Beat the butter, sugar and vanilla until light and creamy. Beat in the eggs, one at a time. Stir the chocolate and milk into the butter mixture.

**2** Sift the flour, cocoa, baking powder, allspice and a pinch of salt into the butter mixture and mix well. Stir the pecans through. Refrigerate for at least 3 hours, or overnight.

**3** Preheat the oven to moderate 180°C (350°F/Gas 4). Roll tablespoons of the mixture into balls and roll each in sifted icing sugar to coat.

**4** Place well apart on the trays to allow for spreading. Bake for 20–25 minutes, or until lightly browned and just firm. Leave on the trays for 3–4 minutes, then cool on a wire rack.

## SWEET PUFF PASTRY TWISTS

Preheat the oven to moderately hot 200°C (400°F/Gas 6). Stir 1 teaspoon cinnamon through 2 tablespoons caster sugar. Brush 2 sheets puff pastry with milk and sprinkle the cinnamon sugar over the pastry. Cut the pastry into 2 cm (¾ inch) strips. Hold the ends of each strip and twist four times. Cover a baking tray with paper and bake a quarter of the strips for 5 minutes, or until golden, turning once. Repeat with the remaining twists. Makes 24.

## GINGER PECAN BISCOTTI

**Preparation time:** 30 minutes + cooling
**Total cooking time:** 1 hour 20 minutes
**Makes** about 20

1 cup (100 g/3¹/₂ oz) pecans
2 eggs
²/₃ cup (155 g/5 oz) soft brown sugar
1 cup (125 g/4 oz) self-raising flour
³/₄ cup (90 g/3 oz) plain flour
100 g (3¹/₂ oz) glacé ginger, finely chopped

**1** Preheat the oven to warm 160°C (315°F/ Gas 2–3). Spread the pecans on a baking tray and bake for 10–12 minutes, or until fragrant. Tip onto a chopping board to cool, then roughly chop. Cover the baking tray with baking paper.
**2** Put the eggs and sugar in a bowl and beat with electric beaters until pale and creamy. Sift the flours into the bowl and add the nuts and ginger. Mix to a soft dough, then place on the tray and shape into a 9 x 23 cm (3¹/₂ x 9 inch) loaf.
**3** Bake for 45 minutes, or until lightly golden. Transfer to a wire rack to cool for about 20 minutes, then carefully cut into 1 cm (¹/₂ inch) slices with a large serrated bread knife. It will be crumbly on the edges, so work slowly and, if possible, try to hold the sides as you cut. Arrange the slices on baking trays and bake again for about 10 minutes each side. Don't worry if they don't seem fully dry as they will become crisp on cooling. Cool completely before storing in an airtight container.

## CARDAMOM LIME CRESCENTS

**Preparation time:** 40 minutes
**Total cooking time:** 20 minutes per batch
**Makes** 30

¹/₂ cup (60 g/2 oz) slivered almonds
250 g (8 oz) butter, softened
¹/₄ cup (30 g/1 oz) icing sugar, sifted
2 tablespoons brandy
1 teaspoon finely grated lime rind
2¹/₂ cups (310 g/10 oz) plain flour
1 teaspoon ground cardamom
4 cups (500 g/1 lb) icing sugar, to dust

**1** Preheat the oven to moderate 180°C (350°F/ Gas 4). Line two baking trays with baking paper. Put the almonds on another baking tray and bake for 5 minutes, or until lightly golden. Allow to cool, then finely chop.
**2** Beat the butter and sugar in a bowl until light and creamy. Gently mix in the brandy, lime rind and almonds.
**3** Sift the combined flour and cardamom onto a sheet of baking paper and gradually fold into the butter mixture to form a soft dough.
**4** Shape level tablespoons of mixture into small crescents and place on the lined baking trays. Bake for 15–20 minutes, or until lightly golden. Place the trays on a wire rack and allow the biscuits to cool. To serve, sift a heavy coating of icing sugar over the biscuits to cover them completely. If storing the biscuits, place in a tin or plastic box and cover entirely with the remaining sifted icing sugar.

*ABOVE: Ginger pecan biscotti*

# LIQUEUR FRUITS

These liqueur-infused fruits are luscious with cream or ice cream, waffles or crepes.

They are also great with brioche or panettone spread with ricotta or mascarpone.

### PEARS IN MULLED WINE

Put 2 cups (500 g/1 lb) sugar and 3 cups (750 ml/24 fl oz) red wine in a large pan. Stir over low heat until the sugar has dissolved. Add 1.25 kg (2½ lb) peeled, halved and cored small pears, 1 cinnamon stick, 6 cloves, 6 whole allspice and 2 strips each of orange and lemon rind. Cover with a plate to keep the pears submerged. Bring to the boil (at least 90°C), then reduce the heat and simmer for 10 minutes. Arrange the pears in a heatproof, warm, sterilized 1 litre (32 fl oz) jar. Boil the syrup for 15 minutes, then mix ½ cup (125 ml/ 4 fl oz) syrup with ½ cup (125 ml/ 4 fl oz) brandy and 3 cloves. Pour over the pears to cover, seal and invert for 2 minutes. Store in a cool, dark place for up to a month before using. Refrigerate after opening. Fills a 1 litre (32 fl oz) jar.

### DRUNKEN PRUNES

Put 750 g (1½ lb) pitted prunes in a heatproof, warm sterilized 1 litre (32 fl oz) jar. Cut a vanilla bean in half lengthways and add to the jar. Add 2 cups (500 ml/16 fl oz) tawny port to cover the prunes, seal and invert for 2 minutes. Leave for at least 1 month before using. Store for up to 6 months. Refrigerate after opening. Fills a 1 litre (32 fl oz) jar.

## CLEMENTINES OR CUMQUATS IN LIQUEUR

Cut a cross in the tops of 500 g (1 lb) cumquats or clementines and pack into heatproof, warm sterilized jars. Place 1 cup (250 g/8 oz) sugar and ¾ cup (185 ml/6 fl oz) water in a saucepan and boil for 1 minute. Stir in ¼ cup (60 ml/2 fl oz) orange liqueur, then pour over the fruit. Screw on the lids loosely—do not tighten. Place layers of cloth on the base of a deep, heavy-based saucepan. Put the jars on top and cover with hot water to reach the shoulders of the jars. Bring the water slowly to simmering point, then reduce the heat and simmer for 20 minutes, or until the fruit starts to look clear. Remove the jars. Immediately tighten the lids fully with a tea towel. Cool, label and date. Store in a cool, dark place for 2 months before using, turning the jars upside-down every 2 weeks.

Will keep for 6 months. Refrigerate after opening. Fills a 750 ml (24 fl oz) jar.

## PEACHES IN SPICED SAUTERNES

Cut 4–6 kg (8–12 lb) ripe freestone peaches in half, discard the stones and pack the peaches, with 1 cinnamon stick and 1 star anise into a heatproof, warm sterilized 2 litre (64 fl oz) jar. Place 2 cups (500 g/1 lb) sugar in a large saucepan, add 2 cups (500 ml/16 fl oz) water and stir over low heat until all the sugar has dissolved. Bring to the boil (at least 90°C) and boil for 5 minutes, then pour the hot syrup over the peaches and top with 1 cup (250 ml/4 fl oz) Sauternes. Following the cumquat instructions, simmer in the jar for 10 minutes, or until the peach syrup reaches 90° (check with a thermometer). Keep in a cool, dark place for at least 2 weeks before using. Will keep for

6 months. Refrigerate after opening. Fills a 2 litre (64 fl oz) jar.

## CHERRIES IN VANILLA BRANDY

Prick the skins of 750 g (1½ lb) cherries with a fine skewer. Heat 1½ cups (375 g/ 12 oz) sugar with ½ cup (125 ml/4 fl oz) each of brandy and water in a pan, stirring until all the sugar has dissolved. Add the cherries and a vanilla bean and heat until boiling (90°C). Place the cherries and syrup in a heatproof, warm, sterilized jar, seal while hot and invert for 2 minutes. Store in a cool place for 6 weeks, turning every couple of days for the first 2 weeks. Serve the cherries in the liqueur. Refrigerate after opening. Fills a 1 litre (32 fl oz) jar.

*FROM LEFT: Pears in mulled wine; Drunken prunes; Clementines in liqueur; Peaches in spiced Sauternes; Cherries in vanilla brandy*

*ABOVE: Pineapple and mango jam*

juice, and sugar in a large heavy-based saucepan. Stir over low heat until all the sugar has completely dissolved.

**2** Bring to the boil, then reduce the heat and simmer, stirring often to prevent from sticking to the pan, for 30–40 minutes, or until setting point is reached. Remove any scum during cooking with a skimmer or slotted spoon. Stir across the base of the pan to check that the jam is not sticking or burning. Be careful, the jam will froth. When the jam falls from a tilted wooden spoon in thick sheets without dripping, start testing for setting point.

**3** Remove the pan from the heat and test for setting point by placing a little jam on one of the cold plates and allow to cool. A skin will form on the surface and the jam will wrinkle when pushed with your finger when setting point is reached. Remove any scum from the surface.

**4** Pour immediately into clean, warm jars (see Note on next recipe) and seal. Turn upside-down for 2 minutes, then invert and cool. Label and date. Store for 6–12 months in a cool, dark place. Refrigerate after opening for up to 6 weeks.

**NOTE:** To warm the sugar, place it in a deep-sided baking tray in a slow (150°C/300°F/Gas 2) oven for 10–15 minutes, stirring occasionally, or until it is warmed through.

## PINEAPPLE AND MANGO JAM

**Preparation time:** 30 minutes
**Total cooking time:** 45 minutes
**Makes** 1 litre (32 fl oz)

★ ★

1 ripe pineapple
2 large mangoes
1 teaspoon grated lemon rind
1/3 cup (80 ml/2 3/4 fl oz) lemon juice
1.2 kg (2 lb 6 1/2 oz) sugar, warmed (see Note)

**1** Place two small plates in the freezer. Discard the skin and the tough eyes from the pineapple. Cut into quarters lengthways, remove the core and cut the flesh into 1 cm (1/2 inch) pieces. Peel the mangoes and cut each mango cheek from the stone. Cut into 1 cm (1/2 inch) pieces. Put the pineapple, mango, any juices, lemon rind and

## APRICOT AND GINGER JAM

**Preparation time:** 15 minutes + overnight standing
**Total cooking time:** 1 hour
**Makes** 1 litre (32 fl oz)

★ ★

500 g (1 lb) dried apricots
200 g (6 1/2 oz) preserved ginger in syrup, drained and thinly sliced
3 3/4 cups (935 g/1 lb 14 1/2 oz) sugar, warmed (see Note)
2 tablespoons lemon juice
1/2 cup (60 g/2 oz) slivered almonds

**1** Place two small plates in the freezer. Place the apricots in a large bowl, cover with 1.25 litres (40 fl oz) water and soak overnight.

**2** Transfer the apricots and water to a large heavy-based saucepan. Bring to the boil, reduce the heat and simmer, covered, for 15 minutes, or until the apricots are tender.

**3** Add the ginger, sugar, and juice to the saucepan. Stir constantly over low heat until

the sugar has dissolved. Bring to the boil, reduce the heat slightly and boil, uncovered, for 25–30 minutes, or until setting point is reached. Remove any scum during cooking with a slotted spoon. Stir across the base of the pan occasionally to check the jam is not sticking. Be careful as the jam will froth. When the jam falls from a tilted wooden spoon in thick sheets without dripping, start testing for setting point. Remove the pan from the heat and test by placing a little of the jam on a cold plate and allow to cool. A skin will form on the surface and the jam will wrinkle when pushed with your finger. Remove any scum from the surface. Leave the jam for 2 minutes.

**4** Stir the almonds into the jam. Spoon into clean, warm jars (see Note) and seal. Turn upside-down for 2 minutes, then invert and cool. Label and date the jars.

**NOTE:** To warm the sugar, place it in a deep-sided baking tray in a slow (150°C (300°F/Gas 2) oven for about 10–15 minutes, stirring occasionally, until it is warmed through.

To ensure clean jars, preheat the oven to very slow 120°C (250°F/Gas ½). Wash the jars and lids in hot, soapy water and rinse well with boiling water. Put the jars on baking trays and place in the oven for 20 minutes, or until you are ready to use them. Dry fully in the oven.

## PASSIONFRUIT CURD

**Preparation time:** 15 minutes
**Total cooking time:** 20 minutes
**Makes** 3 cups (750 ml/24 fl oz)

4 eggs
3/4 cup (185 g/6 oz) caster sugar
1/3 cup (80 ml/2 3/4 fl oz) lemon juice
3 teaspoons finely grated lemon rind
1/2 cup (125 g/4 oz) passionfruit pulp
200 g (6 1/2 oz) unsalted butter, chopped

**1** Beat the eggs well, then strain into a heatproof bowl, and stir in the sugar, lemon juice, lemon rind, passionfruit pulp and butter. Place the bowl over a saucepan of simmering water and stir constantly with a wooden spoon over low heat for about 15–20 minutes, or until the butter has melted and the mixture thickly coats the back of the wooden spoon.

**2** Transfer the curd to a clean heatproof jug and pour into clean, warm jars (see Note on previous recipe). Seal while hot. Turn the jars upside-down for 2 minutes, invert and cool, then refrigerate. Refrigerate for up to 1 month.

**PASSIONFRUIT**
There are 350 members of the *Passiflora* species but only three of them are commonly available. Banana passionfruit have a long yellow fruit with a less acidic fruit and juice. Common passionfruit have deep-purple skin, a red pith and a much more orangey fruit with small black seeds. Yellow passionfruit have a much smoother skin and a yellower colour, but have a less intense flavour. When a recipe calls for passionfruit, it usually refers to the purple passionfruit. The pulp is scooped out for eating or using in desserts. For some recipes, the pulp is pushed through a sieve and the seeds discarded.

*ABOVE: Passionfruit curd*

267

# OILS & VINEGARS

Great for gifts, most oils and vinegars will keep for up to 6 months if you sterilize

the storage jars by washing, rinsing with boiling water and drying in a warm oven.

### RASPBERRY VINEGAR

Place 2¹/₃ cups (290 g/10 oz) fresh or thawed frozen raspberries in a non-metallic bowl and crush gently with the back of a spoon. Warm 2 cups (500 ml/16 fl oz) white wine vinegar in a saucepan over low heat. Add the vinegar to the raspberries and mix well. Pour into a 2 cup (500 ml/16 fl oz) sterilized glass bottle and leave in a warm place for about 2 weeks, shaking regularly. Strain through a muslin-lined sieve into a small pan. Add 2 teapoons caster sugar and stir over medium heat until dissolved. Pour into the clean, warm sterilized bottle. Add 2–3 raspberries, if desired, then seal, label and date. Store in a cool, dark place. Makes 2 cups (500 ml/16 fl oz).

### TARRAGON VINEGAR

Warm 2 cups (500 ml/16 fl oz) white wine vinegar in a saucepan over low heat. Gently bruise 25 g (³/₄ oz) fresh tarragon leaves in your hands and put into a 2 cup (500 ml/16 fl oz) sterilized glass bottle. Pour in the vinegar, seal with a non-metallic lid and shake well. Leave to infuse in a warm place for about 2 weeks. Strain and return to the clean, warm sterilized bottle. Add a fresh sprig of tarragon, then seal, label and date. Store in a cool, dark place. Makes 2 cups (500 ml/16 fl oz).

## CHILLI OIL

Place 6 dried chillies and 1 teaspoon chilli powder in a heavy-based saucepan. Add 3 cups (750 ml/24 fl oz) olive oil and stir over medium heat for 5 minutes (if it gets too hot the oil will change flavour). Remove from the heat. Cover with plastic wrap and leave in a cool, dark place for 3 days. Strain into a 3 cup (750 ml/24 fl oz) sterilized bottle. Discard the chillies and add new chillies. Seal, label and date, then store in a cool, dark place. Makes 3 cups (750 ml/24 fl oz).

## SPICED MALT VINEGAR

Pour 2 cups (500 ml/16 fl oz) malt vinegar into a saucepan. Add a 1 cm (1/2 inch) piece fresh ginger, quartered, 10 whole cloves, 1 cinnamon stick, 2 teaspoons allspice berries, 1/2 teaspoon black peppercorns, 1 teaspoon brown mustard seeds and warm over low heat.

Pour into a warm, sterilized 2 cup (500 ml/16 fl oz) glass bottle and seal with a non-metallic lid. Leave in a warm place for 2 weeks. Strain the vinegar and return to the clean, warm bottle with some black peppercorns. Seal, label and date, then store in a cool, dark place. Makes 2 cups (500 ml/16 fl oz).

## PARMESAN OIL

Combine 2 cups (500 ml/16 fl oz) olive oil and 100 g (3 1/2 oz) finely grated Reggiano Parmesan in a small pan. Stir the oil mixture over low heat for 10–15 minutes, or until the Parmesan starts to melt and clump together. Remove from the heat and allow to cool. Strain into a sterilized 2 cup (500 ml/16 fl oz) bottle and add 20 g (3/4 oz) shaved Parmesan. Seal, label and date, then store in a cool, dark place. Makes 2 cups (500 ml/16 fl oz).

## SPICED APPLE AND CINNAMON VINEGAR

Combine 2 cups (500 ml/16 fl oz) white wine vinegar, 1/3 cup (30 g/1 oz) finely chopped dried apple slices, 1/4 teaspoon black peppercorns, 2 bay leaves, 1/4 teaspoon yellow mustard seeds, 2 cinnamon sticks, 2 sprigs fresh thyme or a sprig of fresh tarragon and 1 peeled garlic clove in a sterilized 2 cup (500 ml/16 fl oz) bottle. Seal and leave in a cool, dark place for 2 weeks. Strain the vinegar and return to the warm sterilized bottle. Seal, label and date, then store in a cool, dark place. Makes 2 cups (500 ml/16 fl oz).

*FROM LEFT: Raspberry vinegar (2); Tarragon vinegar (2); Chilli oil; Spiced malt vinegar; Parmesan oil (2); Spiced apple and cinnamon vinegar (with tarragon); Spiced apple and cinnamon vinegar (with thyme)*

glædelig

✝ Joyeux N

Fröhliche Weihna

Merry Christ

Buon Nat

# AROUND THE WORLD

One of the best things about Christmas is knowing that a wonderful feeling of goodwill is being shared all over the world. Of course, every country has its own Christmas traditions but the essence of this celebration is the same: togetherness. And eating! In Italy people enjoy freshly baked panettone and the marvellously dense panforte, in Scotland they tuck into Dundee cake and Scottish black bun and in Russia, cranberry kissel and nesselrode are devoured enthusiastically. At this magical time of year, the world is united in savouring the delicious cooking smells wafting from the family kitchen.

PANETTONE

The yeast mixture is ready when it is foamy. If it doesn't foam, it is dead and you will have to start again.

Knead the dough on a lightly floured surface until smooth and elastic.

Spread half the fruit mixture over the flattened dough and fold over the edges to cover the fruit.

Put the dough in the tin, brush with melted butter, then cut a slash in the shape of a cross on the top.

*ABOVE: Panettone*

## PANETTONE (ITALIAN)

**Preparation time:** 30 minutes
  + 4 hours rising
**Total cooking time:** 50 minutes
**Makes** 1

★ ★ ★

1/2 cup (90 g/3 oz) candied mixed peel
1/2 cup (80 g/2³/4 oz) sultanas
1 teaspoon grated lemon rind
1 teaspoon grated orange rind
1 tablespoon brandy or rum
7 g (1/4 oz) sachet dried yeast
220 ml (7 fl oz) warm milk
1/4 cup (60 g/2 oz) caster sugar
3¹/4 cups (400 g/13 oz) white bread flour
2 eggs
1 teaspoon vanilla essence
150 g (5 oz) unsalted butter, softened
20 g (1/2 oz) unsalted butter, melted, to glaze

**1** Put the peel, sultanas and grated rind in a small bowl. Add the alcohol, mix well and set aside.
**2** Put the yeast, warm milk and 1 teaspoon sugar in a small bowl and leave in a warm place for 10–15 minutes, or until foamy. Sift 200 g (6¹/2 oz) flour and 1/2 teaspoon salt into a large bowl, make a well in the centre and add the yeast mixture. Mix together with a large metal spoon to form a soft dough. Cover the bowl and leave to 'sponge' and rise in a warm place for 45 minutes, or until frothy and risen.
**3** Add the eggs, remaining sugar and vanilla and mix. Add the butter and stir until well combined. Stir in the remaining flour and mix well. Knead well on a floured surface until the dough is smooth and elastic. You may need to add up to 1/2 cup (60 g/2 oz) flour to the dough as you knead. Place the dough in a lightly greased bowl, cover with plastic wrap and leave in a warm place for 1¹/2–2 hours, or until doubled.
**4** Lightly grease a 15 cm (6 inch) round cake tin and line the base and side with a double thickness of baking paper, ensuring the collar extends above the rim of the tin by 10 cm (4 inches).

**5** Knock back the dough and turn out onto a floured work surface. Roll into a 30 x 20 cm (12 x 8 inch) rectangle. Drain the fruit mixture and spread half the fruit over the surface of the dough. Fold over the short edges like an envelope to cover the fruit. Roll again and repeat the process to incorporate all the fruit. Gently knead the dough for 2–3 minutes and shape into a neat ball. Place in the tin, brush with the melted butter, then slash a cross on the top with a sharp knife and leave to rise again in a warm place for 45 minutes, or until doubled in size.

**6** Preheat the oven to moderately hot 190°C (375°F/Gas 5). Bake for 50 minutes, or until golden brown and a skewer inserted into the centre comes out clean. Leave in the tin for 5 minutes, then transfer to a wire rack to cool.

**NOTE:** This yeast cake is a speciality of Milan but is enjoyed throughout Italy at festive times such as Christmas and Easter. It can be made in all different sizes, ranging from an individual cake (see page 250) to a large one.

## CERTOSINO (ITALIAN)

**Preparation time:** 30 minutes
**Total cooking time:** 1 hour 30 minutes
**Makes** 1

★★

3 cups (375 g/12 oz) plain flour

1 teaspoon ground cinnamon

1/2 teaspoon ground nutmeg

1 1/2 teaspoons bicarbonate of soda

100 g (3 1/2 oz) unsalted butter

1 cup (350 g/11 oz) honey

3/4 cup (205 g/6 oz) apple sauce

2/3 cup (110 g/3 1/2 oz) sultanas

170 g (5 1/2 oz) blanched almonds, coarsely chopped

1/3 cup (50 g/1 3/4 oz) pine nuts

75 g (2 1/2 oz) dark chocolate, coarsely chopped

1 cup (185 g/6 oz) mixed peel

1 tablespoon rum

2 tablespoons apricot jam

icing sugar, for serving

**1** Preheat the oven to warm 160°C (315°F/Gas 2–3). Lightly grease a 23 cm (9 inch) springform cake tin and cover the base with baking paper.

**2** Sift the flour, spices, bicarbonate of soda and 1/4 teaspoon salt into a large bowl. Make a well.

**3** Combine the butter, honey and 2 tablespoons water in a saucepan over low heat, stirring until the butter has melted. Remove from the heat and pour into the well in the flour. Add the apple sauce, sultanas, nuts, chocolate, peel and rum and mix well.

**4** Spoon the mixture into the tin and bake for 1 1/4–1 1/2 hours, or until the cake is golden brown, feels firm and a skewer comes out clean when inserted into the centre. Cool in the tin for 20 minutes before turning out onto a wire cake rack to cool.

**5** Stir the jam and 1 tablespoon water in a small saucepan over low heat until hot, then strain and brush all over the warm cake. Just before serving, dredge the top with icing sugar.

**NOTE:** This cake matures and mellows if stored so try to make it a week early and store in foil.

*ABOVE: Certosino*

## PANFORTE (ITALIAN)

**Preparation time:** 20 minutes
**Total cooking time:** 40 minutes
**Makes** 1

✷ ✷

²/₃ cup (100 g/3¹/₂ oz) blanched almonds
³/₄ cup (105 g/3¹/₂ oz) roasted, skinned hazelnuts
¹/₂ cup (95 g/3 oz) candied peel, chopped
¹/₂ cup (100 g/3¹/₂ oz) chopped candied pineapple
¹/₄ cup (30 g/1 oz) cocoa powder
¹/₂ cup (60 g/2 oz) plain flour
¹/₂ teaspoon ground cinnamon
¹/₄ teaspoon mixed spice
¹/₃ cup (90 g/3 oz) sugar
¹/₃ cup (115 g/4 oz) honey
icing sugar, for dusting

 **1** Line a 20 cm (8 inch) springform tin with baking paper and grease well with butter. Toast the almonds under a hot grill until brown, then leave to cool. Put the nuts in a bowl with the peel, pineapple, cocoa powder, flour and spices and toss them all together. Preheat the oven to slow 150°C (300°F/Gas 2).

**2** Put the sugar and honey in a saucepan and melt them together over low heat. Cook the syrup until a little of it dropped into cold water forms a soft ball when moulded between your finger and thumb. The colour will turn from golden to brown.

**3** Pour the syrup into the nut mixture and mix well, working fast before it stiffens too much. Spoon straight into the tin, press firmly and smooth the surface. Bake for 35 minutes. Unlike other cakes this will neither firm up nor colour as it cooks at all so you need to time it carefully.

**4** Cool in the tin until the cake firms enough to enable you to remove the side of the tin. Peel off the paper, turn the cake over onto another piece of paper and leave to cool completely. Dust the top heavily with icing sugar before serving.

**NOTE:** This fruity, spicy flat cake with a dense texture originated in Siena in Tuscany. It can be refrigerated in foil for up to 6 weeks.

*ABOVE: Panforte*

CHRISTMAS COLOURS
The colours red, green and white have for a long time been associated with Christmas. Red, the most exciting colour of the three, represents charity, blood and fire. Green symbolizes nature, youth and the hope of eternal life. Green holly is said to remind us of Christ's crown of thorns. The sharp pointed leaves represent his wounds and the red berries, his blood. White depicts light, purity, joy and glory. It is seen in the robes of the angels and in decorations and, in many countries, snow.

# HONEY CAKE
## (UKRAINIAN)

**Preparation time:** 15 minutes
**Total cooking time:** 1 hour 20 minutes
**Makes** 1

3 cups (375 g/12 oz) self-raising flour

1 cup (250 g/8 oz) sugar

2 teaspoons ground ginger

1 teaspoon ground cloves

1 teaspoon ground cinnamon

1 teaspoon bicarbonate of soda

1 teaspoon vanilla essence

2 eggs, lightly beaten

1 cup (350 g/11 oz) honey

1 cup (250 ml/8 fl oz) sunflower oil

1 Preheat the oven to warm 170°C (325°F/ Gas 3). Lightly grease a 24 x 9 x 10 cm (9 x 3½ x 4 inch) loaf tin and line the base with baking paper.

2 Sift the flour into a large bowl, make a well in the centre and add all the remaining ingredients. Pour in 1 cup (250 ml/8 fl oz) hot water, stir thoroughly to mix, then beat until quite smooth.

3 Spoon the mixture into the prepared loaf tin and lightly tap the tin on the bench to remove any air pockets. Bake for 1 hour 20 minutes, or until a skewer inserted into the centre comes out clean. If the cake starts to brown too much, cover loosely with foil halfway through cooking. Leave to cool in the tin for 20 minutes, then invert onto a wire rack and cool completely.

*LEFT: Honey cake*

# CHRISTOPSOMO (GREEK)

**Preparation time:** 30 minutes + 2 hours proving
**Total cooking time:** 45 minutes
**Makes** 1

★★★

1 tablespoon sesame seeds

7 g (¹/₄ oz) sachet dry yeast

2 teaspoons sugar

2¹/₂ cups (310 g/10 oz) plain flour

2 teaspoons whole aniseeds

2 tablespoons unsalted butter, melted

¹/₂ cup (125 ml/4 fl oz) milk, warmed

1 tablespoon ouzo

1 egg, lightly beaten

2 tablespoons chopped walnuts

1 tablespoon whole blanched almonds, chopped

4 dried figs, chopped

1 teaspoon sesame seeds, extra

2 tablespoons honey

**1** Grease a 20 cm (8 inch) round cake tin lightly with oil. Sprinkle the sesame seeds over the base and side of the tin.
**2** Place the yeast, sugar and ¹/₄ cup (90 ml/3 fl oz) warm water in a small bowl and leave in a warm place until foamy. (If the yeast doesn't foam, it is dead and you will have to start again.)
**3** Sift the flour into a large bowl, add the aniseeds and stir to combine. Make a well in the centre and add the yeast mixture and combined butter, milk and ouzo. Mix together to form a soft dough, then turn onto a lightly floured surface and knead for about 10 minutes, until smooth and elastic.
**4** Place the dough in a large greased bowl. Cover and leave in a warm place for 45–60 minutes, or until the dough has doubled. Turn the dough onto a floured surface and knead until smooth. Break off a small portion of dough about the size of a lime and reserve. This portion will be used for decorating the bread.
**5** Shape the larger piece of dough into a round to fit in the cake tin. Brush lightly all over with some of the beaten egg. Roll the reserved ball of dough into two thin sausage shapes and form an equal-armed cross on the top of the dough, brushing with a little more beaten egg. Arrange the nuts and figs on top of the dough and sprinkle with extra sesame seeds. Cover and leave in a warm place for about 45 minutes, or until the dough has doubled in size.

**6** Preheat the oven to moderately hot 190°C (375°F/Gas 5). Bake the bread for 45 minutes, or until it is golden brown and sounds hollow when tapped on the base. Cover loosely with foil if the top is over-browning. Turn onto a wire cake rack and brush with honey while still hot.
**NOTE:** This rich, sweet bread has a slightly denser texture than normal bread.

# KOURABIETHES (GREEK)

**Preparation time:** 20 minutes
**Total cooking time:** 20 minutes
**Makes** about 40

★★

250 g (8 oz) butter, softened

1 cup (125 g/4 oz) icing sugar

1¹/₂ teaspoons vanilla essence

¹/₂ teaspoon finely grated orange rind

1 egg yolk

1¹/₂ tablespoons brandy

2¹/₂ cups (310 g/10 oz) plain flour

1 teaspoon baking powder

¹/₃ cup (30 g/1 oz) ground almonds

¹/₃ cup (40 g/1¹/₄ oz) slivered almonds, finely chopped

2 tablespoons orange flower water

1¹/₂ cups (185 g/6 oz) icing sugar, extra, for dusting

**1** Preheat the oven to warm 160°C (315°F/Gas 2–3). Line two baking trays with baking paper.
**2** Beat the butter, icing sugar, vanilla essence and orange rind in a bowl with electric beaters until light and creamy. Gradually add the egg yolk and brandy and beat until combined.
**3** Sift the flour and baking powder into a large bowl, stir in the ground and chopped slivered almonds, then stir into the butter mixture. Form walnut-sized pieces into crescent shapes and place on the trays, leaving a little room for spreading. Bake for 20 minutes, or until just lightly coloured. Cool for 5 minutes, then lightly brush with the orange flower water. Roll in icing sugar to coat and set aside on wire racks to cool.
**4** When cool, dredge the remaining icing sugar heavily over the top of the kourabiethes.
**NOTE:** Large quantities of these mouthwatering little shortbread cakes are made in Greek homes at Christmas time.

**XMAS**
The spelling of Christmas as 'Xmas' comes from the Greek letter 'x' (*shi*), the first letter of Xristos, meaning Christ. Scribes, who abbreviated words to save time and cut down on the use of parchment, often used this letter 'X' for Christ. Eventually, the usage became traditional in many places. Later, some people mistakenly believed that the 'X' represented a St Andrew's cross, while others thought Jesus Christ's name was too sacred to be written in full.

*OPPOSITE PAGE:*
*Christopsomo (top);*
*Kourabiethes*

*ABOVE: Creamed rice with hot cherry sauce*

## CREAMED RICE WITH HOT CHERRY SAUCE
### (DANISH)

**Preparation time:** 15 minutes + cooling
**Total cooking time:** 50 minutes
**Serves** 6

1 cup (220 g/7 oz) short-grain rice
1 litre (32 fl oz) milk
1 tablespoon vanilla sugar
2 tablespoons caster sugar
1¼ cups (315 ml/10 fl oz) cream
2 tablespoons whole blanched almonds

**Dark cherry sauce**

3 teaspoons cornflour
425 g (14 oz) can stoneless black cherries
　in syrup

**1** Put the rice and milk in a saucepan, cover and cook over low heat for 40–45 minutes, or until the rice is cooked and the mixture is thick and creamy. Stir occasionally to prevent the rice forming lumps and sticking to the pan. Remove from the heat and stir in both the sugars. Spoon into a large bowl, cover the top of the rice with plastic wrap and allow to cool at room temperature, stirring occasionally.

**2** When the rice is cool, stir to separate the grains. Beat the cream in a bowl with electric beaters until soft peaks form. Fold into the creamed rice. Reserve 1 whole almond and roughly chop the rest. Fold into the creamy rice and stir in the whole almond. Refrigerate the rice while preparing the sauce.

**3** For the sauce, blend the cornflour with 2 tablespoons water in a small bowl. Pour the cherries and their juice into a small saucepan, add the cornflour mixture and stir over medium heat until the mixture boils and thickens. Remove from the heat. Spoon the rice into serving bowls and top with the hot sauce.

**NOTE:** Traditionally, the person who gets the whole almond receives a small gift or token from the host.

# KLEJNE
## (DANISH)

**Preparation time:** 25 minutes + 1 hour
30 minutes refrigeration
**Total cooking time:** 15 minutes
**Makes** about 50

4 cups (500 g/8 oz) plain flour
1¼ teaspoons baking powder
¼ teaspoon bicarbonate of soda
½ teaspoon ground cinnamon
½ cup (125 g/4 oz) caster sugar
1 teaspoon finely grated lemon rind
100 g (3½ oz) butter, melted
1 cup (250 ml/8 fl oz) milk
oil, for deep-frying
icing sugar, for dusting

1 Sift the flour, baking powder, bicarbonate of soda and cinnamon into a large bowl and stir in the sugar and lemon rind. Make a well in the centre and stir in the butter. Gradually add enough milk to make a soft dough. Turn onto a lightly floured surface and press together until the dough comes together. Pat into a ball, wrap in plastic wrap and refrigerate for 1 hour to firm.

2 Roll the dough on a lightly floured surface into a rectangular shape about 5 mm (¼ inch) thick. Trim the edges. Cut into strips at 3 cm (1¼ inch) intervals, then cut each strip on the diagonal into 8 cm (3 inch) lengths.

3 Cut a slit in each strip leaving 1 cm (½ inch) at each end. Poke one end through the slit and carefully pull out the other side to form a twist in the pastry. Take care when pulling through as it may split. Repeat with the remaining dough. Place the shapes on a tray covered with baking paper and refrigerate for 30 minutes, or until firm.

4 Fill a deep heavy-based saucepan one third full of oil and heat to 180°C (350°F), or until a cube of bread dropped into the oil browns in 15 seconds. Fry the biscuits in batches until well browned and cooked through. Drain on crumpled paper towels. Place on a tray covered with baking paper, cool to warm and dust lightly with icing sugar. Best eaten warm but can be eaten cold.

**NOTE:** Originally German, these are now a favourite at Danish Christmas celebrations.

## KLEJNE

When the dough starts to come together, gather together into a ball and wrap in plastic wrap.

Roll in a rectangle shape until thin, then cut into strips, then cut again on the diagonal into short lengths.

Poke one end through the slit and carefully pull out the other side to form a twist in the pastry.

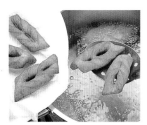

When the biscuits are well browned, remove from the oil with a slotted spoon.

*LEFT: Klejne*

**To decorate**

toasted flaked almonds

selection of glacé cherries (cut in halves),
angelica, crystallized violets or sugared
grapes, fresh fruit or sugared rose petals

1 cup (250 ml/8 fl oz) cream, extra,
whipped, optional

**1** Beat the egg yolks and sugar together in a small bowl with electric beaters until pale, thick and fluffy. Pour half the cream into a saucepan and heat until almost boiling. Gradually pour onto the eggs and sugar, mixing well. Strain the mixture back into the clean pan and place over low heat.

**2** Using a wooden spoon, stir constantly around the base and sides of the pan until the custard thickens slightly and coats the back of the spoon. Do not boil or the custard will curdle. Remove from the heat and stir in the vanilla and brandy. Add the chestnut purée and beat well to combine. Strain the mixture and allow to cool.

**3** Beat the remaining cream in a bowl until soft peaks form and fold into the custard mixture.

**4** Put the currants and sultanas in a bowl and cover completely with warm water.

**5** Pour the cream mixture into a shallow metal tray and freeze for 2–3 hours, or until the mixture is just starting to freeze. Transfer to a large bowl or food processor, beat until smooth, then pour back into the tray and return to the freezer. Repeat this step three times. Before the final freezing, add the glacé cherries, mixed peel and the well-drained currants and sultanas, then mix thoroughly.

**6** Lightly oil a 2 litre (64 fl oz) charlotte mould, line with plastic, then pour in the cream mixture Cover the surface with a piece of plastic and freeze for at least 8 hours, or until firm.

**7** Invert the pudding onto a serving plate and carefully peel away the plastic. Decorate the sides with evenly spaced lines of toasted almonds, pieces of angelica, halved glacé cherries, crystallized violets or sugared fruits. The nesselrode can be put back in the freezer after it is decorated. When ready to serve, pile whipped cream over the top, then top that with piped whipped cream.

# NESSELRODE
## (RUSSIAN)

**Preparation time:** 25 minutes + freezing
**Total cooking time:** Nil
**Serves** 8

★★★

5 egg yolks

3/4 cup (185 g/6 oz) caster sugar

1 litre (32 fl oz) cream

1 teaspoon vanilla essence

1 tablespoon brandy

1/2 cup (165 g/5 1/2 oz) chestnut purée

1/2 cup (75 g/2 1/2 oz) currants

1/2 cup (80 g/2 3/4 oz) sultanas

1/4 cup (60 g/2 oz) glacé cherries, chopped

1/2 cup (95 g/3 oz) mixed peel

*ABOVE: Nesselrode*

# CRANBERRY KISEL
## (RUSSIAN)

**Preparation time:** 15 minutes
 + 2 hours refrigeration
**Total cooking time:** 15 minutes
**Serves** 4

2 lemons
1 1/2 cups (375 g/12 oz) caster sugar
2 cinnamon sticks
600 g (1 1/4 lb) cranberries
    (fresh or frozen)
2 teaspoons cornflour
2 teaspoons orange juice

**Yoghurt cream**

1 cup (250 ml/8 fl oz) cream
1/2 cup (125 ml/4 fl oz) natural yoghurt
1/2 cup (115 g/4 oz) soft brown sugar

**1** Remove the peel from the lemons in large strips with a vegetable peeler, avoiding the white pith. Place the peel, sugar, cinnamon sticks and 1 1/2 cups (375 ml/12 fl oz) water into a saucepan and stir over low heat until the sugar has dissolved. Bring to the boil, reduce the heat and simmer for 5 minutes.
**2** Rinse the cranberries (not necessary if frozen) and remove any stems. Add the cranberries to the hot syrup, return to the boil and simmer for 10 minutes, or until the skins have split. Remove from the heat and set aside to cool.
**3** When cool, remove and discard the peel and cinnamon sticks. Remove about 1/2 cup of the berries and reserve. Blend or process the remaining mixture until smooth, return to the saucepan and add the reserved whole berries. Blend the cornflour and orange juice in a small bowl, add to the purée then stir over medium heat for 5 minutes, or until the mixture boils and thickens. Serve cold or warm with yoghurt cream.
**4** For the yoghurt cream, beat the cream in a bowl until soft peaks form, then fold the yoghurt through. Transfer to a small bowl and sprinkle with the sugar. Refrigerate, covered, for 2 hours.

**KISEL**
Kisel (or kissel) is a fruit dessert with a soup-like consistency. The word means sour, so tart berries such as cranberries or raspberries are best, but other fruits such as red or white currants, plums or rhubarb can also be used. The dish is delicious when served with pancakes or waffles and is sometimes used in savoury sauces in the same way you would use redcurrant jelly.

*LEFT: Cranberry kisel*

KOEKSISTERS

Simmer the sugar, cinnamon stick, lemon juice and water in a saucepan over low heat until thick and syrupy.

Mix the dough with a flat-bladed knife, using a cutting action, until the mixture comes together in clumps.

Use a sharp, long knife to cut the dough in half crossways, then cut each half into quarters.

## KOEKSISTERS (SOUTH AFRICAN)

**Preparation time:** 20 minutes + 1 hour resting
**Total cooking time:** 15 minutes
**Makes** about 12

★ ★

### Syrup

3¹/₂ cups (875 g/1 lb 12¹/₂ oz) caster sugar
1 cinnamon stick
2 teaspoons lemon juice

3¹/₂ cups (435 g/14 oz) self-raising flour
1 teaspoon ground cinnamon
1 tablespoon caster sugar
50 g (1³/₄ oz) butter, chopped
2 eggs, lightly beaten
1 cup (250 ml/8 fl oz) milk
oil, for deep-frying

1 Combine the sugar, cinnamon stick, lemon juice and 1¹/₂ cups (375 ml/12 fl oz) water in a saucepan and stir over medium heat until the sugar has dissolved. Bring to the boil, then reduce the heat and simmer for 5–7 minutes, or until thick and syrupy. Remove and leave until cold.

2 Sift the flour and cinnamon into a large bowl, stir in the sugar and add the butter. Rub the butter into the flour with your fingertips until the mixture resembles fine breadcrumbs. Make a well in the centre, add the eggs and milk and mix with a flat-bladed knife, using a cutting action, until the mixture comes together in clumps. Gather together and knead on a lightly floured surface for 1 minute, or until smooth. Place in a large lightly oiled bowl, cover and leave for 1 hour.

3 Roll the dough out into a 30 x 40 cm (12 x 16 inch) rectangle. Cut the dough in half crossways, then cut each half into quarters. Cut each quarter into nine 10 cm (4 inch) long strips. Plait 3 strips together, pinching the ends firmly to seal. Repeat with the remaining strips.

4 Fill a deep heavy-based saucepan one third full of oil and heat to 170°C (325°F), or until a cube of bread dropped into the oil browns in 20 seconds. Fry the plaits in several batches for about 2–3 minutes, or until well browned and cooked though. Drain on crumpled paper towels. While still hot, dip each into the cold syrup for about 5 seconds, turning to coat evenly. Drain on a wire cake rack over a baking tray. Although best eaten on the day they are made, they can be eaten the next day, heated and brushed with any remaining syrup.

*ABOVE: Koeksisters*

# GALETTE DES ROIS (FRENCH)

**Preparation time:** 25 minutes + 30 minutes refrigeration
**Total cooking time:** 35 minutes
**Makes** 1

✱ ✱

2 x 375 g (12 oz) blocks ready-made puff
   pastry, thawed
3/4 cup (75 g/2 1/2 oz) ground almonds
1/3 cup (90 g/3 oz) caster sugar or vanilla sugar
1 tablespoon cornflour
1 teaspoon finely grated orange rind
100 g (3 1/2 oz) unsalted butter, softened
3 egg yolks
1/2 teaspoon almond essence
1 tablespoon rum or kirsch
1 dried haricot bean or ceramic token
1 egg, lightly beaten, for glazing

**1** Roll 1 block of pastry out on a lightly floured surface to 5 mm (1/4 inch) thick and cut into a 22 cm (9 inch) circle. Repeat with the other block of pastry. Line a baking tray with baking paper and top with one of the circles.

**2** In a bowl, combine the almonds, sugar, cornflour and rind. Add the butter, egg yolks, essence and rum and mix well. Spread over the pastry on the tray, poking in the bean or token and leaving a 2 cm (3/4 inch) rim. Brush the rim with some beaten egg, taking care not to brush the cut edges as this will prevent the pastry puffing.

**3** Place the second circle of puff pastry over the first, pressing gently around the edge to seal. Using a sharp knife, make swirling patterns from the centre, fanning outwards in the pastry, taking care not to cut all the way through. Brush the top with beaten egg and refrigerate for 30 minutes. Preheat the oven to moderately hot 200°C (400°F/Gas 6). Bake for 30–35 minutes, or until well puffed and golden. Serve warm or cold. Remember to tell everyone about the bean or token in the filling.

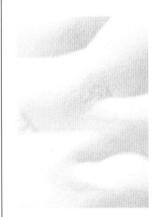

**GALETTE DES ROIS**
This is a traditional French cake served at Christmas and in winter holidays. The bean or token represents the baby Jesus and whoever is lucky enough to find it becomes the King or Queen for the day. The cakes are sometimes sold (topped with a gold crown) in patisseries.

*LEFT: Galette des rois*

## GINGER CHRISTMAS TREE BISCUITS (SWEDISH)

**Preparation time:** 20 minutes + 4 hours refrigeration
**Total cooking time:** 25 minutes
**Makes** about 45

★ ★

1 cup (185 g/6 oz) soft brown sugar
1/2 cup (175 g/6 oz) molasses
2 teaspoons ground ginger
1/2 teaspoon ground cinnamon
1/2 teaspoon ground cloves
185 g (6 oz) unsalted butter, cubed
1 egg, beaten
5 cups (625 g/1 1/4 lb) plain flour, sifted
2 teaspoons baking powder

1 Put the sugar, molasses, ginger, cinnamon and cloves in a small saucepan and bring to the boil over medium heat. Remove from the heat, add the butter, then pour into a heatproof bowl and stir until the butter melts and the mixture is combined. Cool slightly, then mix in the beaten egg. Stir in the sifted flour and baking powder in two batches, mixing thoroughly. Press together on a lightly floured board for 2 minutes, then wrap in plastic wrap and refrigerate for at least 2–4 hours. Preheat the oven to moderate 180°C (350°F/Gas 4).

2 Divide the dough into 3 and roll out 1 portion to a thickness of 3 mm (1/8 inch). Cut into shapes using Christmas-theme cutters. Repeat with the other portions of dough, re-rolling any leftover dough. Place on a baking tray lined with baking paper, then make a hole in the top of each biscuit with a skewer and bake in batches for 5–6 minutes, or until lightly coloured and firm.

3 While the biscuits are still warm reinforce each hole with the skewer (they may have closed during baking). Cool on a wire rack, then thread the biscuits with ribbon and store in an airtight container until ready to hang on your Christmas tree. The biscuits will last hanging on the tree for up to 1 week, after which they will soften.

**NOTE:** These biscuits also look great decorated with icing.

*ABOVE: Ginger Christmas tree biscuits*

# STOLLEN (GERMAN)

**Preparation time:** 30 minutes
+ 1 hour 45 minutes rising
**Total cooking time:** 40 minutes
**Makes** 1

1/3 cup (80 ml/2³/4 fl oz) lukewarm milk
2 teaspoons sugar
7 g (³/4 oz) sachet dried yeast
125 g (4 oz) unsalted butter, softened
1/3 cup (90 g/3 oz) caster sugar
1 egg
2 teaspoons vanilla essence
1/2 teaspoon ground cinnamon
3 cups (375 g/12 oz) plain flour
1/2 cup (80 g/2³/4 oz) raisins
1/2 cup (75 g/2¹/2 oz) currants
1/2 cup (95 g/3 oz) mixed peel
1/2 cup (60 g/2 oz) slivered almonds
30 g (1 oz) butter, melted
icing sugar, for dusting

**1** Combine the milk, sugar and yeast with 1/3 cup (80 ml/2³/4 fl oz) warm water in a small bowl and leave in a warm place for 10 minutes, or until foaming. Meanwhile, beat the butter and sugar with electric beaters until light and creamy, then beat in the egg and vanilla essence.

**2** Add the yeast mixture, cinnamon and almost all the flour and mix to a soft dough, adding more flour if necessary. Turn out onto a lightly floured surface and knead for 10 minutes, or until the dough is smooth and elastic. Place in a lightly oiled bowl, cover with plastic wrap and leave for 1 hour 45 minutes in a warm place, or until doubled in volume. Preheat the oven to moderate 180°C (350°F/Gas 4). Lightly grease a baking tray.

**3** When the dough has risen, tip it out of the bowl onto a floured work surface and punch it to expel the air. Press it out to a thickness of about 1.5 cm (⁵/8 inch). Sprinkle the fruit and nuts over the dough, then gather up and knead for a few minutes to mix the fruit and nuts evenly through the dough.

**4** Shape the dough into an oval about 18 cm (7 inches) wide and 30 cm (12 inches) long. Fold in half lengthways, then press down to flatten slightly, with the fold slightly off centre on top of the loaf. Place on the tray and bake for 40 minutes, or until golden brown. As soon as it comes out of the oven, brush with the melted butter, allowing each brushing to be absorbed until you have used all the butter. Cool on a wire rack. Dust with icing sugar before cutting.

**STOLLEN**
Stollen is a rich fruit bread from Germany that is now known internationally as a special Christmas treat. Sometimes a filling such as marzipan is put in the centre. The oval shape, with a ridge down the middle, is meant to represent the Christ Child in swaddling clothes. Stollen is sometimes given the name *Christstollen*.

*LEFT: Stollen*

## SPECULAAS (GERMAN/DUTCH)

**Preparation time:** 20 minutes
  + 45 minutes refrigeration
**Total cooking time:** 12 minutes per tray
**Makes** about 48

★ ★

3¼ cups (405 g/13 oz) plain flour

1 teaspoon ground cinnamon

¼ teaspoon ground nutmeg

¼ teaspoon ground cloves

¼ teaspoon ground cardamom

160 g (5½ oz) unsalted butter,
  softened

1⅓ cups (310 g/10 oz) soft brown sugar

1 egg

⅓ cup (80 ml/2¾ fl oz) milk

¼ cup (45 g/1½ oz) ground almonds

milk, extra, for glazing

*ABOVE: Speculaas*

**1** Preheat the oven to moderately hot 200°C (400°F/Gas 6). Cover baking trays with baking paper. Sift the flour, spices and ¼ teaspoon salt together into a large bowl.
**2** Beat the butter and sugar together in a bowl until pale and creamy. Beat in the egg, mixing well, and then the milk. Fold in the almonds, then the sifted flour and spices and mix well. Wrap in plastic and refrigerate for 45 minutes.
**3** Divide the mixture into 4 portions and roll each portion out on a lightly floured surface to 4 mm (⅛ inch) thick. Cut into shapes using Christmas-theme cutters (stars, trees, candy canes or bells). Place on the baking trays, leaving room for spreading. Brush with milk and bake for 12 minutes, or until light brown. Repeat with the remaining dough, returning any scraps to the refrigerator to chill before re-rolling. Cool the biscuits on wire racks. When cold, store in airtight containers.
**NOTE:** This Christmas biscuit is from the Rhine area in Germany and neighbouring Holland.

# CHOCOLATE PFEFFERNUSSE
## (GERMAN)

**Preparation time:** 50 minutes
+ 2 hours refrigeration
**Total cooking time:** 15 minutes per tray
**Makes** 65

200 ml (6¹/₂ fl oz) honey

100 ml (3¹/₂ fl oz) treacle

²/₃ cup (155 g/5 oz) soft brown sugar

150 g (5 oz) unsalted butter

4 cups (500 g/1 lb) plain flour

¹/₂ cup (60 g/1³/₄ oz) cocoa powder

1 teaspoon baking powder

¹/₂ teaspoon bicarbonate of soda

1 teaspoon ground white pepper

1 teaspoon ground cinnamon

¹/₂ teaspoon ground nutmeg

²/₃ cup (100 g/3¹/₂ oz) blanched almonds,
   chopped

1 teaspoon finely grated lemon rind

¹/₄ cup (45 g/1¹/₂ oz) mixed peel

2 eggs, lightly beaten

300 g (10 oz) dark chocolate, chopped

1 Cover baking trays with baking paper. Combine the honey, treacle, brown sugar and butter in a small saucepan. Place over medium heat and bring to the boil, stirring occasionally.

2 Remove from the heat and set aside to cool a little. Sift the flour, cocoa, baking powder, bicarbonate of soda, spices and ¹/₄ teaspoon salt into a large bowl. Stir in the almonds, lemon rind and mixed peel and mix thoroughly. Make a well in the centre. Pour in the honey mixture and the eggs and mix until well combined.

3 Cover the mixture and refrigerate for 2 hours. Preheat the oven to moderate 180°C (350°F/ Gas 4). Roll level tablespoons of the dough into balls. Place on the trays, allowing room for spreading. Bake for 12–15 minutes, until slightly coloured and firm to the touch. Transfer to a wire rack to cool.

4 To decorate, put the chocolate in a heatproof bowl. Bring a pan of water to the boil, then remove from the heat. Sit the bowl over the pan, making sure the base of the bowl doesn't sit in the water. Stir occasionally until the chocolate melts. Dip the tops of the biscuits in chocolate (up to the base), allow excess to drain off, then place on baking paper to set.

### GERMAN CHRISTMAS
In Germany, preparations for Christmas start weeks before the day. Things such as advent wreaths, candles and calendars put everyone in the mood. The enduring tradition of the Christmas tree began in the sixteenth century but is said to have been popularized much later by the Germans, to whom it symbolized eternal life. In the nineteenth century, they decorated their trees with fruits and biscuits which couldn't be eaten until after the Twelfth Night when the tree was taken down.

*LEFT: Chocolate pfeffernüsse*

**BLACK BUN**

Mix the dough with a flat-bladed knife, using a cutting action, until the mixture forms small clumps.

Divide another portion of the dough into 3 and roll each piece to line the side of the tin.

Stir the flour, spices and salt with the sugar, fruit peel, nuts and rind in a large bowl until well mixed.

Fold the pastry edges over the filling and brush the pastry with beaten egg.

*OPPOSITE PAGE: Black bun (top); Cinnamon stars*

# BLACK BUN (SCOTTISH)

**Preparation time:** 45 minutes + 30 minutes refrigeration + 20 minutes standing
**Total cooking time:** 2 hours 30 minutes
**Makes** 1

2¹/₂ cups (310 g/10 oz) plain flour
¹/₂ teaspoon baking powder
150 g (5 oz) butter, chilled and grated
1 egg, beaten

**Filling**

³/₄ cup (90 g/3 oz) plain flour
¹/₂ teaspoon grated nutmeg
¹/₂ teaspoon ground coriander
¹/₂ teaspoon mixed spice
1 teaspoon ground cinnamon
1 teaspoon ground ginger
¹/₂ cup (115 g/4 oz) soft brown sugar
3²/₃ cups (590 g/1¹/₄ lb) raisins, chopped
1¹/₂ cups (240 g/7¹/₂ oz) sultanas
2¹/₃ cups (350 g/11 oz) currants
¹/₂ cup (95 g/3 oz) mixed peel
²/₃ cup (100 g/3¹/₂ oz) blanched almonds, chopped
2 teaspoons finely grated lemon rind
2 eggs
2 tablespoons brandy
3 tablespoons treacle
2 tablespoons milk

**1** Grease a 24 cm (9 inch) springform cake tin. Sift the flour, baking powder and ¹/₄ teaspoon salt into a bowl. Mix the butter into the flour with your fingertips. Make a well, add up to ¹/₃ cup (80 ml/2³/₄ fl oz) water and mix with a flat-bladed knife, using a cutting action, until the mixture comes together in clumps (you may need extra water). Gather together and lift onto a lightly floured surface. Press into a ball, cover with plastic wrap and refrigerate for 30 minutes.
**2** Divide the dough into 3 portions. Roll out a portion, on a lightly floured surface, to fit the base of the tin. Divide another portion into 3 and roll each piece to line the side of the tin. Refrigerate the tin and the remaining portion of dough while preparing the filling.
**3** Preheat the oven to slow 150°C (300°F/ Gas 2). For the filling, sift the flour, spices and ¹/₄ teaspoon salt into a large bowl, then stir in the sugar, fruit, peel, almonds and rind. Mix well.

**4** Lightly beat the eggs with the brandy, treacle and milk in a bowl, then mix into the fruit. The mixture should come together, but not be too wet.
**5** Spoon the mixture into the pastry-lined tin and press into the base. The mixture will only come about three-quarters up the sides. Fold the pastry edges over the filling and brush the pastry with beaten egg. Roll the remaining pastry out, on a lightly floured surface, until large enough to cover the top. Trim to fit and press down firmly to seal. Prick the pastry top a few times with a fork. Brush with beaten egg and bake for 2–2¹/₂ hours. The top should be golden brown. If the pastry is over-browning, cover loosely with foil. Place the tin on a wire rack for 20 minutes to cool, then remove the side of the springform tin, and cool completely. When cold, store in an airtight container. Serve thin wedges.

# CINNAMON STARS (GERMAN)

**Preparation time:** 15 minutes + setting time
**Total cooking time:** 10 minutes per batch
**Makes** about 30

2 egg whites
2¹/₄ cups (280 g/9 oz) icing sugar
1¹/₂ cups (145 g/5 oz) ground almonds
1¹/₂ tablespoons ground cinnamon

**1** Beat the egg whites lightly with a wooden spoon in a large bowl. Gradually stir in the sifted icing sugar to form a smooth paste. Remove ¹/₃ cup (100 g/3¹/₂ oz), cover and set aside. Add the almonds and cinnamon to the remaining icing and gently press together with your hands. Add 1 teaspoon water if the mixture is too dry. Press together well before adding any water as the warmth of your hands will soften the mixture.
**2** Lightly dust a work surface with icing sugar and roll out the mixture to about 3 mm (¹/₈ inch) thick. Spread with a thin layer of the reserved icing. Leave, uncovered, at room temperature for 30–35 minutes, or until the icing has set. Preheat the oven to slow 150°C (300°F/Gas 2).
**3** Cut out shapes using a star cutter (about 45 mm/2 inches across from point to point). Dip the cutter in icing sugar to help prevent sticking. Place the stars on a baking tray covered with baking paper and cook for 10 minutes, or until just firm. Turn the tray around after 5 minutes. Cool on the tray. Store in an airtight container up to 2 weeks.

*ABOVE: Saffron buns*

## SAFFRON BUNS
### (SWEDISH)

**Preparation time:** 30 minutes + 2 hours rising
**Total cooking time:** 10 minutes per tray
**Makes** 16

★★

2 x 7 g (¼ oz) sachets dry yeast
2 cups (500 ml/16 fl oz) milk
½ teaspoon saffron threads
150 g (5 oz) unsalted butter, chopped
7 cups (875 g/1 lb 12½ oz) white bread flour
1 teaspoon salt
⅔ cup (160 g/5½ oz) sugar
1 cup (160 g/5½ oz) raisins
2 eggs, lightly beaten

**1** Combine the yeast with ½ cup (125 ml/ 4 fl oz) warm milk and the saffron in a small bowl. Set aside for 5 minutes, or until foamy. Melt the butter in a small saucepan, add the saffron and remaining milk and stir over low heat until warm. Remove from the heat and cover.
**2** Sift the flour into a large bowl, stir in the frothy yeast, salt, sugar and half the raisins, then make a well in the centre. Add the just warm saffron milk mixture and 1 of the eggs. Mix with a flat-bladed knife, using a cutting action, until the mixture comes together to form a soft dough.
**3** Turn the dough onto a lightly floured work surface and knead for 5–7 minutes, or until the dough is smooth. Place the dough in a large, lightly oiled bowl, cover with plastic wrap or a damp tea towel, and leave for 1–1½ hours in a warm place or until doubled in size.
**4** Turn out the dough onto a lightly floured work surface and knead for 5 minutes. Cut into 16 portions. Roll each portion into a sausage shape about 20 cm (8 inches) long and form each into an 'S' shape. Place on a greased baking tray. Cover loosely and stand in a warm place for 30 minutes, or until doubled in size. Preheat the oven to moderately hot 200°C (400°F/Gas 6).
**5** Brush with the remaining beaten egg and decorate with the remaining raisins, placing them gently into the 'S' shape, being careful not to deflate the buns. Bake for 10 minutes, or until the tops are brown and the buns feel hollow when tapped underneath. Transfer to a wire rack to cool. Serve warm or cold, plain or buttered.
**NOTE:** These buns are also popular in England.

# OLIEBOLLEN
## (DUTCH)

**Preparation time:** 20 minutes
+ 30 minutes proving
**Total cooking time:** 15 minutes
**Makes** about 48

 ✷ ✷

7 g (¼ oz) sachet dry yeast
1 tablespoon caster sugar
1 cup (250 ml/8 fl oz) milk, warmed
2¼ cups (280 g/9 oz) plain flour
¾ cup (120 g/4 oz) raisins, chopped
1 green apple, peeled and diced
¼ cup (45 g/1½ oz) mixed peel
2 eggs, lightly beaten
2 teaspoons finely grated
   lemon rind
oil, for deep-frying
caster sugar, for coating

**1** Place the yeast, 1 teaspoon of the sugar and ¼ cup (60 ml/2 fl oz) of the milk in a bowl and stir. Leave in a warm place for about 10 minutes, until frothy. (If the yeast doesn't froth it is dead and you will need to start again.)
**2** Sift the flour into a large bowl and stir in the remaining sugar, raisins, apple and peel. Make a well in the centre and pour in the remaining milk, the yeast mixture, eggs and lemon rind. Mix with a flat-bladed knife to a soft sticky batter. Cover and leave to prove for 30 minutes. Stir the mixture thoroughly before cooking. It should drop off the spoon in one thick blob.
**3** Fill a deep heavy-based saucepan one third full of oil and heat to moderate 180°C (350°F), or until a cube of bread dropped into the oil browns in 15 seconds. Drop walnut-sized balls of dough from a tablespoon into the hot oil. Cook in several batches until well browned and cooked through. Drain well on crumpled paper towels, then toss lightly in caster sugar. Serve while still warm.
**NOTE:** For a delicious dessert, you can make large oliebollen and serve them with cream or ice cream.

## OLIEBOLLEN

Mix the dough with a flat-bladed knife until it forms a soft sticky batter.

Drop walnut-sized balls of the dough from a tablespoon into the hot oil.

When the fruity doughnuts are cooked, lift from the hot oil using a slotted spoon and drain on crumpled paper towels.

*LEFT: Oliebollen*

BEIGLI

Lightly knead the dough for about 10 minutes until soft, smooth and shiny.

Spread half the cooled walnut filling onto each rectangle, leaving a border all the way around.

Neatly roll the dough from the short end to enclose the filling.

## BEIGLI (HUNGARIAN)

**Preparation time:** 25 minutes
  + 3 hours 30 minutes rising
**Total cooking time:** 50 minutes
Makes 2

☆ ☆

3/4 cup (185 ml/6 fl oz) milk, warmed

7 g (1/4 oz) sachet dried yeast

1/2 cup (125 g/4 oz) caster sugar

4 cups (500 g/1 lb) white bread flour

220 g (7 oz) butter, at room
    temperature

2 eggs, lightly beaten

1 teaspoon grated lemon rind

1 egg, lightly beaten, extra

### Walnut filling

3 1/4 cups (400 g/13 oz) walnuts

2/3 cup (160 g/5 1/2 oz) sugar

1/2 cup (75 g/2 1/2 oz) currants

1 teaspoon finely grated lemon rind

*ABOVE: Beigli*

**1** Pour 1/3 cup (80 ml/2 3/4 fl oz) warm milk into a small bowl. Sprinkle the yeast and a teaspoon of sugar over the surface, stir to dissolve and leave for 10 minutes, or until foamy.

**2** Sift the flour into a large bowl and rub in the butter with your fingertips until the mixture resembles fine breadcrumbs. Make a well, add the yeast mixture, remaining milk and sugar, the eggs and lemon rind. Mix with a flat-bladed knife until the mixture comes together. Turn onto a lightly floured work surface and knead lightly for 10 minutes. You may need to knead in up to 1/2 cup (60 g/2 oz) extra flour so the mixture is no longer sticky. Return to a clean bowl, cover with plastic wrap and leave in a warm place for 2 hours, or until doubled.

**3** Meanwhile, for the filling, roughly chop the walnuts in a food processor, then transfer to a large bowl. Combine the sugar and 1 cup (250 ml/8 fl oz) water in a saucepan and stir over medium heat until the sugar has dissolved. Bring to the boil, reduce the heat and simmer for 10 minutes to reduce and thicken slightly. Remove from the heat and add to the ground walnuts. Stir in the currants and lemon rind and mix well. Set aside to cool.

**4** Knock back the dough and knead on a lightly floured surface for 2–3 minutes. Divide into two and roll each portion into a rectangle about 22 x 36 cm (9 x 14 inches). Spread half the filling onto each, leaving a 2.5 cm (1 inch) border on all sides. Roll up from the short end to enclose the filling and place on a greased baking tray with the seam underneath. Cover with a tea towel and leave in a warm place for 1½ hours, or until doubled in size.

**5** Preheat the oven to moderately hot 200°C (400°F/Gas 6). Brush the dough with extra beaten egg and prick the top in six places with a fork. Bake for 35–40 minutes, or until golden brown. Cover loosely with foil if over-browning. Cool on wire racks.

## DUNDEE CAKE (SCOTTISH)

**Preparation time:** 35 minutes
**Total cooking time:** 2 hours 30 minutes
**Makes** 1

★ ★

250 g (8 oz) unsalted butter, softened

1 cup (230 g/7½ oz) soft brown sugar

¼ teaspoon almond essence

2 teaspoons finely grated orange rind

2 teaspoons finely grated lemon rind

4 eggs, lightly beaten

1⅔ cups (250 g/8 oz) currants

2 cups (320 g/11 oz) sultanas

½ cup (80 g/2¾ oz) raisins, chopped

⅓ cup (60 g/2 oz) mixed peel

⅔ cup (100 g/3½ oz) blanched almonds, coarsely chopped

¾ cup (75 g/2½ oz) ground almonds

1½ cups (185 g/6 oz) plain flour

½ cup (60 g/2 oz) self-raising flour

½ teaspoon ground cinnamon

2 tablespoons whisky

⅔ cup (100 g/3½ oz) whole blanched almonds, for decoration

**1** Preheat the oven to slow 150°C (300°F/ Gas 2). Lightly grease a 20 cm (8 inch) round cake tin and line as shown on pages 224–5.

**2** Beat the butter, sugar, essence and rinds in a small bowl with electric beaters until light and fluffy. Add the eggs gradually, beating well after each addition. Transfer to a large bowl, stir in the dried fruits, mixed peel and chopped nuts,

then the ground almonds, sifted flours, cinnamon and whisky. The batter should be just soft enough to drop from a spoon when shaken, so if it is too dry add 1–2 tablespoons milk. Spread into the tin and smooth the surface. Wrap newspaper around the tin as shown on pages 224–5.

**3** Arrange whole almonds on top of the cake in a spiral pattern. Place the tin on several layers of newspaper on the oven shelf. Bake for 2–2½ hours, or until a skewer comes out clean when inserted into centre of the cake. Cover the top with a sheet of baking paper then cover tightly with foil and wrap in a thick tea towel. Cool completely in the tin, then store in an airtight container for up to 3 months.

*ABOVE: Dundee cake*

# INDEX

Page numbers in *italics* refer to photographs.  Page numbers in **bold** type refer to margin notes.

Cover illustration: Individual Bourbon Christmas Cakes, page 232

# ACKNOWLEDGEMENTS

HOME ECONOMISTS: Alison Adams, Laura Ammons, Miles Beaufort, Anna Beaumont, Anna Boyd, Wendy Brodhurst, Kerrie Carr, Rebecca Clancy, Bronwyn Clark, Michelle Earl, Maria Gargas, Wendy Goggin, Kathy Knudsen, Michelle Lawton, Michaela Le Compte, Ben Masters, Melanie McDermott, Beth Mitchell, Kerrie Mullins, Kate Murdoch, Justine Poole, Tracey Port, Kerrie Ray, Jo Richardson, Maria Sampsonis, Christine Sheppard, Margot Smithyman, Dimitra Stais, Michelle Thrift, Angela Tregonning, Alison Turner, Jody Vassallo, Maria Villegas

RECIPE DEVELOPMENT: Roslyn Anderson, Anna Beaumont, Wendy Berecry, Janelle Bloom, Wendy Brodhurst, Janene Brooks, Rosey Bryan, Rebecca Clancy, Judy Clarke, Amanda Cooper, Anne Creber, Michelle Earl, Stephanie Elias, Jo Glynn, Jenny Grainger, Lulu Grimes, Margaret Harries, Eva Katz, Coral Kingston, Kathy Knudsen, Jane Lawson, Michelle Lawton, Barbara Lowery, Rachel Mackey, Voula Mantzouridis, Tracey Meharg, Rosemary Mellish, Kerrie Mullins, Kate Murdoch, Sally Parker, Jacki Passmore, Rosemary Penman, Tracey Port, Jennene Plummer, Justine Poole, Wendy Quisumbing, Kerrie Ray, Jo Richardson, Tracy Rutherford, Stephanie Souvilis, Dimitra Stais, Beverly Sutherland Smith, Alison Turner, Jody Vassallo, Maria Villegas, Lovoni Welch

PHOTOGRAPHY: Jon Bader, Paul Clarke, Craig Cranko, Joe Filshie, Roberto Jean François, Andrew Furlong, Chris Jones, Andre Martin, Luis Martin, Andy Payne, Hans Sclupp, Peter Scott

STYLISTS: Anna-Marie Bruechert, Marie-Hélène Clauzon, Georgina Dolling, Kay Francis, Mary Harris, Donna Hay, Vicki Liley, Rosemary Mellish, Lucy Mortensen, Sylvia Seiff, Suzi Smith, Maria Villegas

The publisher wishes to thank the following for their assistance in the photography for this book:
The Bay Tree Kitchen Shop, NSW;
Chief Australia;
Christoflé Paris Retail, NSW;
Made in Japan, NSW;
MEC-Kambrook Pty Ltd, NSW;
Hale Imports Pty Ltd, NSW;
Orson & Blake, NSW;
Royal Doulton Australia Pty Ltd, NSW;
Ruby Star Traders Pty Ltd, NSW;
Sheldon & Hammond;
Southcorp Appliances;
Villeroy & Boch Australia Pty Ltd, NSW;
Waterford Wedgwood Australia Ltd, NSW.